Managing Risk:
Methods for Software Systems Development

Elaine M. Hall, Ph.D.

ADDISON–WESLEY

Boston • San Francisco • New York • Toronto • Montreal
London • Munich • Paris • Madrid
Capetown • Sydney • Tokyo • Singapore • Mexico City

Software Engineering Institute

The SEI Series in Software Engineering

Many of the designations used by manufacturers and sellers to distinguish their products are claimed as trademarks. Where those designations appear in this book and we were aware of a trademark claim, the designations have been printed in initial capital letters or all capitals.

The authors and publisher have taken care in the preparation of this book, but make no expressed or implied warranty of any kind and assume no responsibility for errors or omissions. No liability is assumed for incidental or consequential damages in connection with or arising out of the use of the information or programs contained herein.

The publisher offers discounts on this book when ordered in quantity for special sales. For more information please contact:

Pearson Education Corporate Sales Division
One Lake Street
Upper Saddle River, NJ 07458
(800) 382-3419

corpsales@pearsontechgroup.com

Visit AW on the Web at *www.awl.com/cseng/*

Library of Congress Cataloging-in Publication Data

Hall, Elaine M.
    Managing risk: methods for software systems development / Elaine
M. Hall.
        p. cm.–(SEI series in software engineering)
    Includes bibliographical references and index.
    ISBN 0-201-25592-8
    1. Computer software.   2. Risk management.   I. Title.
    II. Series.
    QA76.754.H346   1997
    005.1'068'1–DC21   97–24703
                                                                    CIP

Text printed on recycled and acid-free paper.

ISBN 0201255928

4 5 6 7 8 9 MA   04 03 02 01

4th Printing   April 2001

FOR MY HUSBAND

CONTENTS

FOREWORD: RUNNING TOWARD RISK

Running away from risk is a no-win strategy. Unless your organization has been sound asleep for the past 30 years, all the relatively risk-free opportunities have long since been exploited. The remaining high-opportunity areas are rife with risk. It is in these areas and these alone where you need to focus your attentions, skills, and resources.

Consider, for example, projects that implemented the first Web-based stock trading systems: E*TRADE, e.Schwab, and Fidelity's Web Xpress. These endeavors forced their respective teams into previously uncharted waters. They had to come to grips with Java and PERL, secure sockets, 128-bit encryption, CGI scripts and server-side technology, multiplatform support, help desks, and hitherto unimagined kinds of audits and checks. Their competitors glanced uneasily at these horrors and decided to pass: "Um, let's just convert another one of our back-office systems to client-server mode instead; that is something we've finally learned to do pretty well." In the short run, that decision might have seemed sensible, but in the long run, it is a disaster. It is only by coping with risks today that you have a chance of achieving market distinction tomorrow.

Moving aggressively after opportunity means running *toward* rather than *away from* risk. But running successfully toward risk requires more than just competent process and an ability to think on your feet. It requires discipline. The discipline that enables you to prosper in such circumstances is called risk management.

Like other uncertainty-based disciplines, risk management is somewhat anti-intuitive. That means you cannot count on common sense alone to guide you. Common sense, for example, might suggest that positive thinking is the key to achieving anything really ambitious, but risk management schools us to consider certain forms of negative thinking as well. Common sense might suggest that the bigger and more ambitious the effort, the more essential it is to "plan the work and work the plan." But risk management tells us something entirely different: the plan will never work. It is only by accepting and quantifying the essential fallibility of our plans that we gain effective control over the effort.

Since it is more than just common sense, the newcomer to risk management needs an intelligent guide. It is in this role that Elaine Hall's *Managing Risk: Methods for Software Systems Development* excels. This book provides a set of practical and well-delineated processes for implementation of the discipline.

I end with an observation about the linked nature of risk and challenge. When software people tell me about what matters to them in their work, they almost always mention challenge. Work without challenge, they seem to be saying, would be as unsatisfactory as work without pay. But there can be no real challenge without risk. Risk management, in this light, is seen for what it really is: a tool for taking on challenge. *Managing Risk: Methods for Software Systems Development* will be just that for you; it will enable you to confront greater challenges than you might have without it, and it will give you the confidence and capability to achieve them.

Tom DeMarco
The Atlantic Systems Guild Inc.
Camden, Maine

PREFACE

The growing pains of the software community continue with the increased demand for software systems. The fact that software, the code developed to execute in a computing system, is pervasive in society is both a problem and an opportunity for managers and engineers. Many software professionals see the problems, but only a few see the opportunities. Problems that cause projects to be late, over budget, or of poor quality are collectively known within the community as the *software crisis*. Application of traditional problem-solving methods to solve the software crisis has been ineffective for the most part. The source of the software crisis is the project, process, and product risk that turns into problems because risk management is not done. Risk management differs from traditional problem solving for the simple reason that a risk is not a problem. By analogy, risk management is to a risk what an algorithm is to a problem. Whereas problems may be solved by the application of algorithms, a risk may be resolved by application of risk management.

Software risk management is a practice designed to resolve risks that affect the software project, process, or product. The goal of *Managing Risk* is to help people responsible for software systems acquire the knowledge necessary to apply software risk management. This book provides a handy reference to help busy professionals assess and control software risks.

This book will help you answer the following questions:

1. What does it take to manage software risk?
2. What is my ability to manage software risk?
3. How can I increase my ability to manage software risk?

This book is a practical, easy-to-use guide for managing software risk that describes an approach based on proved practices. Whether your level of expertise in managing risk is novice, beginner, intermediate, advanced, or expert, the five stages of risk management evolution ensure that you know where to start your journey.

Because *risk* is defined as the possibility of loss, traditional works often portray it with a negative connotation. This book however, has a broad and positive perspective on risk. Risk has long been associated with unmet reliability, safety, and security requirements. Although these requirements are important applications of risk concepts, they do not preclude managing risk to satisfy any other requirement, such as profitability, reusability, and quality. This book makes no assumptions about what your requirements are; it simply encourages you to take a broad view of managing risk to satisfy your requirements and achieve your goals. This book does not judge the consequence of a risk. Instead, it reframes risk in a positive manner, and views opportunity cost as a loss. A broad and positive perspective of risk challenges us to exceed expectations through thinking about the possibilities. How can we manage risk to benefit from the enormous opportunity that exists today in the field of software?

Audience

This book is written for people who manage and develop software systems, including those who hold the responsibilities for oversight and improvement of a software project, product, or process. I assume that you are a busy professional, interested in maintaining a competitive advantage for yourself and your organization. Your job could be one of these:

- ❏ Senior manager, responsible for management of an organization that has a core competency in software.
- ❏ Engineering manager, responsible for functional management of technical staff who develop or maintain software systems.
- ❏ Project manager of software systems acquisition, development, or maintenance.
- ❏ Software manager, responsible for directing software teams.
- ❏ Systems engineer, responsible for meeting the technical requirements of software systems.

❏ Software engineer, responsible for large-scale software development or maintenance.

❏ Quality assurance specialist, responsible for verification of process and product compliance using risk identification and problem prevention as a proactive strategy.

❏ Measurement analyst, responsible for either short-term or long-term measurement of software projects.

❏ Engineering process group or process action team member, responsible for organizational technology transfer, process definition, and process improvement.

❏ Change agent, working with software organizations as a corporate trainer.

❏ Process consultant, performing risk assessment and risk management for clients within the government or commercial software sector.

❏ College professor, teaching software project management or risk management.

Book Overview

The book is divided into five parts that describe a risk management road map designed to take you from crisis to control of software projects. The path to increasing your ability to manage risk is shown through progress in four synergistic dimensions of people, process, infrastructure, and implementation. These dimensions provide a separation of responsibility and focus that map to the specialization of the roles required on a software project. Parallel efforts in each dimension may speed the transition of risk management in your organization.

Each book part begins with a brief overview that summarizes the key topics covered in each chapter and why they are important.

Part I, "Risk Management Discovery," lays the foundation for understanding the role of risk management in software engineering. The chapters describe the relationship of six disciplines that illustrate where risk fits in to managing product development and the factors that contribute to the ability to manage software risks. The Risk Management Map, Personal Risk Management Matrix and the Ten-Point Game Plan are presented to provide understanding and motivation for improvement.

Part II, "Risk Management Process," elaborates the activities to perform risk management using a standard process definition notation. Process steps, inputs, and outputs are fully defined. Methods and tools used by the process are shown by example. The process dimension describes the steps to predictable risk management results in terms of *what* and *how*. Engineering process group or process action team members and process consultants can appreciate this reusable process component.

Part III, "Risk Management Infrastructure," sets out the organizational foundation that supports the establishment of a risk-aware culture. Training metrics help you provide just enough information just in time. Techniques for project oversight are included, as well as a method for establishing a baseline for quantitative process improvement. Without infrastructure, there is no strategic plan in place to institutionalize risk management. Senior managers, engineering managers, and change agents should benefit from these organizational building blocks.

Part IV, "Risk Management Implementation," instantiates the standard process within a software project. Risk management activities throughout the life cycle are planned, budgeted, scheduled, and staffed. The implementation dimension describes *who, where, when,* and *why.* The details of the risk management plan are presented, with tailoring suggestions for the standard process, especially useful for project managers, software managers, systems engineers, and software engineers behind schedule.

Part V, "People in Crisis and Control," describes actual project teams whose practices formed the basis of the risk management evolution stages. These case studies provide a wealth of experiences, ancedotes, and benchmark data from the 1990s. I had the opportunity to survey and study people's perceptions of the performance and importance of their risk management practices and identified effective and ineffective practices used by project managers, engineering managers, configuration managers, quality assurance specialists, systems engineers, software engineers, test engineers, and customers. These insights and lessons learned should be invaluable to people struggling to manage software systems risk.

How to Read This Book

The approach for reading this book depends on your job category, and your risk management ability. Everyone should read Part I, which provides the background for the rest of the book. If you are a risk management novice read Chapter 1 completely. Read Chapter 2 to learn the success formula for managing risk. Read Chapter 3 to understand the road map to increase your risk management ability. Depending on your job category, Parts II through IV will apply. Read Part II if you are responsible for risk management process definition or execution; Part III if you are responsible for establishing risk management policy, training, compliance, verification, or process improvement; and Part IV if you are responsible for planning, tailoring, or performing risk management on a project. Everyone should read the case studies in Part V to benchmark their personal, project, and organizational risk management capability.

These case studies are based on a range of software projects. Read them to determine whether your risk management process is above or below the levels described. Use them to define the steps needed to mature your risk management ability. Technical terms in boldface are explained in the Glossary. You might read a section out of order and find a term defined a few chapters back. The questions at the end of each chapter support retention and learning.

Acknowledgments

I acknowledge those software risk management pioneers who built a body of fundamental knowledge. Barry Boehm, Robert Charette, and the Software Engineering Institute (SEI) inspired me to develop this practical set of risk management methods applicable to the entire software community.

Several managers were responsible for my process improvement experience at Harris Corporation. Phil Henderson, as general manager of the Information Systems Division, established the Software Process Team and funded the Software Engineering Process Group (SEPG) to improve the software process. Hank Eyster, division director and steering committee representative on the Software Process Team, supported training and the use of project risk assessment and risk management. Gary Natwick, SEPG manager, recognized my enthusiasm for risk management and allowed me time to write articles and present papers. Those who worked with me on the Software Risk Management Action Team were Clay Eberle, Jane Eden, Gary Natwick, Lon Hixson, Russ Hooper, and Steve Morris. Their cross-functional perspectives helped to evaluate and expand the current documented policy for risk management with a focus on practical project implementation.

The benefits derived from the SEI efforts in technology transfer cannot be overstated. I was able to leverage this expertise to assist pursuits, proposals, and project teams in establishing effective risk management practices. Ken Dymond, Walt Lamia, and George Pandelios at the SEI Risk Program provided my early training in risk assessment. I am grateful to them and others who contributed to the SEI Risk Program. Those with whom I worked to write a key process area for risk management were Robert Charette, George Kambic, Roy Kimbrell, George Pandelios, and Charlie Weber. Those who made the SEI/Harris technical collaboration agreement possible included Julia Allen and Clyde Chittister. For help in streamlining the risk assessment process, I thank Carol Ulrich and Marvin Carr. Thanks to Mike Dedolph and Julie Walker for on-the-job training in software risk evaluation and Audrey Dorofee for training in the Risk Clinic.

My involvement in systems engineering process improvement through the International Council on Systems Engineering (INCOSE) has broadened my perspective on risk management. I thank those who discussed ideas with me, including George Friedman, Jerry Lake, Jim Brill, and Larry Brekka, former chair of the INCOSE Risk Management Working Group. Members who shared their experiences in risk management with me include Bob Shishko, Art Gemmer, John Hazelwood, and Rudy Elam. Thanks also to members who contributed technical papers on risk practices to the national symposium, especially Dennis Beude for enlightening me on tools for risk analysis.

Many organizations contributed to the Department of Defense's Software Acquisition Best Practices Initiative. Those that shared risk practices included Aerospace Corporation, C&C Associates, Ceridian Corporation, Harris Corporation, Mitre Corporation, and Unisys. Norm Brown, initiative coordinator and director of the Software Program Managers Network (SPMN), deserves the credit for condensing industrial-strength software management strategies from the reported best practices. At the SPMN, I learned commercial best practices and the need for them to help meet defense needs at lower cost. The Airlie Software Council, especially opinion leader Tom DeMarco, deserves the credit for encouraging consensus that the number one best practice in software acquisition is formal risk management.

I thank the attendees of my Software Risk Management seminars at the Defense Systems Management College, and in London, Orlando, New Zealand, and Washington, D.C., for sharing their risks, questions, and improvement suggestions.

Peter Gordon, my sponsoring editor, provided the opportunity to share my knowledge and experiences. Reviewers who contributed distinctly different perspectives are Barry Boehm, John D. Eikenberry, Tom Gorsuch, Susan Tinch Johnson, J. Richard Newman, Richard Rubinstein, Professor Wade H. Shaw, David Siefert, and Hank Stuebing. Thanks to those at Addison-Wesley who made this book possible, and especially to Helen Goldstein, who made it a delight.

Elaine M. Hall
Indialantic, Florida

ABOUT THE AUTHOR

Elaine Hall is founder of Level 6 Software, the leading consulting group in discovery methods for software engineering. She conducts training seminars and supports the implementation of software risk management for both government and industry clients worldwide. Dr. Hall is chair of the International Council on Systems Engineering (INCOSE) risk management working group.

As Director of Risk Management and Metrics at Computer & Concepts Associates, Hall assisted top officials at the Department of Defense in their Software Acquisition Management Best Practices Initiative at the Software Program Managers Network. She presented training on MIL-STD-498 for the Joint Logistics Commanders direct satellite broadcast. At Harris Corporation, Hall was a member of the SEPG responsible for achieving SEI Level 3 and International Standards Organization (ISO) 9001 Registration. She led a technical collaboration between the SEI and Harris Information Systems Division to develop and use effective risk assessment methods. She wrote database software for the Joint Surveillance Target Attack Radar System (J-STARS) that flew operationally in the Persian Gulf War. As a certified software developer for Apple Computer she authored two medical software applications that were sold commercially with zero defects. As an assistant professor at the Florida Institute of Technology, she taught graduate-level software project management.

Hall's electronic mail address is DrEHall@aol.com.

PART I

Risk Management Discovery

I am used to thinking three or four months in advance about what I must do, and I calculate on the worst. If I take so many precautions it is because it is my custom to leave nothing to chance.
—Napoleon I, in a conversation with Marshall Murat, March 14, 1808

Part I establishes the context for understanding risk as an important part of how we think and how you can develop the ability to manage software systems risk.

Chapter 1, "Software Risk Management," defines software risk management and describes the need for it in the software community. It then presents a six-discipline model that integrates risk into the way we think. Read Chapter 1 to understand the essence of software risk management.

Chapter 2, "P^2I^2 Success Formula," discusses what it takes to manage risk in the context of a project and an organization. Read Chapter 2 to understand the major factors that affect risk management capability and to glean a success formula for managing software risk.

Chapter 3, "Risk Management Map," outlines a risk management road map designed to improve your ability to manage risk. Read Chapter 3 to understand how to increase your ability to manage risk through progress in four synergistic dimensions of risk management.

With the knowledge of software risk management and the road map provided in Part I, you will be ready to assess and develop your ability to manage risk.

1

1

Software Risk Management

In the middle of difficulty lies opportunity.
—Albert Einstein

The quest for an effective approach to managing software development is as sought after today as the Holy Grail was in medieval times. Just as the grail remained elusive to errant knights, the panacea for the **software crisis** has yet to be discovered by the software community. We continue to search for our grail in new and improved standards, languages, methods, and tools. In our failure to discover it, we blame people, process, technology, and management. Focus in any single area will not provide the synergy required to help the software community. Only a requisite set of properly coordinated disciplines can lead the crusade on software risk.

In this chapter, I define **software risk** and describe the need for **software risk management**. I describe a six-discipline model that integrates risk into the way we think. I discuss how we create opportunity by applying persistence to the possibilities.

This chapter answers the following questions:

❏ What is software risk management?

❏ Why is risk management necessary for software systems development?

❏ How does risk fit into the big picture of managing product development?

1.1   Foundations

At the foundation of modern life in engineering, finance, insurance, medicine, and science is the mastery of risk. Peter Bernstein, a Wall Street economist, argues that the notion of bringing risk under control is one of the central ideas that distinguishes modern times from the more distant past [Bernstein96].

1.1.1   Risk

Risk as a science was born in the sixteenth-century Renaissance, a time of discovery. The word *risk* derives from the early Italian *risicare*, which means "to dare." Games of chance led to the discovery of the theory of probability, the mathematical heart of risk. Today we define risk as the possibility of loss [American85]. We obtain an instance of a risk by specifying values for the risk attributes of probability (the possibility) and consequence (the loss). **Probability** is the likelihood that the consequence will occur. **Consequence** is the effect of an unsatisfactory outcome. I use the notation L^2 to denote that we measure **risk exposure** by multiplying likelihood times loss.

Blaise Pascal and Daniel Bernoulli significantly contributed to defining risk. In 1654, the French mathematician Blaise Pascal solved a puzzle for gamblers. His solution of how to divide the stakes of an unfinished game of chance, called *balla*, led to the discovery of the theory of *probability*, which provides a method to calculate uncertainty. Pascal worked inductively to create Pascal's Triangle for determining the probability of possible outcomes [David62]. This type of systematic method for measuring probability in terms of numbers is the cornerstone of modern insurance.

In 1738, in a paper titled "Exposition of a New Theory on the Measurement of Risk" [Bernoulli38], Swiss mathematician Daniel Bernoulli introduced the concept of **utility**, a measure of the *consequences* of an outcome in valuing risk. Bernoulli recognized that utility is dependent on the particular circumstances of the person valuing risk. He defined a procedure for introducing these subjective considerations into decisions that have uncertain outcomes. (A **decision** is the passing of judgment on an issue under consideration.) He suggested that our desire for wealth is inversely proportionate to the quantity of goods possessed. Bernoulli's emphasis was on decision making based on a desire for wealth and opportunity rather than mathematical probability. Utility theory provides the basis for the law of supply and demand in economics.

1.1.2   Risk Management

Risk management can be traced to the eighteenth century era of Enlightenment, a time of searching for knowledge and exploring the unknown. Today we use **risk management** as a general procedure for resolving risks. Risk management is said to resolve a risk if, when it is applied to any instance, the possible consequences are all acceptable. **Acceptable risk** means that we can live with the worst-case outcome. There are two major activities in any risk management process. The first activity, **risk assessment**, defines the risk. Risk assessment is a discovery process of identifying sources of risk and evaluating their potential effects. The second activity, **risk control**, resolves the risk. Risk control is a process of developing risk resolution plans, monitoring risk status, implementing risk resolution plans, and correcting for deviations from the plan. You do not need to know what the risks are to begin risk management. It is normal to start the risk management process with fuzzy issues, concerns, doubts, and unknowns. The process of risk management transforms this uncertainty into acceptable risk.

Risk management transcends modern management theory, such as Total Quality Management (TQM) [Kolarik95] and Business Process Reengineering (BPR) [Champy95], because it is basic to decision making. Risk management is based on theories that provide different strategies for decision making under probabilistic conditions. All strategies attempt to improve the quality of decisions on the evaluation of two or more alternative courses of action [Clemen91].

Nine theories for decision making are fundamental to the practice of risk management.

Bayes theorem describes how to blend new information into old. In 1763, English minister Thomas Bayes's *Essay Towards Solving a Problem in the Doctrine of Chances* was published [Bayes63]. Bayes addresses the dynamic nature of risk by providing a method to alter judgment as events unfold. Under conditions of uncertainty, there can be no static answer. The Bayesian system of inference is a learning process used in risk management to account for new information. It is fitting that Bayes himself is characterized in business statistics literature as "enigmatic" [Groebner93]. Risk management often begins with **enigma**: information that is mysterious, ambiguous, puzzling, paradoxical, and obscure.

Chaos theory tells us that chaos and uncertainty are market opportunities. We should take a competitive situation as given and learn to thrive on it. Winners of tomorrow will deal proactively with chaos. They will look at the chaos as the source of market advantage, not as a problem to get around [Peters87].

Creativity theory asserts that our brain processes information at a level that is not accessible to our conscious thought. Creativity theory attempts to understand the individual needs and motivations that are critical to creative solutions [Clemen91]. With creativity, we can generate opportunities by using knowledge and imagination to develop ideas that are either original (previously unknown) or novel (extensions of known). One theory divides creativity into four stages: preparation, incubation, illumination, and verification. Preparation and verification stages use *convergent thinking:* the ability of the left brain to deduce correct answers logically. Incubation and illumination stages, the heart of the creative process, use *divergent thinking:* the ability of the right brain to discover new answers through synthesis, imagery, and fantasy. It is in the incubation stage that ideas, associations, and relationships percolate beneath the creator's conscious awareness. In fact, the right brain is most active when we are dreaming. Highly creative people are intensely observant, have a tolerance for ambiguity, and thrive on complexity and confusion [Fincher89].

Decision theory provides techniques to solve difficult problems—ones that are complex, have uncertain aspects, have multiple objectives, or encompass different perspectives. Decision theory uses probabilities to determine outcomes. Techniques to structure difficult problems include decision trees and computer simulation.

Game theory uses heuristics to determine which alternatives to explore in large search spaces. For example, artificial intelligence research uses the techniques of game theory. Much of what we call intelligence resides in the heuristics humans use to solve problems. The presence of an opponent in game playing adds an element of unpredictability to the game and the need to consider psychological as well as tactical factors in game strategy [Luger89]. Game theory presents life as a contest in which people seek to maximize rewards and minimize risks, while others do the same, often with conflicting objectives.

Portfolio theory is based on the assumption that **diversification** reduces risk. Putting all your eggs in one basket is an unacceptably risky strategy [Markowitz52]. Applying this theory to software development, this means not to rely heavily on one customer, vendor, method, tool, or person to fulfill project needs. Instead, build a balanced approach that stresses mastery of software project fundamentals.

Probability theory defines probability as a degree of certainty and uses a quantifiable probability to forecast an outcome. Through an estimation of probability before the fact, probability theory determines the probability of an outcome prior to the event's occurrence. As an instrument for forecasting, probability theory depends on the quality of information that forms the basis of probability estimates.

Uncertainty theory uses probability to model unknown, uncertain, or subjective decision problems. Uncertainty results when there is a lack of adequate information to make a decision [Giarratano89]. The probability distribution of an uncertain event reflects the probability sets of all possible outcomes. Probability distributions are expressed as expected values, variance, and standard deviation.

Utility theory models people's preference and attitude toward risk. Individuals have different tolerances for risk, which affects the way we make decisions.

Utility theory selects the alternative that maximizes the expected-utility function. A **utility function** can reveal whether the decision maker is risk averse, risk seeking, or risk neutral.

We reason about the probability of risk using aspects of portfolio, probability, and uncertainty theories. Using aspects of chaos, creativity, game, and utility theories, we explore our desires regarding the consequence of risk. The combination of probability and consequence over time yields dynamic risk, which leads to the choices of risk management. We can better understand these choices through the use of Bayes theorem and the techniques of decision theory. These theories and their underlying principles form the basis of the risk management methods explored in this book.

1.1.3   Software Risk

Software risk is a measure of the likelihood and loss of an unsatisfactory outcome affecting the software project, process, or product.

1. **Software project risk**. This category defines operational, organizational, and contractual software development parameters. Project risk is primarily a management responsibility. Project risk includes resource constraints, external interfaces, supplier relationships, or contract restrictions. Other examples are unresponsive vendors and lack of organizational support. Perceived lack of control over project external dependencies makes project risk difficult to manage. Funding is the most significant project risk reported in risk assessments.

2. **Software process risk**. This category includes both management and technical work procedures. In management procedures, you may find process risk in activities such as planning, staffing, tracking, quality assurance, and configuration management. In technical procedures, you may find it in engineering activities such as requirements analysis, design, code, and test. Planning is the management process risk most often reported in risk assessments. The technical process risk most often reported is the development process.

3. **Software product risk**. This category contains intermediate and final work product characteristics. Product risk is primarily a technical responsibility. You may find product risk in the requirements stability, design performance, code complexity, and test specifications. Because software requirements are often perceived as flexible, product risk is difficult to manage. Requirements are the most significant product risks reported in risk assessments.

Figure 1.1 illustrates a useful hierarchy of responsibility for each type of software risk found on software projects. This top-level classification scheme

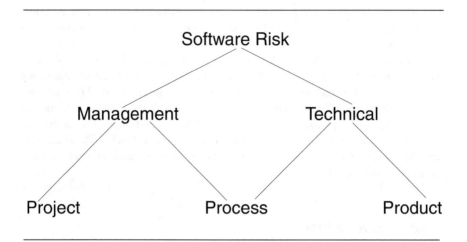

FIGURE 1.1   Software risk classification. Risks may be classified into categories to better understand the nature of the risk. *Management* contains project and management process risks. *Technical* contains product and technical process risks. *Project* is a major risk category that includes customer relationships. *Process* includes tools to produce a product. *Product* includes intermediate work products. The top-level classification should be used as a minimum to classify a risk (e.g., Risk.Technical.Process). (This hierarchy is an abstraction of the Software Engineering Institute risk taxonomy [Carr93].)

for software risk explicitly shows the multiple inheritance of process risk from both management and technical processes.

Each software system is unique with its own particular set of risks. There are many software risks but fewer consequences that we care to avoid. Perhaps that is why we often discuss software risk in terms of the potential cost, schedule, and technical consequences. These three consequences are significant, because they could prevent a software project from meeting its cost, schedule, and technical goals. Goals are important because they define the success criteria for the project. To be successful, software projects must meet their technical requirements within cost and schedule constraints. Software risk is perilous because it can prevent software project success.

1.1.4   Software Risk Management

Software risk management is the practice of assessing and controlling risk that affects the software project, process, or product. You can discover software risks by working backward. First, define your goals and objectives. Then describe the risk in terms of uncertainty, loss, and time. The more clearly you define the goal and the associated risk, the more easily you can communicate these to other team members. Difficult choices often arise when collective team goals compete for the same scarce resources (most often time and money). Consideration of risk information helps teams sort out their priorities and provides the knowledge to make intelligent decisions.

The basic concepts of software risk management are these.

- **Goal**. We manage risk in relation to a specific goal and can affect only the work that remains to achieve the goal. What is the risk in the plan? What is the risk in the remaining work? A clearly defined goal with measurable success criteria bounds acceptable risk.

- **Uncertainty**. Uncertainty is that which we do not know. It is inherent in all of our assumptions and the future itself. There is always a degree of uncertainty in risk occurrence. We can be certain that the probability of risk occurrence is greater than zero and less than 100 percent. This means that we do not know whether the risk will (100 percent probability) or will not (probability of zero) occur. The likelihood that a loss will occur helps to determine the relative priority of the risk.

- **Loss**. Unless there is a potential for loss, there is no risk. The loss can be either a bad outcome or a lost opportunity. An unsatisfactory outcome might be a product with an unacceptable latent defect rate, or failure to meet the desired delivery date. **Opportunity** is the chance of a good outcome; **opportunity cost** is the loss of a missed opportunity. Opportunity cost can be calculated in lost customer satisfaction (delivering a buggy product) and lost profits (failing to beat the competition to market).

- **Time**. We need time to anticipate and prevent problems. Time is a great equalizer because every day we each have the same amount. Although a valuable resource, we cannot accumulate time. As time goes by, viable options tend to decrease. By managing risk, we reduce wasted time by using it to our advantage.

- **Choice**. Unless there is a choice, there is no risk management. Sometimes we believe we cannot control risk, or do not feel empowered to select from the available options. Doing something or doing nothing should be a conscious choice. Understanding the goal, and the risk of not achieving the goal, helps us to make the right choice.

We can discover the risk of software risk management by first defining its goals.

- **Make intelligent decisions.** We make intelligent decisions based on awareness, insight, and understanding of risk. Risk management provides a process to communicate risk information and provide visibility into software risks at all project levels.

- **Resolve risk.** We develop and execute a risk action plan to resolve risk. The key to resolving risk is finding risk when there is time to take action and knowing when to accept a risk. It is possible that your risk resolution strategy is not to minimize risk but to maximize opportunity. Acceptable risk is defined by the decision maker.

❏ **Prevent problems.** Resolution of software risk prevents problems and surprises. Risk management is a proactive strategy to reduce the problem of costly rework.

The risk of software risk management can be described by the uncertainty and loss that might occur if the goals of software risk management are not met. For example, the likelihood of making a bad decision without proper attention to the risk component of the decision is high. The loss caused by a bad decision would not be satisfactory when it could have been prevented. The risk of software risk management is that of making foolish decisions, accepting unsatisfactory outcomes, and paying for costly rework. If you can make a choice to prevent these risks from occurring, then you have time for risk management.

1.1.5   Need for Software Risk Management

Software practitioners have been challenged to make the transition from programmers who write projects in an ad hoc fashion to software engineers who develop high-quality software in a disciplined way. **Software engineering** is defined as the establishment and use of sound engineering principles in order to obtain economically software that is reliable and works efficiently on real machines [Naur69]. Software engineering encompasses methods, tools, and procedures that enable managers to control the process and provide practitioners with a foundation for building high-quality software in a productive manner [Pressman92].

There are many reasons that risk management is currently in use on software projects. The ability to manage uncertainty on projects is a requirement designed to deal with scarce resources, advances in technology, and the increased demand for complex systems in a rapidly changing environment. Given the current business climate of shrinking profit margins, the global economy and its uncertain market conditions, and the competitive forces pressured by rapid technology advances, we can all use a coping mechanism. To respond to this need, risk management methods have been tailored for use by software managers and engineers.

Risk management techniques were introduced to the software community in the 1980s. The father of software risk management is Barry Boehm, whose contributions include the **Spiral Model**, a software life-cycle model that is iterative and risk driven [Boehm88]. The U.S. government has been a major player in defining software risk management to reduce the acquisition risk for software-intensive systems. The Department of Defense (DoD) has provided guidance and funding in this area to the following organizations.

❏ **Defense Systems Management College (DSMC).** A memorandum from the deputy secretary of defense in 1981 required DoD action to improve the acquisition process. One initiative was to increase the visibility of technical risk in budgets of weapon systems acquisition projects and incorporate the use of budget funds for technological risk. In response, the DSMC wrote a handbook to familiarize project management personnel with the concepts and techniques of quantitative risk assessment to assist them in internal management decision making [DSMC83].

❑ **Air Force Systems Command (AFSC).** Since 1983, the Software Development Integrity Program has used the Software Development Capability/Capacity Review question set to lower the risk of weapon systems acquisition by determining contractors' software capability [Babel90]. The Air Force has several publications on risk, including the landmark AFSC/AFLC Pamphlet 800-45 on software **risk abatement** [AirForce88]. The Air Force has developed the Software Development Capability Evaluation (SDCE) model as a basis for the state of practice in software development [Frankford93]. The primary purpose of the SDCE is to reduce the acquisition risk for software-intensive systems.

❑ **Software Engineering Institute (SEI).** In 1984, the DoD awarded the Carnegie Mellon University (CMU) a contract to establish the SEI. The SEI Risk Program was chartered in 1990 to develop risk methods and transfer the technology to industry. Two important contributions of the SEI Risk Program are the Risk Management Paradigm and the Taxonomy-Based Questionnaire. The Risk Management Paradigm [VanScoy92] is a model of how the different elements of a risk management process interact. Taxonomy-Based Risk Identification [Carr93] is a repeatable method for identifying risk in software projects using a software risk taxonomy and associated questionnaire.

❑ **Software Program Manager's Network (SPMN).** The SPMN was established in 1992 to help DoD software acquisition managers with the difficulties they face in managing complex systems. The SPMN mission is to focus the defense software acquisition community on employing high-leverage management practices that enable competitive software development. These proven practices were shared by successful organizations in the DoD's Software Acquisition Best Practices Initiative. A **best practice** is a routine activity that enables excellent performance. The SPMN led this initiative to seek out the practices that improve software productivity and quality while reducing cost and risk. The Airlie Software Council, a group of industry software experts, was brought together to review and achieve consensus on the best practices. The council agreed that risk is inherent in all large software systems. They concluded that if you are told there is no risk, there probably is high risk because of risk that is overlooked until too late. After a rigorous collection and analysis process, SPMN reported **formal risk management** as the number one best practice [Hall95].

1.2   Risk in the Large

Any professional developing complex software in a team environment can appreciate the concept of *programming in the large*. If you have had the experience of personally writing a software program to satisfy an academic course requirement, then you understand the concept of *programming in the small*. Similarly, the distinction can be made between *risk in the large* and *risk in the small*.

Those who practice risk management agree that it must be performed regularly throughout the life cycle of a software system. Risks are dynamic, meaning that they change over time. As a project progresses, there is growth in staffing, an increased awareness of project issues, and a different life cycle focus that contribute to the need for routine risk management. Two perspectives hinder routine risk management.

1. *Risk viewed as extra activity*. Risk management is an extra activity layered on assigned work. The danger in perceiving risks as less important than assigned work is that we may not address risks when work priorities escalate.

2. *Risk viewed as outside activity*. Risk management is an outside activity that is not *your* responsibility. The pitfall in perceiving risk as someone else's responsibility is that when that person is not around, risk management will cease.

When risk management is implemented as a mainstream function in the development process, the project is helped the most. Risk is neither more nor less important than work; it is, instead, a part of the effort remaining. There is not a "risk season" [VanScoy92] or a separate team to perform risk management. Risk management is not tied to a planning phase that is completed early in the project life cycle. For simplicity, most process descriptions show an isolated risk management process—what I call *risk in a box*. In fact, I use this depiction in discussing the risk management process in Part II. Although this is a convenient way to describe the process itself, it does not provide the understanding of risk in the larger context. My search to understand how risk fits into the big picture of managing product development led to my conclusion that existing management models lacked the ability to describe risk adequately.

1.2.1   The Six-Discipline Model

Two models of managing product development are based on the work of W. Edwards Deming, the father of statistical process control and the Japanese quality revolution. The first, *continuous process improvement*, is based on evolutionary key process areas of the SEI Capability Maturity Model^{SM} for

Software (SW-CMM^{SM})[1] [Paulk93]. The second, *reengineering*, is based on revolutionary innovation [Hammer93]. Both approaches have their roots in Deming's quality work [Deming86]. The Plan-Do-Check-Act (PDCA) cycle popularized by Deming is a closed-loop approach for process optimization. The Deming cycle is an evolutionary model based on the scientific method [Basili95]. The systematic flow of Deming's evolutionary model for product improvement based on process modification is unquestioned in contemporary quality literature.

Deming's PDCA cycle defines four disciplines of human behavior. A **discipline** is a body of theory and technique that must be studied and put into practice to be mastered. It has a developmental path for acquiring certain skills or competencies. To practice a discipline is to be a lifelong learner. You spend your life mastering disciplines [Senge90]. The adaptation of Deming's manufacturing process to software development is lacking a known discipline to develop vision that Deming described but did not diagram in the PDCA cycle. Developing vision is included in my model as the fifth discipline, *Envision*. In this section, I introduce a sixth discipline, *Discover*, which extends the Deming cycle by adding the ability to reveal risk and opportunity. These six disciplines are essential to managing development of software systems [Hall97], and together they form a new six-discipline model. The **Six-Discipline (6-D) Model**, presented in Figure 1.2, describes the relationship among the disciplines required to manage software systems development successfully. Deming's PDCA disciplines are preserved within the 6-D Model as Plan-Work-Measure-Improve (PWMI). Three terms were updated to reflect the focus at successive SEI CMM levels, which correspond to each of Deming's disciplines. For example, we do not *check* the software process, we *measure* it.

Envision.   This discipline means transforming ideas into goals and objectives. Deming's chain reaction begins with the creation and communication of organizational vision.[2] First, management demonstrates its commitment to the vision statement. Then everybody in the organization learns the new philosophy. For a software project, a statement of need, such as "on-time delivery" or "flight safety," can become the vision. Apple Computer developed the user-friendly Macintosh out of Steven Jobs's vision of the computer as a household appliance. The vision of the U.S. Air Force that drove the development of the SEI CMM was to

---

[1] Capability Maturity Model and CMM are service marks of Carnegie Mellon University.

[2] Deming's *chain reaction* was a revolutionary concept that showed how an improvement in quality causes productivity to improve. At that time, management believed that quality and productivity were traded off. Deming must have realized the fallacy of the logic in asking the customer, "Which would you prefer: quality or productivity?" His quality philosophy is described in fourteen points that drive the chain reaction.

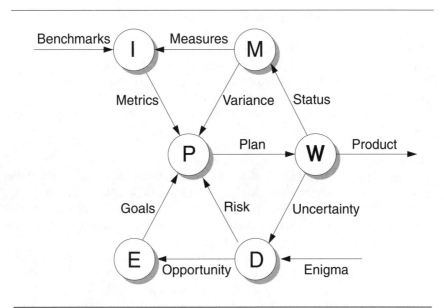

FIGURE 1.2   Six-Discipline Model. (E) *Envision*. Develop a vision for a software product. (P) *Plan*. Plan the project by mapping resources to the goals established for the software. (W) *Work*. Produce the product based on the current plan. (M) *Measure*. Report the variance between expected and actual results to update the plan. (I) *Improve*. Analyze benchmarks and organization project measures to improve processes and metrics. (D) *Discover*. Assess the uncertainty of our work and external enigma for risk and opportunity, which we manage through changes to the plan and vision.

identify capable contractors. The power of the SEI CMM lies in its ability to create a vision of a mature process for the software industry. An organization at SEI CMM Level 1 must have management commitment to *Envision* process improvement.

Plan.   This discipline refers to mapping available resources to requirements, which are derived from project goals and objectives. Although management is responsible for high-level project planning, everyone plans with respect to accomplishing assigned work. We estimate the resources required to perform work based on historical performance data, sequence the planned work in a schedule, and develop standards and procedures such as the software development plan. SEI CMM Level 2 provides key process areas for the *Plan* discipline.

Work.   This discipline refers to implementing the plan to produce the product (Deming's "Do"). Work is any activity to produce the product, including intermediate and disposable work products (e.g., derived requirements, design documents, and test drivers). By-products of work are status and uncertainty, which develop as you make progress. Work includes identifying the unknowns in the intermediate work product (e.g., incomplete requirements) and uncertainty in the work environment (e.g., unfamiliar tools). If we cannot resolve the uncertainty, we must report it through communication channels designed to inform the appropriate people. Products remain in work until they satisfy the quality criteria. SEI CMM Level 3 provides key process areas for the *Work* discipline.

Measure.   This discipline refers to comparing expected and actual results (Deming's "Check"). We track our results over time and determine progress by comparing status (Where are we?) to the plan (Where should we be?). We analyze the variance and recommend corrective action. We report the variance between the estimates in the plan and the actual status to allow for midcourse corrections. We update the plan based on variance data from measurements of work status. SEI CMM Level 4 provides key process areas for the *Measure* discipline.

Improve.   This discipline refers to learning from past experience (Deming's "Act"). We analyze **benchmarks** and project measures for reporting and improving organizational processes and metrics. Internal measures and external benchmarks help us to know how to change our plan. We retain long-term organizational memory by maintaining process asset libraries, reuse repositories, and organizational metrics. We gather lessons learned to support continuous improvement. SEI CMM Level 5 provides key process areas for the *Improve* discipline.

Discover.   The sixth discipline means becoming aware of the future. We seek to know by investigating what we do not know. We assess the uncertainty of our work for risk, which we manage through changes to the plan. We become cognizant of external enigma that puzzles us. We search for an explanation to ambiguous information by questioning and doubting what we think we know. We uncover opportunity by realizing the answer to the riddle. The significance of the sixth discipline is that it provides the input required to change the vision.

1.2.2   Future Awareness

Many computer companies suffer when senior management fails to read the future direction of the software industry. Even Microsoft chairman Bill Gates, a student of business history, reacted to the explosion of the World Wide Web. As Microsoft sales rocketed to $3.8 billion and staff soared from 5,600 to 14,400 in the early 1990s, chaos from cyberspace was around the corner [Rebello96]. Microsoft engineers worried about their own lack of responsiveness to the new age of Internet computing, yet management seemed asleep at the wheel. How did they manage to wake up in time to avert disaster? The breakthrough for Microsoft came at an executive retreat focused on the Internet as a critical issue. Later, Gates said, "I don't know of any examples where a leader was totally energized and focused on the new opportunities where they totally missed it" [Gates95].

Future awareness is *reasoning about possibilities*. Possibilities have uncertain outcomes that may be good or bad. Opportunities are possibilities that have good outcomes; risks are possibilities that have bad outcomes. The sixth discipline, Discover, is the key to accessing future awareness *because it resolves enigma that comes from the environment.* In Microsoft's case, past awareness would not have helped solve the 1990 Internet enigma. At that time, Microsoft owned the operating system for the world's most popular computer, the PC, and its engineers were busy improving their operating system, which shipped as Windows95. No productivity measures or return-on-investment indicators could have told Microsoft management to change its plan. Only attention to the Discover discipline could help Microsoft leaders with the enigma that contradicted their belief that the Internet was free: there was no money to be made in cyberspace.[3] By struggling with these issues, Microsoft came to understand the opportunity and risk of the Internet, which radically changed their game plan and, most important, led them to a new vision.

Whoever changes the rules wins the game. Question: What could take the place of the PC? Answer: The Internet. Because the owner of the preferred operating system of the Internet is TBD (to be determined), Microsoft and the rest of the software community can benefit from learning the disciplines for future awareness. The power of future awareness lies in its ability to provide opportunity for innovation. Innovation introduces something new, which changes the rules within the software community. Consider the changes associated with the invention of Web browsers on the Internet. Web browsers caused new rules for software development, distribution, technical support, marketing, and sales. When a new paradigm appears, everyone must go back to zero [Barker87]. After innovations occur, a new cycle of **continuous improvement** begins (e.g., better Web browsers). Future awareness and the risk of competition can be the stimulus that drives development of unprecedented software systems, which are radically innovative and fundamentally change the way we live. In this sense, the concept of risk can be revolutionary.

All six disciplines[4] are requisite to managing and developing software systems successfully. As shown in Figure 1.3, the disciplines for future awareness are Plan, Work, Discover, and Envision. The disciplines for past awareness are Plan,

---

[3] Today we understand that the Internet is worth billions of dollars.

[4] One acronym for the six disciplines is PM-WIDE, which reminds us to use them programwide.

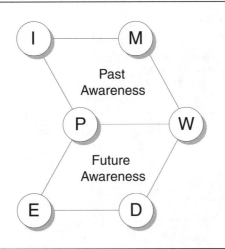

FIGURE 1.3   Disciplines for awareness. Past awareness (PWMI) is achieved through planning, working, measuring, and improving. Future awareness (PWDE) is achieved through
planning, working, discovering, and envisioning.

Work, Measure, and Improve. Many software organizations support either continuous improvement (a model based on past awareness) or reengineering (a model
based on future awareness). The fallacy in the logic of choosing between these two
management models is that one without the other ultimately creates a dysfunc-
tional organization. Only through the coexistence of past and future awareness can
we optimize existing products and capitalize on new opportunities.

1.3   Risk in the Small

In this section, I discuss how individuals within the software community
should think about risk. The six disciplines of the 6-D Model form four quadrants
of awareness—known, past, unknown, and future—that together describe everything that we can consciously discern (see Figure 1.4).

❑ *Known.* The Plan, Work, and Measure disciplines provide a short-term perspective of understanding where we are in relation to our plan. With these three
disciplines, we can recognize discrepancies between the plan and our work.

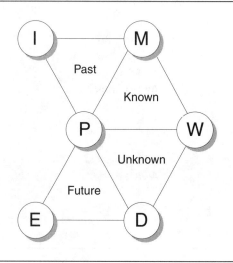

FIGURE 1.4   Quadrants of awareness. The six disciplines form four quadrants of awareness: Known (PWM); Past (PMI); Unknown (PWD); and Future (PDE).

- *Past.* The Plan, Measure, and Improve disciplines provide a long-term perspective of prior experience. With these three disciplines, we can use lessons
  learned on preceding projects to establish realistic expectations for our current project.
- *Unknown.* The Plan, Work, and Discover disciplines provide a short-term
  perspective of those pieces of the plan or work that remain to be investigated.
  With these three disciplines, we can explore hidden requirements or new
  technology to reveal possible effects on our plans.
- *Future.* The Plan, Discover, and Envision disciplines provide a long-term
  perspective of prospective circumstances. With these three disciplines, we
  can perceive an opportunity and capitalize on it.

1.3.1   Personal Awareness

Deming's disciplines are found within the context of software development at the
organization, project, and personal levels. Watts Humphrey states that "the Personal Software Process[5] is a self-improvement process (*Improve*). We are each
blessed with unique talents and opportunities. We need to decide what to do with

---

[5] Personal Software Process and PSP are service marks of Carnegie Mellon University.

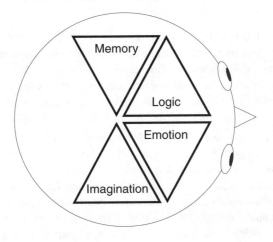

FIGURE 1.5   Quadrants of personal awareness. The six disciplines logically connect four quadrants of our brain. Logic and memory constitute the left brain, emotion and imagination the right brain.

them (*Plan*). Consistent high performance takes persistent effort (*Work*), an understanding of your own abilities (*Measure*), and a dedication to personal excellence (*Envision*)" [Humphrey95].

The 6-D Model is also powerful at the personal level. In fact, a personal perspective of the 6-D Model is conceptually more powerful than a Turing machine.[6] Consider this: What could be more powerful than a computer? The mind of the computer's creator. Further, the human brain is the most powerful parallel processor on earth. Called the *ultimate enigma*, the brain perplexes all who presume to take its measure [Fincher89].

The 6-D Model is a requisite set of properly coordinated disciplines because *it describes the four quadrants of the human brain*: memory, logic, imagination, and emotion.[7] (Figure 1.5 illustrates these four quadrants of personal awareness.) Past awareness requires logic and memory, which constitute the left brain. Future

---

[6] In 1936, Alan Turing described a simple mathematical model of a computer. The Turing machine is equivalent in computing power to the digital computer as we know it today [Hopcroft79].

[7] Contributed by engineering manager Tom Gorsuch. As part of a leadership workshop, Tom used the Herrmann Brain Dominance Instrument to create a metaphorical model of his thinking cap. Ned Herrmann's whole brain theory allocates the brain's specialized modes into four physiological structures [Herrmann96].

awareness requires emotion and imagination, which constitute the right brain. The quadrants of personal awareness are these.

❏ **Logic**. Cerebral left performs the disciplines of Plan, Work, and Measure. Logic helps you understand technical work and precisely measure variance from the plan. Using logic, we can reason about what we know. Cerebral left is the portion of the brain that gathers facts, analyzes issues, and solves problems logically. Words that describe people who prefer to use their cerebral left brain include *factual, logical, rational, theoretical*, and *mathematical*.

❏ **Memory.** Limbic left performs the disciplines of Plan, Measure, and Improve. Memory helps you develop detailed plans and procedures, organize and keep track of essential data, and maintain a standard of consistency. Using memory, we can learn from our experience. Limbic left is the portion of the brain that approaches problems practically and implements projects in a timely manner. Words that describe people who prefer to use their limbic left brain include *ordered, detailed, sequential, controlled*, and *conservative*.

❏ **Emotion.** Cerebral right performs the disciplines of Plan, Work, and Discover. Emotion helps you challenge established policies, solve problems in intuitive ways, and recognize new possibilities. Using emotion, we can interpret our feelings about what we do not know. We can determine our fear of the unknown and develop valuable insight through these perceptions. Cerebral right is the portion of the brain that reads signs of coming change, tolerates ambiguity, helps you see the big picture, and integrates ideas. Words that describe people who prefer to use their cerebral right brain include *musical, spiritual, talkative, emotional*, and *empathetic*.

❏ **Imagination**. Limbic right performs the disciplines of Plan, Discover, and Envision. Imagination helps you develop a vision based on your discovery. Using imagination, we can conceive new ways of living. Limbic right is the portion of the brain that anticipates how others will feel, considers values, and engenders enthusiasm. Words that describe people who prefer to use their limbic right brain include *artistic, holistic, flexible, imaginative*, and *synthesizing*.

1.3.2 Risk and Personal Progress

Risk is a consequence of the uncertainty in our work, not a reflection of our own ability. As shown in Figure 1.6, software risk exists in the uncertainty of what it will take to complete an assigned task. For any given task, risk is bounded by the progress made toward task completion and the actual task completion. Progress is the movement toward a goal. Risk, like status, is relative to a specific

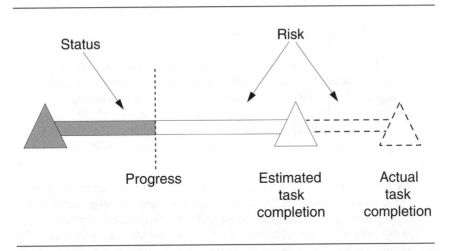

FIGURE 1.6   Risk and scheduled task completion. Risk exists in the unknowns of the work remaining to complete a task. Risk also exists in the work plan, because the plan approximates the time and effort required for task completion. This diagram shows how a task estimated to take three months to accomplish may actually take four months to complete without risk management.

goal (in this example, the goal is task completion). Whereas status is a measure of progress toward a goal, risk is a measure of the probability and consequence of not achieving the goal (an unsatisfactory outcome). Risk is neither more nor less important than work, but rather is one of the obstacles remaining to achieve the goal. *We make no progress without conquering risk.* This means that if risk has not been resolved in previous work, the reported progress may be at risk. Although we may believe that our status is correct, risk exists whether or not we acknowledge it.

Our professional goals usually include meeting technical requirements and managing project constraints. As a practitioner, I was given three months to design software for a fingerprint-matching subsystem. My goal on the project was to architect this functionality according to the given schedule. My risk was anything that could prevent me from achieving my project goal. To achieve the project goal, I had to use an engineering process, a development system, and my knowledge. Whether your goal is making money from software or making fully functional software, risk is an important concept. Thus, risk management is essential to software managers and technical staff—teams and individuals—who inherit risk as an attribute of their assigned work. To be successful, we must manage software risks.

1.4   Consequences of Knowledge

From the study of risk in software development come awareness and improved understanding in how we think about risk. What are the consequences of this knowledge? What is the opportunity provided by this knowledge?

Knowledge of the 6-D Model and its implication for effective behavior requires an orientation of organizational priorities toward using the six disciplines and recognizing individual intelligence. These priorities are briefly described as follows.

❏ **Six disciplines.** An orientation toward mastery of the six basic disciplines. These fundamentals support all project roles. Specialization requires that there is a manager who plans, an engineer who works, and a measurement analyst who measures. This specialization does not abdicate our responsibility for learning and using the six disciplines regardless of our assigned task. At the individual level, we use all six disciplines to function each day. We should evolve a basic capability in each discipline concurrently, rather than attempt to master the disciplines one at a time.[8]

❏ **Individual intelligence.** An orientation toward the use of individual preference in work assignments. Trying to fit "square" people into "round" jobs reduces the effectiveness of both the individual and the organization. Individual contribution is the key to high-performance teams and profitable organizations. Organizations must recognize the strengths of people who make a contribution by using their brains. People's brain dominance (either left or right hemisphere) determines their preference, which ultimately determines their capability. From utility theory we know that preference also determines our tolerance for risk, which affects the way we make decisions under uncertainty. We must understand our own preference and that of our coworkers, because at work we rarely resolve risk in isolation.

Knowledge of the sixth discipline, Discover, requires an orientation of personal priorities toward utilizing a creative process and risk management. These priorities are briefly described as follows:

❏ **A creative process.** An orientation toward repeatable creativity. The next "killer app" (that is, awesome software application program) will more likely be the result of creativity than a scientific experiment. People who prefer to use their right brain can use a creative process for repeatable results. People who prefer to use their left brain can use this process to expand their thinking and achieve results that are similar to their creative counterparts.

---

[8] This approach to education is similar to learning successive grade levels of English, math, and science in elementary school.

❑ **Risk management.** An orientation toward awareness of the future and our ability to bring the desired future into reality. Time spent understanding the past has diminishing returns when rapid change renders the past obsolete. While software risk exists independent of our individual ability, how we manage that risk does reflect our level of intelligence. The remainder of this book is a practical guide to software risk management.

1.5 Consequences of Ignorance

There was a time when I did not consider risk management as a valuable practice. Unfortunately, I realized the value too late, having invested wealth from my software business poorly due to a lack of financial risk management. From my personal loss, I gained a passion to apply risk management to all areas of my life and to help others understand the consequences of life without risk management. But many people remain in the dark ages and are unaware of the knowledge of risk in software development. What are the consequences of this blissful ignorance? What is the opportunity that is lost by this lack of knowledge? By not doing risk management, you risk the following:

❑ **Lack of skills.** You will miss the knowledge of risk management principles, methods, and tools to grapple with risk.

❑ **Lost opportunity.** You miss an opportunity because you are unable to perceive it. Without knowing the risk, you cannot assess the opportunity.

❑ **Suffer from mistakes.** You increase your chances of blundering into a bad situation because you do not control your risks. You become more afraid to take needed chances. Eventually you stop trying—the only sure way to fail.

❑ **Pain of regret.** You make a conscious decision to remain in the dark ages. One day, the pain of regret will weigh more than the pain of learning and practicing risk management.

1.6 Summary

In this chapter, I used the simple notation L^2 to denote that we measure risk exposure by multiplying likelihood times loss. I defined software risk management as a practice of assessing and controlling risk affecting the software project, process, or product. Since the advent of the risk-driven Spiral Model, risk management has been recognized as an important activity for software projects. Software risk management is necessary for managing and developing software systems.

❏ Software risk is inherent in our work.

❏ Software risk increases as system complexity increases.

❏ Software risk prevents us from achieving our goals and objectives.

Risk fits into the big picture of managing product development as an input to the planning discipline. That is why risk is closely associated with the planning process. The discipline to transform uncertainty into risk is a discovery process, which is quite different from a planning process. I described the Six-Discipline (6-D) Model that enhances W. Edwards Deming's evolutionary improvement model *by addressing the revolutionary concept of risk*. The six disciplines of the 6-D Model follow.

1. Envision the product.

2. Plan the work.

3. Work the plan.

4. Measure the work.

5. Improve the process.

6. Discover the possibilities.

I showed how to create opportunity by applying persistence to the possibilities. You may discover the possibilities by searching for them. Perhaps you will find the possibilities in the middle of your difficulty—your risks. You need only to manage them to create opportunity—your good outcomes.

1.7   Questions for Discussion

1. Do you think you should perform software risk management regularly throughout a project life cycle? Explain your answer.

2. What is a discipline? Describe the two disciplines of the 6-D Model that integrate risk into product development.

3. In what way is risk assessment a discovery process? List three items you might observe in a risk assessment at each phase of software development: requirements, design, code, and test. Give an example of a risk for each item you have observed.

4. Compare and contrast risk and risk management. Do you agree that software risk is independent of our individual ability? Discuss why you do or do not agree.

5. In your opinion, what is the power of the 6-D Model at the personal level? Describe your preference for using your left or right brain. Discuss the disciplines that are your

strengths. Explain how an understanding of personal strengths can help a person find the right career path.

6. What is the relationship between risk and progress? Do you agree that you need to manage risk to make progress? Discuss why you do or do not agree.

7. Does the 6-D Model change how you think about risk? If so, what difference do you think that will make in the way you work?

8. Who should use risk management? How would software engineers benefit from applying risk management to their work?

9. Why should risk management be used? Identify the benefits of using risk management on software projects. Discuss the extent to which you need risk management in your current assignment.

10. What is the difference between risk and opportunity? Explain your answer.

1.8 References

[AirForce88] Air Force. *Software Risk Abatement*. AFSC/AFLC pamphlet 800-45. Wright-Patterson Air Force Base, OH: Air Force Systems Command, Air Force Logistics Command, 1988.

[American85] *The American Heritage Dictionary*. 2d college ed., Boston: Houghton Mifflin, 1985.

[Babel90] Babel P. *Software Development Integrity Project*. Video. Herndon, VA: Software Productivity Consortium, 1990.

[Barker87] Barker J. *Discovering the Future: The Power of Vision*. Video. Burnsville, MN: Chart House Int., 1987.

[Basili95] Basili V. "The Experience Factory and Its Relationship to Other Quality Approaches." *Advances in Computers*, Vol. 41. Academic Press, 1995.

[Bayes63] Bayes T. "An Essay Towards Solving a Problem in the Doctrine of Chances." *Philosophical Transactions*. Essay LII. 1763.

[Bernoulli38] Bernoulli D. "Specimen Theoriae Novae de Mensura Sortis (Exposition of a New Theory on the Measurement of Risk)." Translated from the Latin by Louise Sommer in *Econometrica*, 22:23–36, 1954.

[Bernstein96] Bernstein Peter L. *Against the Gods: The Remarkable Story of Risk*. New York: Wiley 1996.

[Boehm88] Boehm B. "A Spiral Model of Software Development and Enhancement." *IEEE Computer* 21(5) (1988): 61–72, 1988.

[Carr93] Carr M, Konda S, Monarch I, Ulrich F, Walker C. Taxonomy Based Risk Identification. Technical report CMU/SEI-93-TR-6. Pittsburgh, PA: Software Engineering Institute, Carnegie Mellon University, 1993.

[Champy95] Champy J. *Reengineering Management*. New York: Harper-Collins, 1995.

[Clemen91] Clemen R. *Making Hard Decisions: An Introduction to Decision Analysis*. Belmont, CA: Wadsworth, 1991.

[David62] David. *Games, Gods, and Gambling*. New York: Hafner Publishing, 1962.

[Deming86] Deming W. *Out of the Crisis*. Cambridge, MA: MIT Center for Advanced Engineering Study, 1986.

[DSMC83] Defense Systems Management College. *Risk Assessment Techniques*. Fort Belvoir, VA, 1983.

[Fincher89] Fincher J. *The Brain: Mystery of Matter and Mind*. Washington, DC: U.S. News Books, 1989.

[Frankford93] Frankford R. (ed.). *Software Development Capability Evaluation*. AFMC pamphlet 800-61. Wright-Patterson Air Force Base, OH: Air Force Material Command, 1993.

[Gates95] Gates W. *The Road Ahead*. New York: Viking, 1995.

[Giarratano89] Giarratano J, Riley G. *Expert Systems Principles and Programming*. Boston: PWS-KENT Publishing, 1989.

[Groebner93] Groebner D, Shannon P. *Business Statistics: A Decision-Making Approach*. 4th ed. New York: Macmillan, 1993.

[Hall97] Hall E, Gorsuch T. "A Sixth Discipline for Future Awareness." *Proc.* Seventh International Symposium of the International Council on Systems Engineering, Los Angeles, August 1997.

[Hall95] Hall E. "Formal Risk Management: #1 Software Acquisition Best Practice." *Proc.* 4th SEI Conference on Software Risk, Monterey, CA, November 1995.

[Hammer93] Hammer M, Champy J. *Reengineering the Corporation*. New York: Harper-Collins, 1993.

[Herrmann96] Herrmann N. *The Whole Brain Business Book*. New York: McGraw-Hill, 1996.

[Hopcroft79] Hopcroft J. and Ullman J. *Introduction to Automata Theory, Languages, and Computation*. Reading, MA: Addison-Wesley, 1979.

[Humphrey95] Humphrey W. *A Discipline for Software Engineering*. Reading, MA: Addison-Wesley, 1995.

[Kolarik95] Kolarik W. *Creating Quality: Concepts, Systems, Strategies, and Tools*. New York: McGraw-Hill, 1995.

[Luger89] Luger G, Stubblefield W. *Artificial Intelligence and the Design of Expert Systems*. Redwood City, CA: Benjamin/Cummings Publishing, 1989.

[Markowitz52] Markowitz H. "Portfolio Selection." *Journal of Finance*, Vol. VII, No. 1 (March), pp. 77–91, 1952.

[Naur69] Naur P, Randell B. *Software Engineering: A Report on a Conference Sponsored by the NATO Science Committee*. NATO, 1969.

[Paulk93] Paulk M, et al. Capability Maturity Model for Software. Version 1.1. Technical report CMU/SEI-93-TR-24. Pittsburgh, PA: Software Engineering Institute, Carnegie Mellon University, 1993.

[Peters87] Peters T. *Thriving on Chaos*. New York: HarperCollins, 1987.

[Pressman92] Pressman R. *Software Engineering: A Practitioner's Approach*. New York: McGraw-Hill, 1992.

[Rebello96] Rebello K. "Inside Microsoft." *BusinessWeek*, July 15, 1996.

[Senge90] Senge P. *The Fifth Discipline: The Art & Practice of the Learning Organization*. Garden City, NY: Doubleday, 1990.

[VanScoy92] VanScoy R. Software development risk: Problem or opportunity. Technical report CMU/SEI-92-TR-30. Pittsburgh, PA: Software Engineering Institute, Carnegie Mellon University, 1992.

2

P²I² Success Formula

Failure is often the first necessary step toward success. If we do not take the risk of failing, we will not get the chance to succeed. When we are trying, we are winning.
—Wynn Davis

What does it take to manage software risk? In 1992, I thought I knew the answer to that question. As the leader of a software risk management action team, my objectives, as stated in the process improvement plan, were clear: "Evaluate and enhance risk management practices from both a software and a programwide point of view, incorporate recommendations into command media, and develop training to comply with SEI CMM Level 3." As a full-time member of the Software Engineering Process Group (SEPG), I was charged with improving the software process for the Information Systems Division at Harris Corporation. It would be a challenge to assemble a cross-functional team of division practitioners to agree on risk management practices. That was just the beginning of my role in the software community as a **risk management champion**.

A champion is a change agent: someone who maintains focus on the goal, strives to overcome obstacles, and refuses to give up when the going gets rough [Humphrey89]. As a risk management champion, I have refined risk management practices using my experience in applying an ivory tower–conceived process to software projects within industry and government [Hall95]. The key to sharing lessons learned from this experience is the feedback I have received from people who participated in learning and trying the new methods. From my perspective, both the success and the failure of the methods were significant in providing insight into the success formula for managing software risk that I present in this chapter.

In this chapter, I describe the major factors that affect **risk management capability**, which is the range of expected results that can be achieved by implementing a risk management process within an organization. I provide insights and lessons learned the hard way to help you avoid the pitfalls of adopting risk management.

This chapter answers the following questions:

❑ What are the four major factors in risk management capability?

❑ How can you overcome the barriers to adoption of risk management?

❑ Why is the risk management process necessary but not sufficient?

2.1   Major Factors in Risk Management Capability

Successful project managers maintain a focus on their project's critical success factors [Boehm91]. Similarly, to manage risk successfully, we should maintain focus on the four critical success factors of risk management—people, process, infrastructure, and implementation—denoted by the $\mathbf{P^2I^2}$ **Success Formula** (see Figure 2.1).

People participate in managing risk by implementing the risk management process according to the risk management plan. As long as people engineer software systems, they will be a critical factor in communicating the issues, concerns, and uncertainties in their work that translate to risk. Section 2.2 describes key points of the human side of risk management. Part V of this book details case studies of how people work together to manage software risk.

Process transforms uncertainty (the input) into acceptable risk (the output) through risk management activities. Process is a major factor in risk management capability because it describes the steps to predictable risk management results. Section 2.3 describes key points of the process dimension of risk management. Part II of this book addresses the risk management process in detail.

Infrastructure specifies how the organization requires the use of risk management on projects by establishing policy and standards. Infrastructure is a major factor in risk management capability because it establishes the culture that supports use of risk management. Section 2.4 describes key points of the infrastructure dimension of risk management. Part III of this book addresses the risk management infrastructure in detail.

Implementation is the plan and methodology used to perform risk management on a specific project. Implementation is a major factor in risk management

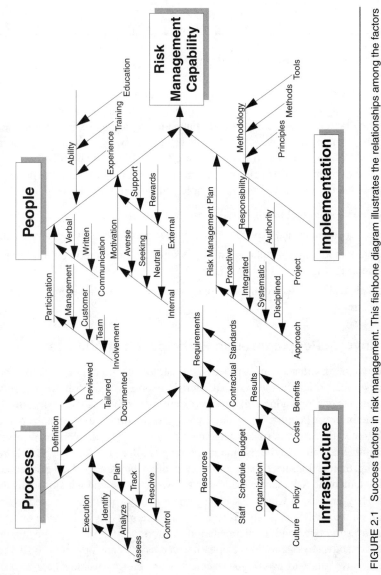

FIGURE 2.1   Success factors in risk management. This fishbone diagram illustrates the relationships among the factors that may influence an organization's ability to manage risk. The success formula P^{2}I^2 denotes these four major factors: people, process, infrastructure, and implementation.

capability because it assigns to the project the responsibility and authority to execute the plan. Section 2.5 describes key points of the implementation dimension of risk management. Part IV of this book addresses the risk management implementation in detail.

2.2   People: The Human Element

The people factors of participation, ability, and motivation describe the human element in managing risk. Participation of management, customer, and technical team is a key factor to the success of communication regarding risk. The ability of individuals in managing risk will vary. Nevertheless, everyone must develop a minimum skill level in order to manage risk effectively. Motivation is the force that drives the continued use of risk management throughout the life of the project. The key points to remember regarding people and risk are the following:

- ❑ Involve people at all levels in risk management activities.
- ❑ Education, training, and experience contribute to people's ability to manage risk.
- ❑ People's motivation for change must be sufficient to overcome the barriers to adopting something new.
- ❑ Individuals have risk preferences that you can use to predict their behavior.

2.2.1   Involve People through Participation at All Levels

People drive the risk management process, infrastructure, and implementation and thus are the most critical factor in managing risk. People who contribute to quality circles, action teams, or engineering process groups may drive the risk management process definition. People in senior management drive the organizational infrastructure with respect to risk management policy. Those who work on projects drive the implementation of the risk management plan. Because different people are contributing, their actions need to be coordinated; often they are not. I have observed people implementing risk management with a flawed process and without adequate training. They may use a vague risk management policy without automated tools, then learn on the job as necessary. Through trial and error, they will figure out the process, infrastructure, and implementation. Unfortunately, most improvement programs for software organizations emphasize process or technology, not people. For a comprehensive guide to people management, I recommend reading *Peopleware: Productive Projects and Teams* [DeMarco87] and *People Capability Maturity Model* (P-CMM[SM]), which provides a focus on developing an organization's talent [Curtis95].

There is no substitute for people. Only people make decisions; without them risk management would not happen.

Assessments of a particular risk vary, depending on job category and level within the project hierarchy. Whereas management is focused on the project profit equation, the technical staff has primary responsibility for the software product. Each person has a specific task assignment, and the risks that concern an individual will be relative to his or her task success criteria. Customers, subcontractors, and end users have different perspectives that may contribute to a more complete picture of the software risk.

People at all levels can contribute to managing risk by identifying the uncertainty with respect to their assigned tasks. An example of communication of risk occurs in group discussions during risk assessments. When project managers are involved in a risk assessment, they usually identify risks in cost and schedule or their customer relations. In their words, aggressive schedules on fixed budgets and lack of customer involvement can be hazardous to the health of their project. Project team members identify technical risks, which are often the source of cost and schedule risks. If you ask the technical staff, they might say changing requirements is a risk. They have an increased awareness of deficiencies in the process, as is evident when they say their risk includes poorly conceived processes and lack of a development methodology.[1] Customers, when they are involved, typically identify risks in the management process, scarce resources, and anticipated requirements growth. Customers have said that the decision-making process is not rigorous and that proper attention is not given to obtaining an accurate estimation of the scope of the work. At lower levels in the project hierarchy, individuals have more detailed information that may not be visible from the top. Knowing the job category of the person to whom you are talking (e.g., quality assurance, configuration management) will give you a good indication of that person's area of concern.

It may be necessary to broaden your definition of team to include all people who have the ability to affect the project. Try communicating risk to this expanded set of team members, and note the short-term and long-term effects. Briefing the customer (also sponsors, investors, clients, or users) and upper management (also functional management, senior management, or board members) on risk assessment results may be a strategic move for project managers. Although there may be initial shock that "the project might not be as easy as we had hoped," expanding the team to encompass customers and upper management will enable cooperative project management (**project management** is the management team responsible

---

[1] Process risk has been consistently one of the top five risks identified during risk assessments in the 1990s, a change from the 1980s [Boehm89], when process was not in the top ten risk list. SEI can be credited with increasing the awareness of the importance of process in developing a quality software product.

for the execution of the project) and allow you to manage risks outside the project locus of control. Including organizational management in the project team worked in the following case study of Project X.

> At the Project X briefing on risk assessment results, the engineering director shook his head with a look of bewilderment on his face. He could not believe that his newest project had over 100 risk issues identified—and less than a month after the contract award. When the initial disappointment had worn off, this director worked closely with the project manager to support the project at the organizational level. One risk identified during the risk assessment was a concern that the team was not physically located together. With the support of the engineering director, the project team moved to a new location.
>
> At project completion, the project manager gave a retrospective review of lessons learned. One was that colocation had worked well for relocated people. Those functions not colocated, product design and drafting, appeared less responsive to the needs of the team. In addition to reporting good project team cooperation and relationship, the project manager also mentioned positive customer attitude and working relationship.

In this case, participation by an extended project team in managing risks had included organizational management and the customer. Although we cannot attribute this project's success to risk management exclusively, we can observe that communication of risk issues may be difficult at first, but may encourage success in the long run.

2.2.2   Develop the Ability to Manage Risk

Education, training, and experience contribute to a person's ability to manage risk. Education begins with the awareness that risk is inherent in all large software systems—and the understanding that an increase in system complexity translates to an increase in risk. Consider the following conversation I had with Ned, a systems engineer and technical leader. After the proposal team assessed its top ten design risks, Ned said to me, "We need another number two risk. If we are SEI Level 3, then software development should not be the number two risk." "Ned," I said slowly, "the customer knows. They know that software development is a risk. That is why they require SEI Level 3 contractors. SEI Level 3 does not make risk go away. It just means that your organization is better prepared to handle the risk."

When people know that risk is present, they can begin to search for it, discover it, and deal with it. Education is general knowledge about risk—including a history of why and how risk management has been applied to software systems. Education might include comparing the uses of risk management concepts in various industries, such as finance and insurance, with uses in the software community. It might also include studies of risks and risk strategies in various software application domains. When would anyone have a use for general knowledge about risk management? When managing risk without precedents. Imagine that you must reconcile a 30 percent probability of failing to meet a success criterion with a customer, who has your company's 100 percent commitment to meet all contractual requirements. How will you justify 30 percent probability when you have no historical sample of similar events?[2] There are numerous perplexities of risk management that require applied intelligence. Education helps us to gain the basics that we need to reason about risks.

Training in basic risk concepts provides a vocabulary that the project team uses to communicate risk issues effectively and conveys specific knowledge about particular risks and known risk strategies. Training should encompass the methods of the risk management process and practice using those methods on current issues facing the project. Such practice doubles as an exercise in team building. In other words, risk management is a productive team-building activity. Advanced training—learning a risk analysis tool or learning how to conduct a risk assessment, for example—should be reserved for individuals performing these specific tasks.

Without proper preparation through education and training, you should not expect any new method to be accepted. Even with preparation, there is no substitute for experience, and experience often results in both success and failure. The key is to learn from your experience by asking three questions: "What worked?" "What did not work?" and "What can be improved?" Documenting the answers to these questions ensures that you will learn from your experience and will be able to share your knowledge to benefit other people.

2.2.3   Provide Motivation to Overcome the Barriers

Your organization's motivation for change to the use of risk management must be sufficient to overcome the barriers to adoption. Even if an organization has many receptive people, change still takes time. Changes in skills or procedures may take only weeks, but changes in structure can take months, and changes in strategy and culture may take years. The longer it takes to change the organization, the harder it is to sustain the change. Compelling reasons that change is needed provide motivation for the use of risk management. Although there are many good reasons to manage risks, simply pushing the positive benefits for change can have the opposite effect. It is often more helpful to remove barriers.

Force field analysis is a technique to help people understand the positive and negative aspects of change. The force field analysis shown in Table 2.1 identifies the positives and negatives of adopting risk management. This technique helps people

---

[2] Never attempt to justify a number that has no basis in reality. Discuss the issue by substituting words (e.g., *unlikely, probably not,* or *little chance*) for the numerical percentage that may not be accurate.

TABLE 2.1   FORCE FIELD FOR RISK MANAGEMENT ADOPTION

Driving Forces	Restraining Forces
Provides a focus on goals	Management lacks commitment
Satisfies customer requirements	People are resistant to change
Increases visibility for high-risk areas	The team has no time for training
Promotes communication of risks	The process levies extra work
Provides for risk-aware decisions	There is a lack of available tools
Helps resolve difficult issues	Attitudes toward risk are negative
Contributes to a more realistic plan	People are already too busy
Helps avoid surprises	Staff support is lacking
Helps prevent problems	Individuals fear retribution
Reduces rework	People fear failure

Note: Driving forces provide the reasons for risk management adoption; restraining forces are the barriers to adoption.

think about making the desired change a permanent one. It encourages them to identify internal and external forces that are drivers for the ideal situation [Brassard94]. In this case, the ideal situation is to manage risk routinely to achieve established goals. Teams should brainstorm their own list of forces to discover their reasons for adopting risk management and what work will be required to remove their barriers to adoption. The team should achieve consensus on the list of forces and their entries' relative rankings. Then the members can work to reinforce the driving forces while eliminating the restraining forces. Driving forces should provide the motivation to overcome the restraining forces.

There are two sources of motivation: internal and external. When they are motivated internally, people behave according to what they perceive is important. When they are motivated externally, they have received support and encouragement from an outside source. People are motivated to different degrees through both internal and external sources. Only people who are appropriately motivated will continue to assess and control software risk. Progress in managing risk should be rewarded through periodic recognition, but the real reward comes from the opportunity to improve the work environment.

2.2.4   Use Risk Preference to Predict Behavior

Risk preference is an attitude toward risk that varies among people. Each person has a natural preference regarding risk that is based on his or her temperament.

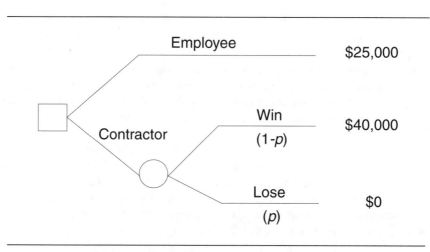

FIGURE 2.2   Decisions are made based on risk preference. This decision tree models one decision (the square) and one uncertain event (the circle). The decision to work as an employee for a guaranteed $25,000 or as a contractor for $40,000 depends on the probability (1-p) of winning a competitive bid. Given that the probability is unknown, you could predict what someone would decide if you knew their risk preference.

Genetics, experience, and body chemistry affect temperament. Temperament determines our behavior, because behavior is how we get what we want [Keirsey84]. Our own disposition is a basic drive that determines our actions, but these internal motivations are rooted in our subconscious desires. Basic temperament determines how an individual perceives risk. To create a risk-aware culture, we must understand and appreciate these differences among people. By knowing a person's risk preference, we can anticipate what choices he or she will make.

An associate recently asked for my advice on whether to accept a three-month assignment as a part-time employee or to work as a contractor. The human resources manager had offered the employee position, but a competitive bid would determine whether he could perform the work as a contractor. Figure 2.2 shows the decision tree that models his decision, the chance event, and the possible outcomes. A **decision tree** is a tool to structure difficult decisions to understand the available options. The tree flows from left to right; the immediate decision is represented by the square at the left side. The branches emanating from the square correspond to the two choices available: work as an employee or bid the job as a contractor. Only one option may be selected. If my associate decides to bid the job as a contractor, the next issue is whether the bid is won or lost. The circle represents this chance event. The branches emanating from the circle represent the possible outcomes. The bid can be either won or lost, but not both, and no other possibilities exist. The values of these outcomes are specified at the ends of the branches. If the bid is accepted, my associate will earn 62.5 percent more for the same work. If the bid is not accepted, he will have to find other work. If he decides to work as an employee, he would earn a more typical salary with standard benefits. These outcomes are shown at the ends of the branches at the right. Which would you choose?

To learn how to recognize your own risk preference, review the decision tree model, select between the two alternatives, and then document the rationale you used to make your decision. Your attitude toward risk can be categorized as *risk averse*, *risk seeking*, or *risk neutral*.

You are **risk averse** if you have a conservative risk attitude with a preference for secure payoffs. People who are risk averse make good middle managers, administrators, and engineers. If you are risk averse, you are practical, accepting, and have common sense. You enjoy facts more than theories, and support established methods of working. Remembering, persevering, and building are activities at which you excel. You agree with the following statements:

- ❏ I like being dependable, and I am usually punctual.
- ❏ I am not likely to take chances.
- ❏ I am responsible and prefer to work efficiently.
- ❏ I am more service oriented than self oriented.
- ❏ I value institutions and observe traditions.

If you are risk averse, your decision in the problem presented in Figure 2.2 will be sensible and realistic: to work as an employee. The unknown probability associated with the choice of working as a contractor would make that decision uncomfortable for you.

You are **risk seeking** if you have a liberal risk attitude with a preference for speculative payoffs. People who are risk seeking make good entrepreneurs and negotiators. If you are risk seeking, you are adaptable and resourceful. You enjoy life and are not afraid to take action. Performing, acting, and taking risks are activities at which you excel. You agree with the following statements:

- ❏ I like action, and I act impulsively at times.
- ❏ I seek excitement for the thrill of the experience.
- ❏ I am resourceful and prefer not to plan or prepare.
- ❏ I am more self oriented than service oriented.
- ❏ I like to anticipate another person's position.

If you are risk seeking, your decision in the problem presented in Figure 2.2 will be optimistic and fearless: to work as a contractor. You may not get the job, but if you do, the payoff will be worth it.

You are **risk neutral** if you have an impartial risk attitude with a preference for future payoffs. People who are risk neutral make good executives, system architects, and group leaders. Risk-neutral types are neither risk seeking nor risk averse, but rather seek strategies and tactics that have high future payoff. If you are risk neutral, you think abstractly and creatively and envision the possibilities. You enjoy ideas and are not afraid of change or the unknown. Learning, imagining, and inventing are activities at which you excel. You agree with the following statements:

- ❏ I trust my intuition, and I am comfortable with the unknown.
- ❏ I think about the future and have long-range objectives.
- ❏ I am naturally curious and often ask, "Why?"
- ❏ I enjoy generating new ideas.
- ❏ I work best when I am inspired.

If you are risk neutral, your decision in the problem presented in Figure 2.2 will be based on what you believe will bring long-term benefits (e.g., career growth or an opportunity to travel). The monetary differential in the short term will not be the deciding factor.

2.3 Process: The Steps to Manage Risk

Process is a set of activities and mechanisms that people use to transform inputs to outputs. The process factors of *definition* and *execution* describe the standard steps to manage risk. The **risk management process** is a systematic and structured way to manage risks that includes the activities and mechanisms used to transform project knowledge into decision-making information. Activities describe the steps to transform uncertainty into acceptable risk. Mechanisms are the means that we use to accomplish each process activity. The key points to remember regarding the risk management process are the following:

- ❏ There are five process elements in the risk management process.
- ❏ The standard process is not one size fits all.
- ❏ The defined process should be flexible.
- ❏ The process execution must be cost-effective.

2.3.1 Learn the Five Process Elements

There are five essential elements of the risk management process:

1. *Identify*—identifying risk and sources of risk. When people have trouble discussing risk, we should ask them instead about their concerns, doubts, issues, and

uncertainties. Because identifying perceived risk is difficult for most people, frame risk in terms of the unknowns that may prevent them from achieving their goals. For example, ask, "What are your assumptions?" instead of "What are your risks?"

2. *Analyze*—analyzing risk based on established criteria. Estimate the probability and consequence of a risk, and evaluate the risk with respect to all the identified risks.

3. *Plan*—planning the next task to resolve a risk. Develop alternative strategies for risk resolution, and define a risk action plan for the selected approach. Establish thresholds that help you determine when to execute a risk action plan.

4. *Track*—monitoring planned thresholds and risk status. Compare thresholds to status to determine variances. Use triggers to provide early warning to implement the risk action plan while there is time to resolve the risk. Report risk measures and metrics.

5. *Resolve*—responding to notification of triggering events, executing the risk action plan, and reporting results of risk resolution efforts until the level of risk is acceptable.

Every risk management process has two primary components: assess and control [Boehm89]. Identify and analyze are process elements of risk assessment. Plan, track, and resolve are process elements of risk control. Risk control is a by-product of successful risk resolution.

2.3.2   Design a Scaleable Process

A standard risk management process is valuable because it serves as a reusable component for an organization and can save projects months of time spent writing procedures. One lesson that I learned by adapting a standard process to projects valued at $10 million to $100 million is that *process is not "one size fits all."* Because projects vary in size, scope, and budget, we cannot expect that one standard process will fit every project. The requirement for flexibility in a reusable process component can be addressed by developing a minimum standard process required of the smallest project in the organization and designing tailoring recommendations that will scale the standard process to meet the needs of the largest project.

2.3.3   Define a Flexible Process

Projects should define a tailored version of the standard process to meet their individual needs. Tailoring allows for flexibility and for unique style. One project I worked on had biweekly videoteleconferencing risk management meetings. Another large project assigned a risk manager to coordinate the identified risks of several integrated product teams. Many innovative process improvements can be made by projects given a flexible process. The standard process is defined when it is described in terms of inputs, activities, outputs, and mechanisms that the project will use. The process definition is reviewed by the people on the project who are required to use the process. The peer review activity uses a checklist of quality criteria to evaluate the process. The process definition determines the effectiveness of the risk management process. There must be a feedback mechanism from the project's process users back to the standard process maintainer, so that the process can be improved for the entire organization.

2.3.4   Execute a Cost-Effective Process

The risk management process must be cost-effective. As shown in Figure 2.3, a cost-effective process balances risk resolution and risk acceptance. We must weigh the cost of risk control against the expected loss without risk control. As risk increases, exposure to loss increases. Risk decreases with the cost of risk control. Even if a cost-effective risk management process exists, the risk and expected loss increase if it is not used. If it is to be cost-effective, a process that is used routinely must be streamlined. An optimal process will minimize total costs.

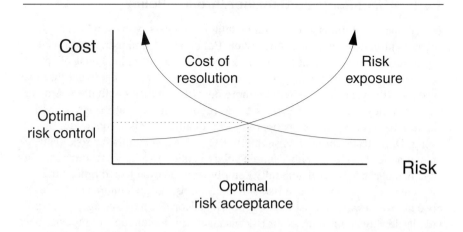

FIGURE 2.3   An optimized risk management process. Overall cost and risk are minimized through cost-effective risk resolution. Without attention to software risk, the exposure to risk increases.

2.4   Infrastructure: The Organizational Foundation

Infrastructure is the organizational foundation that is needed to establish a risk-aware culture. Four infrastructure factors describe the enterprise support required to manage risk:

1. *Organization*—the way that we establish an environment that supports effective working relations.
2. *Requirements*—the minimum standard for projects.
3. *Resources*—the investment required to manage risk.
4. *Results*—the return on investment for managing risk.

The key points to remember regarding the risk management infrastructure are the following:

❑ Senior managers' values affect people's behavior through policies.

❑ Customers and senior managers set expectations for project behavior through requirements.

❑ You resolve risks through the application of resources (e.g., budget, schedule, and staff).

❑ You determine the business case for risk management through cost-benefit analysis.

2.4.1   Affect People's Behavior through Policy

The company culture is a reflection of senior managers' values, which are documented in policies that affect behavior. **Policy** is an administrative procedure or guiding principle designed to influence people to a particular course of action. For example, if senior managers believe that "you can manage what you can measure," the project goals will be more quantitative than qualitative. A documented policy might require risks to be reported at project reviews—with a quantitative risk exposure, as opposed to a qualitative high, moderate, or low rating. Organizational leaders should not set the expectations for risk management practices too low. With a simple policy in place to address risk in a responsible manner, people will generally comply with the established procedure.

Once a policy to manage risk is in place, a risk-aware culture can be developed in several ways. Infrastructure is developed top down by managers, who provide leadership and resources for risk management; bottom up by empowerment of the workforce and rewards for positive results; and sideways by the definition of roles and responsibilities in the organization chart—the horizontal relationships. These relationships may not be defined explicitly in the organization chart, but they usually exist between software engineering and other engineering disciplines (systems, hardware, and test). Integrated product teams (IPTs) help to define the horizontal relationships within a single IPT, but be sure to define how IPTs work together to resolve interrelated risk. A policy for risk management is presented in Chapter 9.

2.4.2 Set Expectations for Project Behavior

Through requirements, customers and senior managers set the expectations for project behavior. Requirements for risk management are often defined by the contract and statement of work, which specify deliverables such as a risk management plan. Systems engineering standards that specify risk management include IEEE 1220 and EIA 632, Processes for Engineering a System.[3] Software development standards that address risk include DoD's MIL-STD-498, ISO 9000-3, and the IEEE Software Project Management Plan.

MIL-STD-498 is a standard for software development and documentation that replaced the document-driven standards DoD-STD-1703, DoD-STD-7935A, and DoD-STD-2167A, which required contractors to document and implement procedures for risk management but was silent on when to perform risk management. MIL-STD-498 is an improvement over its predecessors because it specifically states that risk management is performed throughout development through identification, analysis, and prioritization of technical, cost, and schedule risk areas. MIL-STD-498 states that strategies for risk management must be developed, recorded, and implemented [DoD94].

The U.S. commercial version of MIL-STD-498 is EIA/IEEE J-STD-016 Software Development. The DoD plans to incorporate MIL-STD-498 into an international commercial standard, ISO/IEC 12207 [McPherson95]. The U.S. implementation of this international standard for software life cycle processes is IEEE/EIA 12207. These improved standards preserve the heritage of risk management as a software development requirement.

The ISO 9000 series of standards is a set of documents, promulgated by the International Standards Organization (ISO), a worldwide federation of national standards bodies, that specifies quality system requirements. The ISO 9001 standard applies to software. ISO 9000-3 is a guideline for the application of ISO 9001 to the development, supply, and maintenance of software; it is an international standard for quality management and quality assurance of software. The guidelines are intended to suggest controls and methods for producing software that

---

[3] Development of EIA 632 was accomplished as a joint project of the Electronic Industries Association (EIA), the Institute of Electrical and Electronics Engineers (IEEE), and the International Council on Systems Engineering (INCOSE) [Martin97].

meets requirements by preventing nonconformity at all stages of development. If your software company has a requirement for ISO conformance, then you have a requirement for risk management. Four guidelines specifically address risk:

1. *Corrective action.* The supplier should establish, document, and maintain procedures for investigating the cause of nonconforming products and the corrective action needed to prevent recurrence. It will initiate preventive actions to deal with problems to a level corresponding to the risks encountered.

2. *Contract review.* The supplier should review each contract to ensure that possible contingencies or risks are identified.

3. *Development plan.* The development plan should divide the work into phases, and identify and analyze the potential problems associated with the development phases and the achievement of the specified requirements.

4. *Design reviews.* The design or implementation process should not proceed until the consequences of all known deficiencies are satisfactorily resolved[4] or the risk of proceeding otherwise is known [ISO91].

The Institute of Electrical and Electronics Engineers (IEEE) standard for software project management plans was approved by the American National Standards Institute (ANSI). Risk management is a managerial process identified as follows in the Software Project Management Plan (SPMP):

> This subsection of the SPMP shall identify and assess the risk factors associated with the project. This subsection shall also prescribe mechanisms for tracking the various risk factors and implementing contingency plans. Risk factors that should be considered include contractual risks, technological risks, risks due to size and complexity of the product, risks in personnel acquisition and retention, and risks in achieving customer acceptance of the product. [IEEE88]

2.4.3 Apply Resources to Resolve Risk

Budget, schedule, staff, and other resources must be applied to resolve risk. Implementation of risk action plans may require funds for resolution approaches, such as market research or the use of redundant system components. Use of scarce resources is likely to cause additional stress to the project budget and schedule. Applying risk management helps to make difficult trade-offs to allocate resources effectively. For example, risk assessment findings have shown a correlation between funding risks and inefficient utilization of people. As one project found

---

[4] This instruction from ISO is confusing because we cannot resolve a consequence. I believe the intent is to resolve risk to an acceptable level.

out, using staff time to define roles and responsibilities clearly was a small price to pay for the increase in efficiency on the project.

2.4.4   Analyze Risk Management Costs and Benefits

The business case for risk management is based on **cost-benefit analysis**. If the cost to develop a risk management process is spread over ten projects, then benefits from process reuse can be estimated by the amount of time saved. Savings are measured in resources of time, money, and staff *not* expended on nine of ten projects. Cost is measured by the number of person-hours expended to develop the process. **Return on investment** (ROI) is the ratio of savings to cost that indicates the value provided.[5] The business case to develop a standard risk management process in the above example is justified at 10 to 1 ROI.

Without ROI data, senior managers must rely on testimonials of project managers and staff to judge the perceived benefits of risk management. Reliance on testimonials is built on trust and perception. Trust will erode over time unless perceptions are validated by ROI data. Chapter 8 presents a definition for measuring effectiveness of the risk management process: $ROI_{(RM)}$. Several uses of $ROI_{(RM)}$ are described in Chapter 18. Case studies in Chapters 22 and 23 report ROI using this standard measure.

2.5   Implementation: The Project Execution

Risk management can be implemented by steering committees, senior executives, business area teams, proposal teams, middle management, line management, or individuals. **Implementation**, as I discuss it in this book, is how a particular project executes risk management. The implementation factors of risk management plan and methodology describe how the risks are managed. The **risk management plan** maps resources to risk management activities to satisfy project requirements. **Methodology** is a set of underlying principles and methods particular to a branch of knowledge. Methods include the mechanisms, techniques, and automated tools that support the risk management implementation. The key points to remember regarding the risk management implementation are the following:

❑ Success begins with a high-quality plan.

❑ Projects have a unique personality that their methods reflect.

---

[5] Accountants define ROI as a ratio of **net income** to total assets.

2.5.1   Develop a High-Quality Risk Management Plan

Risk management implementation depends on the people in the project given responsibility and authority to execute the risk management plan. Success begins with a high-quality plan. The procedures for performing risk management on a project may be embodied in a documented risk management plan that describes the approach to managing risk on the project. The best approach is proactive, integrated, systematic, and disciplined.

Proactive.   Performing **proactive risk management** means taking the action required to assess and control risks to prevent problems on software projects [Hall95]. Getting the help you need to assess and control risks also is proactive. Projects beginning to incorporate risk management methods may need a facilitator for independence and motivation.[6] The independence provides an objective view of the project without attribution or blame to individuals whose areas of the project are inherently risky. Motivation is provided to the project in two ways: the facilitator has the knowledge to support a discussion of risks to assess risk situations, and his or her periodic appearance serves as a catalyst for use of risk management to progress toward project goals. You probably need the help of a facilitator when one of the following conditions exist:

- ❑ *Lack of time.* Most team members are too busy handling current problems.
- ❑ *Low ability.* Most team members are not confident assessing risk.
- ❑ *High attribution.* Most individuals are not comfortable discussing risk.

Integrated.   Risk management is integrated in a project when it is implemented as a part of the way that a product is produced. Risk is neither more nor less important than work but, rather, a part of the remaining task.[7] There is no "risk season" [VanScoy92] or a separate team to perform risk management. Risk management is integrated by distribution into routine project activities.

Systematic.   It is not enough to identify risk; you must follow through with risk resolution, or risks will turn into problems. Projects that emphasize risk assessment with no follow-through for risk control will have an unbalanced approach that does not systematically reduce risk. To create a more balanced approach,

---

[6] I recommend a facilitator when you lack the time or ability to do it yourself. Lack of ability may be either low skill level or the inability to be impartial.

[7] Risk exists in our work—our past, present, and future efforts. Past effort may contain the risk of misunderstood requirements, present effort may contain the risk of false assumptions, and our plan for future effort may contain the risk of uncertainty.

spend 20 percent of your time on risk assessment and 80 percent of your time on risk control. It is better to resolve a few risks than it is to identify many risks but do nothing with the risk information.

Disciplined.   A complete strategy is based on the six disciplines of the 6-D Model described in Chapter 1: Envision, Plan, Work, Measure, Improve, and Discover. Each discipline has principles and methods that you can use to develop an effective risk management approach. The developmental path for an individual's acquiring the skills to master any discipline is through unconscious inability, conscious inability, conscious ability, and unconscious ability. The developmental path for organizational learning is through initial contact, awareness, understanding, trial use, adoption, and institutionalization [Conner82].

2.5.2   Choose Methods That Reflect a Project's Personality

The methodology, the means for implementing the risk management process, encompasses specific principles, methods, and tools. *Principles* are the underlying rules used by those who work in a discipline (e.g., diversification). A *method* is a technique or other systematic procedure—for example, the mechanisms that implement the process (e.g., risk management form). *Tools* include the automated mechanisms used to execute risk management efficiently (e.g., risk database). Methods reflect the personality of the project because they are how projects choose to implement the process. Methods are the means to the end; as such, they present a variety of choices that may achieve similar results. The methods may be ad hoc or structured, simple or complex, team oriented or not, depending on how the project chooses to conduct business. The style of the project may mirror the individuals who constitute the project or may conform to the customer's style.

2.6   Summary

In this chapter, I discussed a success formula for managing software risk and described the major factors that affect risk management capability. The success formula for managing software risk is P^2I^2: people, process, infrastructure, and implementation.

People participate in managing risk by implementing the risk management process according to the risk management plan. As long as people engineer software systems, they will be a critical factor in communicating the issues, concerns, and uncertainties in their work that translate to risk.

Process transforms uncertainty (the input) into acceptable risk (the output) through risk management activities. Process is a major factor in risk management capability, because it describes the steps to predictable risk management results.

Infrastructure is the way that the enterprise requires the use of risk management on projects, such as by establishing a policy and standards. It is a major factor in risk management capability because it establishes the culture that supports the use of risk management.

Implementation is the methodology and plan used to perform risk management on a specific project. It is a major factor in risk management capability because it assigns to the project the responsibility and authority to execute the plan.

I used a force field analysis to show how to overcome the barriers to risk management adoption by identifying the positives and negatives of adopting risk management:

- List the driving forces (the reasons for adoption).
- List the restraining forces (the barriers to adoption).
- Reinforce the driving forces (the motivation).
- Eliminate the restraining forces (the effort).

The risk management process is necessary but not sufficient; it takes more than a risk management process to manage risk. Process is shelfware without project implementation. Implementation may not succeed without an organizational infrastructure that supports communication about risk. People are the common denominator in each dimension: process, implementation, and infrastructure. Ultimately, people manage risk.

2.7   Questions for Discussion

1. What are five ways that you could increase your participation, ability, and motivation to manage risk? Do you think this increase in capability to manage risk would change how you work? Explain your answer.

2. Compare and contrast education, training, and experience in risk management. Provide an outline for a lecture on the history of risk management, a hands-on seminar to learn a risk analysis tool, and a meeting agenda for managing software development risk.

3. List your top three barriers to managing risk. Describe a plan to reduce or eliminate each of these barriers. What test criteria would you use to evaluate your success?

4. List your top three reasons for adopting risk management. Describe your reasons in terms of their effect on quality, productivity, cost, and risk of software development.

5. You are the technical lead for a commercially available requirements management tool. Your supervisor has come to you for a make-or-buy decision: In the next tool release, should you develop an object-oriented database in-house, or use an existing third-party object-oriented database package? Use a decision tree to diagram decision, chance event, and outcome nodes. Discuss the parameters of this decision from three perspectives: risk averse, risk seeking, and risk neutral.

6. Do you agree that every risk management process has two primary components: risk assessment and risk control? Discuss why you do or do not agree.

7. Describe how to develop an infrastructure that would support a risk-aware culture from three perspectives: top down, bottom up, and sideways.

8. Develop the business case for risk management. Provide a hypothetical cost-benefit analysis. Was the return worth the investment? Discuss why it was or why it was not.

9. What are the relationships among the four major factors of the P²I² success formula for managing risk? Discuss the dependencies among the factors.

10. Give ten reasons that it is important to involve people at all levels of the project in managing risk. How could you ensure the participation of people at all levels?

2.8   References

[Boehm91] Boehm B. Software risk management: Principles and practices. *IEEE Software*, 8(1):32–41, 1991.

[Boehm89] Boehm B. *IEEE Tutorial on Software Risk Management*. New York: IEEE Computer Society Press, 1989.

[Brassard94] Brassard M, Ritter D. *The Memory Jogger II*. Methuen, MA: GOAL/QPC, 1994.

[Conner82] Conner D, Patterson R. Building Commitment to Organizational Change. *Training and Development Journal*, April, pp. 18–30, 1982.

[Curtis95] Curtis B, Hefley W, Miller S. People Capability Maturity Model. Technical report CMU/SEI-95-MM-002. Pittsburgh, PA: Software Engineering Institute, Carnegie Mellon University, 1995.

[Davis88] Davis, W. *The Best of Success*. Lombard, IL: Great Quotations, 1988.

[DeMarco87] DeMarco T, Lister T. *Peopleware: Productive Projects and Teams*, New York: Dorset House, 1987.

[DoD94] Department of Defense. *Software Development and Documentation*. MIL-STD-498, AMSC NO. N7069, December 1994.

[Hall95] Hall E. *Proactive Risk Management Methods for Software Engineering Excellence*. Doctoral dissertation, Computer Science Department, Florida Institute of Technology, Melbourne, FL, April 1995.

[Humphrey89] Humphrey W. *Managing the Software Process*. Reading, MA: Addison-Wesley, 1989.

[IEEE88] ANSI/IEEE. *IEEE Standard for Software Project Management Plans*. ANSI/IEEE STD 1058.1-1987. October 1988.

[ISO91] American National Standards Institute International Standards Organizations. *Quality Management and Quality Assurance Standards*. ISO 9000–3, 1991.

[Keirsey84] Keirsey D, Bates M. *Please Understand Me*. DelMar, CA: Prometheus Nemesis, 1984.

[Martin97] Martin J, et. al. *EIA Standard Processes for Engineering a System*. Electronic Industries Association, EIA 632, 1997.

[McPherson95] McPherson M, et al. *Guidelines for Successful Acquisition and Management of Software Intensive Systems: Weapon Systems, Command and Control Systems, and Management Information Systems*. Hill Air Force Base, UT: Software Technology Support Center, February 1995.

[VanScoy92] VanScoy R. Software development risk: Problem or opportunity. Technical report CMU/SEI-92-TR-30. Pittsburgh, PA: Software Engineering Institute, Carnegie Mellon University, 1992.

3

Risk Management Map

An effective goal focuses primarily on results rather than activity.
It identifies where you want to be, and, in the process, helps you
determine where you are. It gives you important information on
how to get there, and it tells you when you have arrived.
—Stephen R. Covey

The Capability Maturity Model for Software (CMM) is a de facto model of the software development process, developed by the SEI at Carnegie Mellon University, under the leadership of Watts Humphrey [Humphrey87]. The CMM is a framework that describes the key elements of an effective software process. The CMM describes an evolutionary improvement path from an ad hoc, immature process to a mature, disciplined process [Paulk93b]. The inspiration for the CMM's five levels of software process maturity was Phil Crosby's Quality Management Maturity Grid, a five-stage framework for adopting quality practices [Crosby80]. The software community uses the CMM as a software process–maturity framework to evolve toward software engineering and management excellence. The United States government uses the CMM as the basis for an evaluation method for selecting contractors that will develop software with the lowest overall risk [SCE94]. The foundation of the CMM is continuous process improvement for productivity and quality gains. The CMM is not a **silver bullet** and does not address all the issues important for successful projects [Paulk93a].

A basic assumption of the CMM is that quality increases and risk decreases as maturity levels increase [Humphrey89]. The CMM has helped in the area of process risk, but that is only a fraction of the risks involved with software development. It does not address software technology or human resources issues, for example, which are known sources of software risk [Paulk93c]. It is neither a complete maturity model for risk management, nor does it provide the necessary focus for risk management. CMM v1.1 does identify risk management key practices in several key process areas (KPA). Under the existing CMM architecture, a focus for risk management would require a KPA to be defined at a single maturity level. Working groups at the SEI have discussed the pros and cons of a risk management KPA at Levels 2, 3, and 4. The following quotation is from the CMM v2.0 risk management working group meeting in February 1995:

> The CMM itself is a risk management plan. Its stated purpose is to reduce the risk to a project that a project fails to build the correct software, on schedule and budget. It is highly appropriate that risk management be incorporated as a fundamental aspect of good overall software management. Level 2 organizations would stand to benefit greatly from basic risk management practices. The group did acknowledge that risk management at Level 2 has potentially the greatest impact to the community. The risk management working group concluded that risk management needed the additional emphasis that only a KPA would provide.

As a member of the Risk in the CMM working group, I helped write the Risk Management KPA that was reviewed for inclusion in CMM v2.0. A hotly debated topic at the review meetings, risk management was determined to be orthogonal to the software process and thus would not be incorporated as a separate KPA. The controversy regarding how to address risk management in the CMM continued over two years. In May 1997, a final resolution was made to add a goal in Integrated Software Management and strengthen risk management in other KPAs.

Currently, there are two maturity models that do provide focus for risk management practices—the System Engineering Capability Maturity Model (SE-CMM) [Bate94] and the Software Acquisition Capability Maturity Model (SA-CMM) [Ferguson96]—but neither allows for the maturity of risk management itself. In the software industry, we know that incremental development works, and "big bang" does not work. Similarly, the **evolution** of risk management practice must be understood because, practically, it requires a gradual cultural change. To provide the practical focus needed for risk management, I developed the Risk Management Map, based on evolving the major factors that cause risk management capability. In this chapter, I provide an overview of the map, which is designed to develop your ability to manage risk.

This chapter answers the following questions:

❏ What are the components of the Risk Management Map?

❏ How does the Risk Management Map offer direction?

❏ How can you progress in your ability to manage risk?

3.1   The Road to Risk Management Capability

The **Risk Management Map** charts the course for increasing the capability to manage software risk. As shown in Figure 3.1, the map contains five evolutionary stages: Problem, Mitigation, Prevention, Anticipation, and Opportunity.[1] By following the map and using it at a pace geared to the people's level of commitment and available time, you are assured of a reasonable path for progress. The map provides a detailed plan that can survive in spite of obstacles such as staff turnover and project cancellation. It helps you to do the following.

1. *Lay the foundation.* Each stage builds a capability that is necessary for the next stage. If you have already begun risk management improvement, you can use the map as a checklist to determine where you are and if you have forgotten any steps along the way. You should have a firm footing before proceeding to the next step. Do not overlook foundational steps in your haste to develop capability.

2. *Ease the transition.* The big bang approach is disastrous in software development. Just as an incremental strategy works in software development, it will

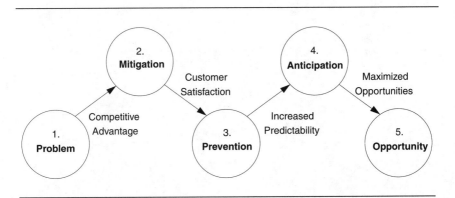

FIGURE 3.1 Risk management map. The map is a practical guide to understanding the path to increasing your ability to manage risk by transitions through five stages. At each stage, a vision provides the direction for your journey.

---

[1] The inspiration for the evolutionary stages is Robert Charette's *Evolution of the Management of Risk* [Charette91], which became known in 1992 as *Charette's Management of Risk Helix.* Charette's innovative diagram illustrates seven levels of increasing capability, from *Crisis Management* to *Management of Change.*

work in developing the capability to manage risk. The map helps to ease into risk management adoption by answering the question "What is the first step to incorporating risk management concepts given our current ability?" Start at the beginning; the map will guide you where you want to go.

3. *Stay the course.* Over time, there is a natural tendency for things to drift off-course. To avoid this entropy and stay the course, you need a detailed plan that can survive the effects of time. Your staff should be skilled in risk management as long as your organization is in business. Your risk management skill will be proportional to your level of commitment. If you are concerned about the quality of your results, you must check the quality of your input. The map helps you track your progress as you improve your practice.

3.2   Risk Management Map Directions

The structure of the map is similar to the arrow of a state-transition diagram that takes you to another node. As shown in Figure 3.2, a "stage" transition takes you to a higher level of risk management capability. To achieve the next stage of development, you need the vision, goals, and strategy provided by the Risk Management Map:

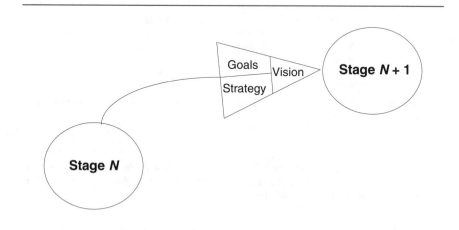

FIGURE 3.2   Map architecture. The underlying structure of the Risk Management Map supports the transition between stages. *Stages* provide incremental enhancements in the capability to manage risk. *Vision* guides the way to the next stage. *Goals* are accomplished to achieve the vision. *Strategy* is the activity that supports goal attainment.

❑ **Vision.** Vision is an ideal state of the practice that guides the journey. It acts as a driving force that provides the motivation required to continue our effort. The Risk Management Map paints a picture of five progressive stages.

❑ **Goals.** We accomplish goals to achieve our vision. Effective goals clearly define where you should be. Once you understand your current position, your goals will determine the scope of your task. The map provides the goals to bring each vision into reality. Parts II through V of this book group goals by the major factors of the P^2I^2 Success Formula (people, process, infrastructure, and implementation), and each subsequent chapter describes one goal of the map.

❑ **Strategy.** Strategy specifies an approach to accomplish the goals. It contains important information on how to achieve goals and yields activity to check for results. If the results do not support goal attainment, you can make tactical adjustments. The Risk Management Map provides a strategy to realize each goal. Subsections of each remaining chapter outline the strategy the map provides and arrange the required activities in their proper order. You can use the Contents to this book as a checklist to assess the completeness of your practice.

The Risk Management Map divides responsibility among the four major factors of risk management capability and provides five goals for each major factor of the P^2I^2 Success Formula. Risk management capability increases through the accomplishment of each goal, which strengthens the ability to manage risk. The book Contents contains a detailed outline of the map, which can be used as a checklist or quick reference. The following sections briefly describe the map goals for each dimension of the P^2I^2 Success Formula: process, infrastructure, implementation, and people.

3.2.1   Directions for the Process

The process relates to activities of performing risk management effectively and efficiently. The first step is to define the process of identifying risk and the source of risk. The next step is to define the process of analyzing the probability and consequence of the risk to determine risk ranking. The process of developing and executing a risk action plan is then defined. The process of capturing, reviewing, and reporting risk status is also defined, along with mechanisms for resolving risk and correcting for variations from plans.

Part II of this book addresses the following goals for the process:

❑ Identify risk.

❑ Analyze risk.

❏ Plan risk.

❏ Track risk.

❏ Resolve risk.

3.2.2   Directions for the Infrastructure

The infrastructure relates to activities of establishing an environment in which the risk management process can be defined, communicated, monitored, and improved. The first step is to develop a policy for performing risk management that is communicated to the entire organization. The next step is to define a standard risk management process that provides a consistent procedure that may be reused within the organization. Training is essential to raise the awareness and understanding of risk management, which provides the motivation and ability to perform the risk management process. An independent audit of the risk management activities, training, and project performance is required to verify risk management compliance. Risk management practice is then systematically improved by assessing the risk management capability and developing and implementing action plans to ensure continuous improvement.

Part III of this book addresses the following goals for the infrastructure:

❏ Develop the policy.

❏ Define standard process.

❏ Train risk technology.

❏ Verify compliance.

❏ Improve practice.

3.2.3   Directions for the Implementation

The implementation relates to activities of the execution of the risk management process to control risks cost-effectively. The first step is to establish a risk management initiative by reviewing requirements from the project and organization. Planning for risk management activities requires allocating budget, schedule, and staff. The next step is to develop a risk management plan detailing the approach, structure, process, methods, and tools used to implement risk management on the project. The risk management process may be tailored from the organization's standard process by addressing the unique aspects of the project, such as size, budget, and structure, to fit a cost-effective process to a particular project. Risks are iteratively assessed and controlled to manage the software risk.

Part IV of this book addresses the following goals for the implementation:

❏ Establish the initiative.

❏ Develop the plan.

❏ Tailor the standard process.

❏ Assess risk.

❏ Control risk.

3.2.4   Directions for the People

People have different beliefs that affect their behavior toward uncertainty and risk. Their beliefs and behaviors can change, depending on their awareness and understanding of risk management. You can think of risk as what you could lose or what you could fail to gain. The choice is yours. The first step is to recognize that risk management is an option for busy people who are tired of fighting fires. The next step is to learn basic risk concepts and become aware of your critical risks. You can then involve more people in preventing risks from becoming problems. When you learn to quantify the risk exposure, you will be able to focus on the right priorities. When you look at risk in a positive way, you can identify your opportunity cost—the risk of missing an opportunity.

Part V of this book addresses the following goals for the people:

❏ Stage 1: Problem.

❏ Stage 2: Mitigation.

❏ Stage 3: Prevention.

❏ Stage 4: Anticipation.

❏ Stage 5: Opportunity.

3.3   Journey from Problem to Opportunity

A **paradigm shift** is a change in a pattern of thinking. Although changes in thinking can occur in a revolutionary manner, more often, our thinking evolves over time, as a result of knowledge and understanding. The Risk Management Map depicts risk management as evolutionary, with a paradigm shift that occurs in the transition from one stage to the next. The map describes how the major factors of the P^2I^2 Success Formula evolve from problem to opportunity in five stages.

3.3.1   Five Stages of Risk Management

Increasing levels of knowledge, commitment, communication, efficiency, and effectiveness cause the transformation through each stage of risk management evolution [Hall94].

The **problem stage** describes the circumstances when risk identification is not seen as positive. It is characterized by a lack of communication, which causes a subsequent lack of coordination. People are too busy solving problems to think about the future. Risks are not addressed until they become problems, because either management was not aware of the risk or inaccurately estimated the risk's probability of occurrence. Since management reaction to hearing risks is typically to shoot the messenger, most people will not deliver bad news. **Crisis management** is used to address existing problems. People learn that firefighting can be exciting, but it causes burnout. Chapter 19 describes a project whose lack of risk management practices are typical of the problem stage.

The second stage, the **mitigation stage**, details the shift from crisis management to risk management. Management now incorporates risk management technology by asking, "What can go wrong?" and "What are the consequences?" This stage is characterized by an introduction to risk concepts. That is, people become aware of risks but do not systematically confront them. Since their knowledge and experience using risk management are limited, they may be unsure of how to communicate risks. In this stage, managers use risk management to reduce the probability and consequence of critical risks by implementing a contingency plan if the original plan fails. Primary emphasis is in the early phases of a software product definition, since major risk reduction leverage occurs in the early phases [Boehm89]. Chapter 20 describes a project whose risk management practices mirror the mitigation stage.

The **prevention stage** discusses the shift from risk management viewed as a manager's activity to a team activity. This third stage is a transitional one, where the approach changes from avoidance of risk symptoms to identification and elimination of the root cause of risk. It is characterized by team and occasional customer involvement, as managers understand that risk management is a dynamic process that cannot be performed in isolation. For risk management to succeed, it must occur at each level within an organization [Charette93]. Instead of focusing on cost and schedule risk (a management perspective, usually a symptom of technical risk), a focus on technical risks leads to a discovery of the source of risk. Prevention is a turning point from a reactive to a more proactive approach to risk management. Most people are experienced and comfortable in risk identification but are unsure how to quantify risks. Chapter 21 describes a project team whose risk management practices are representative of the prevention stage.

The fourth stage, the **anticipation stage**, describes the shift from subjective to quantitative risk management through the use of measures to anticipate predictable risks. It is characterized by the use of metrics to anticipate failures and predict future events. Predictability involves the ability to learn from, adapt to, and anticipate change [Charette92]. The project team and customer use risk management to quantify risks with reasonable accuracy to focus on the right priorities. A proactive approach to attacking risks and assessing alternatives is used. Alternatives are easier to compare using a quantitative approach. Chapter 22 describes a project team whose risk management practices are characteristic of the anticipation stage.

The final stage, the **opportunity stage**, is a positive vision of risk management that is used to innovate and shape the future. Potentially the most powerful paradigm shift is in perceiving risks as chances to save money and do better than planned. Risk, like quality, is everyone's responsibility. The risk ethic involves everyone (project team, customer, and end user), and is a continuous process of identifying, communicating, and resolving risks in an open and nonthreatening environment [Kirkpatrick92]. Professional attitudes of engineering excellence allow for open communication and individual contribution. We admit that there are things that we do not know and allow for their existence using a best-case, worst-case scenario. People understand there is an opportunity cost associated with every choice, and knowing these trade-offs improves their decision-making ability. Risk does not have to be negative [VanScoy92]. Wherever there is a risk, there also exists opportunity [Charette91]. Chapter 23 describes a project team whose risk management practices reflect the opportunity stage.

3.3.2   Personal Risk Management Matrix

As people progress through the five stages of risk management, their attitude changes. The **Personal Risk Management Matrix**, shown in Table 3.1 describes an individual's behavior with respect to risk for each discipline in the 6-D Model. It shows how an individual's sensibility progresses through five stages of risk management in each of the six disciplines. You can use the matrix to assess your current practice. For each of the six disciplines, select the practice that you perform consistently. Give yourself a point from 1 to 5, depending on the stage you currently perform at, and then total your points.

- ❑ *Score 6 or less.* Get the book *Thriving on Chaos* [Peters87]. You are going to need it!
- ❑ *Score 7 to 12.* Awareness makes you uncomfortable, but keep working at it. It gets better.
- ❑ *Score 13 to 18.* You are more proactive than most others and are an asset to any team.

TABLE 3.1   THE PERSONAL RISK MANAGEMENT MATRIX

	Stage 1: Problem	Stage 2: Mitigation	Stage 3: Prevention	Stage 4: Anticipation	Stage 5: Opportunity
Envision	I am tired of fighting fires.	I want to know what can go wrong.	I want to act so that I have no regrets.	I want to know our chances for success.	I want to exceed my own expectations.
Discover	I am too busy solving problems to think about the future.	I am aware of risks, but I am unsure how to tell my supervisor.	I try to find the cause of my potential problems.	I can predict a bad outcome by projecting work status.	I identify chances to do better than planned.
Plan	I am too busy to take on plans for things that might not happen.	I make backup plans.	I make plans to avoid problems.	I quantify risk with reasonable accuracy to focus on the right priorities.	I revise plans as needed to take advantage of current information.
Work	I have no fear.	I do not like to disclose my problems.	I will share my concerns when I am asked.	If risk can be quantified, we can manage it.	What I identify we will conquer.
Measure	I believe risk management is too imprecise to be of value.	I track my critical risks.	I use a personal process, and I collect data on my status.	I use status to trigger the implementation of risk action plans.	I calculate the loss of missed opportunities.
Improve	I am too busy to improve.	I avoid big "career-threatening" mistakes.	I prevent problems and surprises for my team.	I take corrective action to stay on target.	My ideas make a difference.

- ❏ *Score 19 to 24*. You are more quantitative than most others and are an asset to any team.
- ❏ *Score 25 to 30*. You are self-motivated and have a great attitude. Would you like a job?

To arrive at a team score, average the individual scores. Ask your team members to select the practices they should be performing. The gap between what you do and what you think you should do defines your journey. Begin by improving your weakest practice. Periodic assessment provides evidence of your progress. Once you reach your destination, you may find that you want to set higher goals.

3.4   Journey from Novice to Expert

Managing risk is a lot like playing golf. Known risks on a golf course include sand traps and water hazards. We can recognize a golfer's skill level by how the person manages these risks—for example:

- ❏ *Novice*. In a round of golf, novices have no idea how many balls they will lose in the water.
- ❏ *Beginner*. Around the water hazard, beginners play their less expensive balls. They would rather lose old balls than new ones.
- ❏ *Intermediate*. Because they know their capability with each club, intermediates often switch clubs and lay up before they attempt to cross the water.
- ❏ *Advanced*. Those who are advanced determine the length of the water hazard and select the appropriate club. They may push the limits of their capability or play it safe, depending on the margin needed to win.
- ❏ *Expert*. Experts do not see the water as an obstacle. When they take aim, they account for both wind direction and velocity. They visualize the ball landing in the best position *for their next shot*.

No two golf courses or software projects are ever the same. For this reason, software engineers, like golfers, must develop general skills for managing risk through practice. To progress from risk management novice to expert, you can use the following **Ten-Point Game Plan**.

1. *Understand where the hole (or pin) is*. The "hole" is the goal of a quality software system. The pin provides direction when you cannot see the hole. There are times when you tee off that the pin is nowhere in sight. A map provides guidance like a software life cycle model, to scope the dimensions of the course, or project.

2. *Know your capability with each club*. Your personal best will improve as your skill develops. Clubs are like the tools that engineers use to get the software to the goal. Remember that a fool with a tool is still a fool.

3. *Determine the dimensions of the hazards*. Challenging golf courses have water hazards that you must negotiate to keep your score low. The strategy

you develop to get past these hazards will depend on your skill level. A high score, like a high project cost, indicates an unsuccessful risk manager.

4. *Select the appropriate club.* For each leg of the course, a different club may be appropriate. Remember that each club, or tool, has a range. Do not expect your putter to perform like your woods, or you may find yourself lost in the trees.

5. *Aim toward the pin.* Position yourself correctly before you swing. You will reach your goal only if you are headed in the right direction. Aim that is a little off makes a big difference in where your ball will end up.

6. *Focus on the ball.* The ball is like a software development or maintenance activity. Focus on the task at hand, not on the risk or the goal. When you take your eye off the ball, you are not in a position to move the ball forward.

7. *Take a swing.* Regardless of your skill level, the only way to play the game is to take a swing. Some people will slice or hook by accident. The best golfers intentionally slice or hook when the situation calls for it (e.g., the course bends to the left). As you progress in your skill level, you become more proficient at knowing when to take a full swing or a half swing.

8. *Follow through.* The ball will go much farther and straighter if you follow through with your swing.

9. *Assess your shot for improvement.* If you can determine why your ball landed where it did, you can find out what to do differently the next time. Remember that name calling or finger pointing will not change the position of your ball on the course.

10. *Take corrective action as required.* Playing golf, like managing risk or developing software, usually requires corrective action after each shot. After you modify your strategy, you are ready to begin again with Step 1.

3.5 Summary

In this chapter, I provided an overview of the Risk Management Map that is designed to improve your ability to manage risk. The map shows the way to progress in your ability to manage risk. Its components are listed below as the goals for success. Risk management capability increases through the accomplishment of each goal, which provides the enhancement in the ability to manage risk.

Process Goals

❑ Identify risk.

❑ Analyze risk.

❑ Plan risk.

❑ Track risk.

❑ Resolve risk.

Infrastructure Goals

❑ Develop the policy.

❑ Define standard process.

❑ Train risk technology.

❑ Verify compliance.

❑ Improve practice.

Implementation Goals

❑ Establish the initiative.

❑ Develop the plan.

❑ Tailor the standard process.

❑ Assess risk.

❑ Control risk.

Goals for the People

❑ Stage 1: Problem.

❑ Stage 2: Mitigation.

❑ Stage 3: Prevention.

❑ Stage 4: Anticipation.

❑ Stage 5: Opportunity.

The Risk Management Map offers direction through its structure. The map architecture contains the following hierarchical constructs:

❑ *Stage.* Stages describe incremental enhancements in the capability to manage risk.

❑ *Vision.* For each stage, a vision provides direction and inspiration and guides the way to the next stage.

❑ *Goals.* To achieve the vision, you must accomplish goals. Each subsequent chapter describes one goal of the map.

❑ *Strategy.* Strategy is the activity that supports goal attainment. Subsections of each remaining chapter outline the strategy the map provides.

Individuals progress in their ability to manage risk in three simple steps (teams, projects, and organizations must repeat these steps for each person employed):

❑ Step 1. Assess the stage of your current risk management practice using the Personal Risk Management Matrix.

❑ Step 2. Improve your weakest practice.

❑ Step 3. Repeat Steps 1 and 2.

The ability to manage risk is a "use-it-or-lose-it" proposition. You must apply your ability to manage risk to achieve the control, higher return, or opportunities that you envision. If you develop the ability to manage risk but choose not to use this ability, you will lose your competitive edge. Knowledge without action is insufficient to derive the benefits of risk management.

3.6   Questions for Discussion

1. The Risk Management Map provides the vision, goals, and strategy for progress in the ability to manage risk. Define success criteria for each goal of the map to know when you have arrived at the next consecutive stage.

2. The Risk Management Map builds incremental capability in five stages. What is the result that you expect to achieve at each stage? For each stage, give an example that illustrates your ideal results.

3. Explain the utility of a Risk Management Map. How would you use it if you were responsible for increasing your organization's risk management capability?

4. Assess your risk management capability using the Personal Risk Management Matrix. Plot a histogram of the six disciplines. What, if anything, can you infer from the data? List strengths, weaknesses, and your recommendations for improvement.

5. Describe the difference between your personal risk management skills: the current "as is" and future "should be." Define quantitative goals for the "should be." Estimate how long your effort will take to reach your goals. What is the basis of your estimate?

6. Are you a risk management novice, beginner, intermediate, advanced, or expert? How do you know? What skills will you need to advance to the next level? Why is it important for you to increase your ability to manage risk?

7. What is your risk management philosophy? Do you consider your philosophy to be reactive or proactive? Explain the next step you would take to develop your ability to manage risk.

8. What would you do with the ability to manage risk: control existing risk, take on additional risk for potentially higher return, or maximize long-term opportunities? Explain your choice. What would you do if you knew you could not fail?

9. Effective goals focus on results. Why is it important to divide the goals of risk management capability into categories of people, process, infrastructure, and implementation? What is the relationship among the goals of these four categories?

10. Do you think ahead? Do you calculate based on the worst case? Do you take precautions? Discuss why you do or do not.

3.7   References

[Bate94] Bate R, et al. *System Engineering Capability Maturity Model (SE-CMM) Version 1.0*. Handbook CMU/SEI-94-HB-04. Pittsburgh, PA: Software Engineering Institute, Carnegie Mellon University, December 1994.

[Boehm89] Boehm B. *IEEE Tutorial on Software Risk Management*. New York: IEEE Computer Society Press, 1989.

[Charette93] Charette R. Essential Risk Management: Notes from the Front. *Proc*. 2nd SEI Conference on Risk Management, Pittsburgh, PA, March 1993.

[Charette92] Charette R. Building Bridges over Intelligent Rivers. *American Programmer*, 5(7), September 1992.

[Charette91] Charette R. *Risk Management Seminar*. Videotape Version 1.0, SPC-91138-MC. Herndon, VA: Software Productivity Consortium, August 1991.

[Covey89] Covey S. *The 7 Habits of Highly Effective People*. New York: Simon & Schuster, 1989.

[Crosby80] Crosby P. *Quality Is Free*. New York: McGraw-Hill, 1980.

[Ferguson96] Ferguson J, et al. Software Acquisition Capability Maturity Model (SA-CMM) Version 1.01. Technical report CMU/SEI-96-TR-020. Pittsburgh, PA: Software Engineering Institute, Carnegie Mellon University, December 1996.

[Hall94] Hall E. Evolution of essential risk management technology. *Proc*. 3rd SEI Conference on Software Risk, Pittsburgh, PA, April 1994.

[Humphrey89] Humphrey W. *Managing the Software Process*. Reading, MA: Addison-Wesley, 1989.

[Humphrey87] Humphrey W. Characterizing the software process: A maturity framework. Technical report CMU/SEI-87-TR-11, ADA 182895. Pittsburgh, PA: Software Engineering Institute, Carnegie Mellon University, June 1987.

[Kirkpatrick92] Kirkpatrick R, Walker J, Firth R. Software development risk management: An SEI appraisal. In *1992 SEI Technical Review* (R. Van Scoy, ed.). Pittsburgh, PA: Software Engineering Institute, Carnegie Mellon University, 1992.

[Paulk93a] Paulk M, Curtis B, Chrissis M, Weber C. Capability Maturity Model, Version 1.1. *IEEE Software*, 10(4):18–27, 1993.

[Paulk93b] Paulk M, et.al. Key Practices of the Capability Maturity Model, Version 1.1. Technical report CMU/SEI-93-TR-25. Pittsburgh, PA: Software Engineering Institute, Carnegie Mellon University, February 1993.

[Paulk93c] Paulk M, Curtis B, Chrissis M, Weber C. Capability Maturity Model for Software, Version 1.1. Technical report CMU/SEI-93-TR-24. Pittsburgh, PA: Software Engineering Institute, Carnegie Mellon University, February 1993.

[Peters87] Peters T. *Thriving on Chaos*. New York: HarperCollins, 1987

[SCE94] Members of the CMM-Based Appraisal Project. Software Capability Evaluation (SCE) Version 2.0 Implementation Guide. Technical report CMU/SEI-94-TR-05, Software Engineering Institute, Carnegie Mellon University, Pittsburgh, PA, February 1993.

[VanScoy92] VanScoy R. Software development risk: Problem or opportunity. Techinical report CMU/SEI-92-TR-30. Pittsburgh, PA: Software Engineering Institute, Carnegie Mellon University, 1992.

PART II

Risk Management Process

I always tried to turn every disaster into an opportunity.
—John D. Rockefeller

Part II provides the steps to predictable risk management results. As shown in Figure II.1, there are two logical components of the risk management process: risk assessment, described in Chapters 4 and 5, and risk control, described in Chapters 6 through 8. In each chapter I define a process element in terms of what the activities are and how the mechanisms (methods, techniques, and tools) are used to transform inputs to outputs.

Chapter 4, "Identify Risk," defines the process element *Identify Risk*. Read Chapter 4 to learn how to discover risk and communicate identified risk effectively.

Chapter 5, "Analyze Risk," defines the process element *Analyze Risk*. Read Chapter 5 to understand how to estimate the risk exposure and evaluate interrelated risks.

Chapter 6, "Plan Risk," defines the process element *Plan Risk*. Read Chapter 6 to learn how to develop alternative strategies for risk resolution and establish thresholds that help determine when to execute the risk action plan.

Chapter 7, "Track Risk," defines the process element *Track Risk*. Read Chapter 7 to understand how to compare risk status with planned thresholds in order to determine when to trigger risk action plan execution.

Chapter 8, "Resolve Risk," defines the process element *Resolve Risk*. Read Chapter 8 to learn how to resolve risk to an acceptable level, such that the project can live with the worst-case outcome.

With the knowledge of the risk management process provided in Part II, you will be ready to define a standard process and develop supporting methods for reuse within your organization.

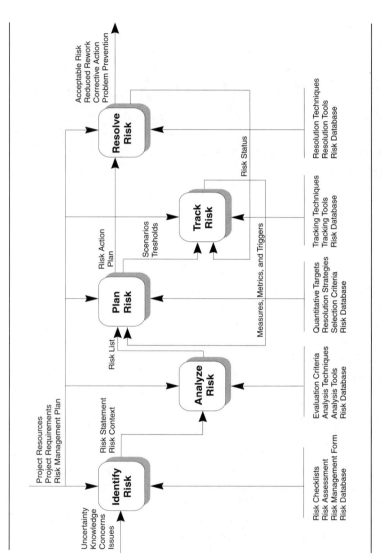

FIGURE II.I Risk management process. The risk management process comprises five process elements. Identify Risk and Analyze Risk contain the activities required to assess risk. Plan Risk, Track Risk, and Resolve Risk contain the practices necessary to control risk.

4

Identify Risk

We are slaves to whatever we do not understand.
—Vernon Howard

In October 1993, Deputy Assistant Secretary of the Air Force Lloyd K. Mosemann wrote in a memo: "It appears that many problems of large-scale software development and maintenance, such as cost overruns, schedule slips, and unmet performance objectives, are in fact the result of the difficulties in effectively managing extremely large and complex undertakings—particularly in the areas of planning and baselining, control, visibility, and risk management. In all likelihood, effective management techniques are not as widely understood or utilized as they could be." Mosemann articulated the very reason that risk management is rarely performed: most people do not know where to start. We can begin by understanding how to identify risks, the first step in the risk management process.

In this chapter, I discuss the **risk identification** process, which defines the activities and methods used to discover risk. I explain the techniques and tools proved to communicate identified risk effectively.

This chapter answers the following questions:

- ❏ What are the activities of the risk identification process?
- ❏ How can you discover unknown risks?
- ❏ Why is a structured risk statement valuable?

4.1   Define the Risk Identification Process

I define risk identification success criteria in terms of the process goals, the results that we expect to achieve by using the process. We describe the risk identification process from two perspectives. The **external view** specifies the process controls, inputs, outputs, and mechanisms. The **internal view** specifies the process activities that transform inputs to outputs using the mechanisms.

4.1.1   Process Goals

The risk identification process is sufficient when it satisfies these goals:

❑ Encourage input of perceived risk from the team.

❑ Identify risk while there is time to take action.

❑ Uncover risk and sources of risk.

❑ Capture risk in a readable format.

❑ Communicate risk to those who can resolve it.

❑ Prevent project surprises.

These goals can be used as a checklist to ensure the process quality.

4.1.2   Process Definition

The risk identification process definition is shown as an **IDEF0** diagram in Figure 4.1. Integrated Computer-Aided Manufacturing Definition (IDEF0) is a function modeling standard established in 1981 for defining manufacturing processes [AirForce81]. IDEF0 is a standard process definition notation used to describe a reusable process component for predictable risk identification. The diagram describes the top-level process by its controls, inputs, outputs, and mechanisms. Control determines when and how the process is executed. Input is an item required for a process transformation that meets the process entry criteria. Output is a result of a process transformation that has been successfully reviewed using process exit criteria. Mechanism determines the methods the process uses.

Process Controls.   Project resources, project requirements, and the risk management plan regulate the risk identification process.

The *project resources* constrain the scope of risk identification in terms of cost, time, and staff. When cost is a constraint, you can use cheaper methods to identify risk. When time is lacking, you can use quicker methods. When staff are

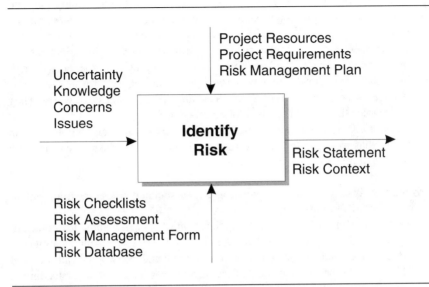

FIGURE 4.1   Risk identification process definition. *Identify Risk* encapsulates the activities of the process that transform inputs to outputs. Controls (at the top) regulate the process. Inputs (on the left) enter the process. Outputs (on the right) exit the process. Mechanisms (at the bottom) support the process.

not available, you can invite fewer people to participate in risk identification. If you cut corners due to project resources, you risk compromising process effectiveness.

Contractual requirements and organizational standards influence the *project requirements* for when to perform risk identification. You can derive requirements for risk identification from organizational standards that require reporting risks at project reviews. Contractual requirements can directly specify requirements for risk assessment, as in the following U.S. Marine Corps statement of work: "The contractor shall perform a continuing assessment of the risks associated with project and contract cost, schedule, and achievement of DemVal phase and project technical requirements."

The *risk management plan* specifies who has the responsibility and authority for risk management activities. It documents the project procedures that specify how to implement the process. (Chapter 15 describes how to develop an effective risk management plan.)

Process Inputs.   Uncertainty, knowledge, concerns, and issues are inputs to the risk identification process.

Uncertainty is what we do not know. It is thus a part of our assumptions and our doubts. For example, requirements that contain the phrase *to be determined* (TBD) are carriers of risk. Similarly, estimates not based on past performance contain more uncertainty (i.e., higher risk) than estimates based on historical data.

Knowledge is what we do know. We must use our previous experience in engineering systems and knowledge of the current project to identify software risk.

Concerns are what we fear. They cause anxiety, uneasiness, or worry. They are the troubles that affect us, which often relate to risk.

An *issue* is a matter that is unresolved with respect to other people. It is an open item that we work together to resolve. Issues can be risks when there are trade-offs that make a decision difficult.

Process Outputs.   A risk statement and its associated risk context are output from the risk identification process.

A **risk statement** is a concise declaration of risk in a standard notation: Issue • probability • consequence. The simplicity of the risk statement makes it easy to read. The risk statement decomposes into the topic and the two main attributes of risk. The value of the risk statement is that it promotes increased understanding in risk communication. Further, it can help to determine whether an issue is a risk. For example, if the probability is 100 percent, there is no risk to resolve. It is too late to prevent the consequence.

The **risk context** provides the collateral information surrounding the risk statement (events, conditions, constraints, assumptions, circumstances, contributing factors, and related issues).

Process Mechanisms.   A risk checklist, risk assessment, risk management form, and risk database are mechanisms of the risk identification process. Mechanisms can be methods, techniques, tools, or other instruments that provide structure to the process activities.

A **risk checklist** contains typical risk areas that relate to the checklist topic. Risk checklists can organize risks by, for example, contract type, maturity level, life cycle model, development phase, organizational structure, project size, application domain, or technology. They help to identify risks in a given area completely. I describe several risk checklists in section 4.2.

Risk assessment is a rigorous method for risk identification that uses a structured risk checklist in an interview-style meeting. I describe a risk assessment method further in section 4.3.

A *risk management form* is a mechanism for addressing risk systematically through a fill-in-the-blank template. I provide a risk management form in section 4.4.

A **risk database** is a repository of identified risks and associated information that logs the risk by assigning the next available sequential number and maintains the history of all identified risks. I outline the data fields of a risk database in section 4.5.

4.1.3   Process Activities

The activities of the risk identification process are the tasks necessary to transform uncertainty into a risk statement:

1. Conduct a risk assessment.
2. Identify risk systematically.
3. Define the risk attributes.
4. Document identified risk.
5. Communicate identified risk.

I discuss the risk identification process activities as sequential steps, but they can be iterative or parallel in execution.

Conduct a Risk Assessment.   The risk assessment identifies risk and evaluates risk based on established criteria (e.g., likelihood of occurrence, consequence, and time frame for action). It provides a baseline of assessed risks that are managed by the project and thus is recommended early in any project. Subsequent risk assessments are recommended at major milestones or as significant project changes occur in areas such as cost, schedule, scope, or staffing. A streamlined risk assessment method [Hall95] is described in section 4.3.

Identify Risk Systematically.   There are many ways to identify risk; several structure input so that it is easier to understand. The methods prescribed in this chapter fall under one or more of the following categories:

- ❑ *Checklist.* Everyone can identify risks by using a checklist as a reminder of the possible risk areas. Section 4.2 defines several checklists used in risk identification.

- ❑ *Interview.* People can identify risks when asked in a group interview session. The value of this method is that the interviewer is not a stakeholder in risk identification and is thus impartial. Moreover, a synergy develops from the discussion.

- ❑ *Meeting.* Periodic meetings, such as weekly staff meetings, monthly team meetings, and quarterly project reviews, are appropriate for dialogue of risk information. Reserve a place for discussion of risk on meeting agendas.

- ❑ *Review.* People can identify risks through a review of plans, processes, and work products.

- ❑ *Routine input.* A risk management form is a template for routine input of identified risk. Forms should be available at any time in both hard copy and soft copy formats. (Section 4.4 defines a template for a risk management form.)

- ❑ *Survey.* Selected categories of people can identify risks quickly and without prior preparation using a survey method. An anonymous survey does not require an individual's name but should provide a job category to understand the perspective of the survey response.

❑ *Working group.* Teams can identify risks by thinking (e.g., brainstorming and meditation) and doing (e.g., modeling and simulation).

Define the Risk Attributes.   After an issue is identified, you can be certain it is a risk by defining the major **risk attributes** of probability and consequence. A simple way to describe the likelihood of risk occurrence is by a subjective phrase. As shown in Figure 4.2, you can map the perceived likelihood to a quantitative probability. To define probability with a margin for error, you can use a range (e.g., 50 to 70 percent). When you have a low confidence in your perceived likelihood, it is best to use a rating system from 1 to 5, or high/moderate/low. Define the consequence in terms of an unsatisfactory outcome that would occur if the risk were realized. We often think of risk consequence as the cost, schedule, and technical effects. Objectives must be clearly stated and prioritized to develop accurate risk consequences. For example, the software design objectives can include flexibility, interoperability, maintainability, portability, reliability, reusability, and testability. Using these objectives, you can define specific technical consequences for a given design risk.

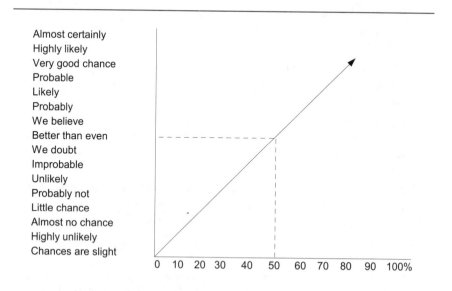

FIGURE 4.2   Perceived probability. A subjective phrase can be used to describe the likelihood of risk occurrence. The perceived probability is then mapped to a quantitative scale, where the probability is a number between 0 and 100 percent. *Source:* [DSMC83]

Document Identified Risk.   The most concise way to specify a risk is to write a statement of risk containing a brief description of the risk issue, the probability, and the consequence in subjective terms. Using a standard format increases the readability of a risk, which makes it appear familiar. When we are comfortable writing risk statements, we have a known frame of reference for describing risk. When we use known techniques such as the risk statement, we feel more confident in our ability to manage the unknown aspects of risk. The value of a structured risk statement is its ability to simplify risk communication. The risk statement captures the essence of the risk. Document identified risk by writing a risk statement and elaborating the associated risk context. The corresponding risk context contains the what, when, where, how, and why of the risk issue.

Communicate Identified Risk.   Communication of identified risk is best when it is both verbal and written. Verbal communication provides a dialogue for clarifying understanding: written communication provides a document for historical purposes. The advantage of verbal risk communication is that it can be heard, in person or over the telephone, and the listener has a chance to clarify the risk communication by asking questions. Face-to-face verbal communication is best the first time that significant risks are identified. A conversation over the telephone provides a personal touch when timeliness is necessary and distance prohibits an appearance in person. The advantage of written risk communication is that it can be read at a fixed location or distributed to a team at different sites. Bulletin boards and status reports are appropriate for a colocated team. E-mail and newsletters are appropriate for a distributed team.

4.2   Develop Risk Checklists

Risk checklists are easy to generate and provide a systematic way to identify risk. You can discover unknown risks that exist on your project by reviewing the project's critical success factors, listing all items on the critical path of your schedule, and itemizing the project interfaces, internal and external. When I asked attendees at my Software Risk Management seminar to create a list of known risks by software development phase, four teams completed checklists for the requirements, design, code, and test phases in 15 minutes. You can avoid this work by using the existing SEI software risk taxonomy[1] or your project work breakdown structure as a checklist.

---

[1] Special permission to reproduce excerpts from Taxonomy Based Risk Identification, CMU/SEI–93–TR–6, © 1993 by Carnegie Mellon University, is granted by the Software Engineering Institute.

TABLE 4.1   SEI SOFTWARE RISK TAXONOMY

Product Engineering	Development Environment	Program Constraints
1. Requirements	**1. Development Process**	**1. Resources**
a. Stability	a. Formality	a. Schedule
b. Completeness	b. Suitability	b. Staff
c. Clarity	c. Process control	c. Budget
d. Validity	d. Familiarity	d. Facilities
e. Feasibility	e. Product control	
f. Precedent		**2. Contract**
g. Scale	**2. Development System**	a. Type of contract
	a. Capacity	b. Restrictions
2. Design	b. Suitability	c. Dependencies
a. Functionality	c. Usability	
b. Difficulty	d. Familiarity	**3. Project Interfaces**
c. Interfaces	e. Reliability	a. Customer
d. Performance	f. System support	b. Associate contractors
e. Testability	g. Deliverability	c. Subcontractors
f. Hardware constraints		d. Prime contractor
g. Nondevelopmental software	**3. Management Process**	e. Corporate management
	a. Planning	f. Vendors
3. Code and Unit Test	b. Project organization	g. Politics
a. Feasibility	c. Management experience	
b. Unit test	d. Project interfaces	
c. Coding/ implementation		
	4. Management Methods	
4. Integration and Test	a. Monitoring	
a. Environment	b. Personnel management	
b. Product	c. Quality assurance	

(CONTINUED)

TABLE 4.1 SEI SOFTWARE RISK TAXONOMY *(CONTINUED)*

Product Engineering	Development Environment	Program Constraints
c. System	d. Configuration management	
5. Engineering Specialties	**5. Work Environment**	
a. Maintainability	a. Quality attitude	
b. Reliability	b Cooperation	
c. Safety	c. Communication	
d. Security	d. Morale	
e. Human factors		
f. Specifications		

4.2.1   Software Risk Taxonomy

The SEI risk taxonomy is a structured checklist that organizes known software development risks from general classes to specific element attributes. The taxonomy provides a framework for identifying technical and programmatic software development risks [Carr93]. The SEI taxonomy[2] is shown in Table 4.1 The taxonomy is organized into three major *classes*, which are further divided into *elements*. Each element is characterized by its *attributes*.

4.2.2   Work Breakdown Structure

The **work breakdown structure** (WBS) provides a framework for identifying specific project risk. A portion of a project WBS is shown in Figure 4.3. Working on activities that are not on the project WBS can be an indication of unknown risk. Any time you perform work not budgeted and scheduled, you detract from planned work. In this case, working on unplanned activities can cause problems, such as schedule slips and cost overruns, in other areas. Unplanned activities, or activities not decomposed properly, will steal time from planned activities. Only activities on the project WBS are visible at the cost accounting level.

---

[2] The SEI risk taxonomy is used in several SEI methods: Software Risk Evaluation [Sisti94], Team Risk Management [Dorofee94], and Continuous Risk Management [Dorofee96].

1	2	3	4	Title	Probability of Occurrence	Consequences at Occurrence	Risk Exposure
01-				TEG-32 Project	Moderate	High	High
01-	01-			Prime Item	Moderate	High	High
01-	01-	01-		GPS	High	High	High
01-	01-	01-	01	Receivers	High	Low	Moderate
01-	01-	02-	01	Interference	Low	High	Moderate
01-	01-	02-	02	Antennas	Moderate	Moderate	Moderate
01-	01-	03-	01	Processor	Low	Moderate	Low
01-	01-	04-	01	Comm Interfaces	Moderate	Low	Low

FIGURE 4.3   Project work breakdown structure. The work breakdown structure can be used as a checklist of risk areas. Known risks are found in the activities listed; unknown risks are found in activities not listed.

4.3   Define the Risk Assessment Method

The risk assessment described in this section is an interview-style method to identify and appraise risks.The risk assessment objectives include training techniques for risk identification that are used throughout the project and providing a baseline of assessed risks for continued risk management. The method is based on concepts developed by the SEI Risk Program [Carr93]. Through collaborative efforts with SEI, a streamlined method of risk assessment was developed [Hall95].

4.3.1   Assessment Preparation

The risk assessment is performed using an assessment team trained in basic risk concepts, the risk assessment method, and the risk management process. The assessment team has a designated leader to coordinate activities with the project. The team reviews the **project profile**, which contains information on topics listed in Table 4.2, to understand the unique aspects of the project. The project profile should present the technical aspects and the current status of the project, including the organization chart and schedule. Existing charts should be used as much as

TABLE 4.2   PROJECT PROFILE CONTENTS

Project Profile	
Company organization	• Organization chart showing relation to the project • Types of systems developed • Domains of technical expertise • Number of engineers
Project data	• Budget • Schedule • Software size estimate • Organization chart • Relationships with government, prime contractor, associate contractors, etc. • Relationship to system engineering, quality assurance, etc. • Subcontractor and vendor responsibilities • Number of people in each function
System description	• Application description • System/software block diagram • Major functions
Project history	• Unexpected events that have occurred on the project • Technical issues that have been put off until later • Major decisions made to keep the project on track • Current issues of concern

possible. The project profile is usually briefed by the project manager or chief software engineer during risk assessment preparation. The individuals from the project selected to participate are informed about the risk assessment purpose and scheduled activities. The assessment preparation comprises the following tasks.

1. Select and train the assessment team.
2. Review the project profile.
3. Select the interview participants.
4. Prepare the risk assessment schedule.
5. Coordinate the meeting logistics.
6. Brief the project participants.

4.3.2   Interview Session

The assessment team conducts interviews of several peer groups using the SEI taxonomy-based questionnaire (TBQ), a risk identification mechanism that will be used throughout the project, and an interview protocol to identify and evaluate risks. The interview protocol creates a nonjudgmental and nonattributive environment so that tentative or controversial views may be voiced in the interview session [Carr93].

During the risk assessment, the assessment team rotates the roles of interviewer, recorder, and observer. The *interviewer* conducts the group discussion using an interview protocol in a question-and-answer format. The project participants identify risks in response to questions posed by the interviewer. The

Introduction	"Welcome. My name is _____, and I will be conducting the risk assessment interview. I personally want to thank you for taking the time to share your thoughts and hope that you find the risk assessment a valuable experience. I would like the rest of the assessment team to introduce themselves and their roles. Now let us get to know the program participants. Please tell us your name and responsibilities on the project."
Purpose	"The objective of this interview is to identify and evaluate risks to a successful project. We will use the SEI risk taxonomy structure to help us systematically think about and identify risks, which are potential problems. We will break at _____. Return promptly at _____, and we will spend the remainder of the time evaluating the identified risks."
Confidentiality	"The findings from all the interviews will be consolidated and briefed to the project at the results briefing. No remarks will be attributed to an individual or interview group. The project will own the findings, and our personal notes will be kept confidential within the assessment team."
Interview process	"Let us begin by reviewing the SEI risk taxonomy structure. As we go through this interview, think about the project as a whole, not just your own work. Feel free to identify risks, issues, or concerns in any area at any time."
Closing	"Thank you for your time and your ideas. The information you have provided will be very useful. The results briefing is on _____, and you are all invited to attend."

FIGURE 4.4   Risk assessment interview script. The interview script should be used as a guide to structure the interview session.

recorder documents risk statements and the results of the preliminary risk analysis, and the *observer* serves as timekeeper and notes details of the discussion, as well as group dynamics and overall process effectiveness.

The interviewer conducts the interview session in accordance with the interview script shown in Figure 4.4. The script ensures consistency among interview sessions and ensures that the interviewer remembers the five major components of the interview session. The interviewer asks the risk assessment team members to introduce themselves prior to conducting the interview session and reminds interviewees that no remarks will be attributed to an individual or interview group to emphasize confidentiality.

The interview session comprises the following tasks:

1. Interview the peer group.
2. Record the risks.
3. Clarify the risk statements.
4. Observe and document the process results.

4.3.3   Preliminary Risk Analysis

The participants assess the risk statements according to defined evaluation criteria. The assessment team evaluates the interview results after the participants have left the meeting room by reviewing the risk statements one at a time and classifying them according to the SEI risk taxonomy. Risks may be entered into the risk database as soon as the information is available.

The preliminary risk analysis comprises the following tasks:

1. Evaluate the identified risks.
2. Evaluate the interview session.
3. Categorize the risks.
4. Enter the risks in the risk database.

4.3.4   Results and Retrospective

Develop viewgraphs to summarize the findings of the interview sessions. Debrief the project manager and ask this person to speak to the project team regarding risk management after the assessment results are presented. Then present the risk assessment process and results to the entire project team, leaving time to respond to questions from the team. The project manager uses the risk database as a baseline of risks or merges it into an existing database. Feedback is documented on the risk assessment evaluation forms that are gathered from the interview participants after the results briefing. The project uses the baselined risks to continue the risk management process throughout the project. Risk management forms are available as the mechanism the project team will use to communicate new risks.

The results and retrospective comprise the following tasks:

1. Prepare the results briefing.
2. Debrief the project manager.
3. Brief the project team.
4. Evaluate the risk assessment.
5. Distribute the risk management form.

4.4   Develop the Risk Management Form

A **risk management form** is used as a risk identification mechanism that anyone may submit at any time to identify risks. The originator enters his or her name, the date, and a brief description of the risk. Figure 4.5 shows a template of a risk management form. A sample risk management form for an active risk is shown in Chapter 15.

4.5   Establish the Risk Database Schema

The risk database contains data fields to describe a risk completely. The database design should include links to requirements and pointers to related risks. The **risk database schema** is the design of the fields for the risk database. As a minimum, the risk database should contain the following data fields:

❑ Log number	❑ Project	❑ Risk resolution strategy
❑ Date	❑ Phase	
❑ Status	❑ Function	❑ Risk action plan
❑ Originator	❑ WBS element	❑ Quantitative target
❑ Risk category	❑ Risk statement	❑ Indicator
❑ Risk title	❑ Risk context	❑ Threshold
❑ Probability	❑ Risk analysis	❑ Trigger
❑ Consequence	❑ Current priority	❑ Cost
❑ Time frame	❑ Previous priority	❑ Savings

Risk Management Form			
Log Number:	Date:	Originator's Name:	Risk Category:
Risk Title:	Probability:	Consequence:	Time Frame:
Project:	Phase:	Function:	WBS Element:
Risk Assessment			
Risk statement:			
Risk context:			
Risk analysis:			
Risk Planning			
Strategy: ❏ Avoidance ❏ Protection ❏ Reduction ❏ Research ❏ Reserves ❏ Transfer	**Risk action plan:**		
Risk Tracking			
Quantitative target:	**Comments:**		
Indicator:			
Threshold:			
Trigger:			
Risk Resolution			
Software Engineer:	System Engineer:	Quality Assurance:	Project Manager:
Date:	Date:	Date:	Date:

FIGURE 4.5   Risk management form.

4.6   Summary

In this chapter, I described the process definition steps for identifying risk:

1. Define the risk identification process.
2. Develop risk checklists.
3. Define the risk assessment method.
4. Develop the risk management form.
5. Establish the risk database schema.

I described the risk identification process, which defines the activities and methods to uncover known and unknown risk. The activities of the risk identification process are as follows:

1. Conduct a risk assessment.
2. Identify risk systematically.
3. Define the risk attributes.
4. Document identified risk.
5. Communicate identified risk.

I identified sources of unknown risks that are inherent in software development. You can discover these risks by reviewing the following project components:

❑ Work breakdown structure.
❑ Critical success factors.
❑ Critical path activities.
❑ External interfaces.

I described techniques and tools proved to communicate identified risk effectively. The value of a structured risk statement is its ability to define a specific risk concisely, increase readability using a standard format, and simplify risk communication.

4.7   Questions for Discussion

1. Describe the risk identification process goals. Why is each goal important? Define quantitative success criteria for each goal.

2. In what way do project resources, project requirements, and the risk management plan regulate the risk identification process? Is there a relationship among these process controls? Discuss why there is or why there is not.

3. What is a risk assessment? Cite three reasons to perform a risk assessment early in the project. Imagine that you were brought in to replace a retiring project manager of a project in the design phase. Would you delegate the task of performing a risk assessment? Discuss the ways a baseline of assessed risks would be valuable to you.

4. List five methods to identify risk. Describe how you would perform a risk assessment using each of these methods. Compare and contrast the methods in terms of their efficiency and effectiveness. For example, if it is more effective to involve more people, then which methods enable more people to participate?

5. List three reasons to categorize risk. Do you think the number of risks identified in a particular category is a significant measure? Discuss why you do or do not think so.

6. Write a risk statement. What are five benefits of using a structured format for documenting risk? How do you think communication of identified risk changes with the use of a risk statement? Explain your answer.

7. You just found out that your software subcontractor has filed for bankruptcy protection. How will you communicate this significant risk to your management? Do you plan to communicate the risk as soon as possible, or take the time to assess it? What information will you communicate to your management?

8. Develop a risk checklist for the requirements, design, code, or test phase of software development. Which phase do you think has the greatest risk? Explain your answer.

9. Discuss the concept of confidentiality in risk assessment. When is confidentiality necessary? In your opinion, what are the advantages and disadvantages of identifying risks in peer groups?

10. How does knowing your risks provide opportunities to manage and improve your chances of success? Explain your answer.

4.8 References

[AirForce81] *Integrated Computer Aided Manufacturing Architecture*, Part II, Vol. IV: *Function Modeling Manual (IDEF0)*. AFWAL-TR-81-4023. Wright-Patterson Air Force Base, OH: Air Force Systems Command, June 1981.

[Boehm89] Boehm B. *IEEE Tutorial on Software Risk Management*. New York: IEEE Computer Society Press, 1989.

[Carr93] Carr M, Konda S, Monarch I, Ulrich F, Walker C. Taxonomy based risk identification. Technical report CMU/SEI-93-TR-6. Pittsburgh, PA: Software Engineering Institute, Carnegie Mellon University, 1993.

[Dorofee96] Dorofee A, et. al. *Continuous Risk Management Guidebook*. Pittsburgh, PA: Software Engineering Institute, Carnegie Mellon University, 1996.

[Dorofee94] Dorofee A, et. al. Introduction to team risk management. Special technical report CMU/SEI-94-SR-001. Pittsburgh, PA: Software Engineering Institute, Carnegie Mellon University, 1994.

[DSMC83] Defense Systems Management College. *Risk Assessment Techniques*. Fort Belvoir, VA, 1983.

[Hall95] Hall E, Natwick G, Ulrich F, Engle C. Streamlining the risk assessment process. *Proc*. Seventh Software Technology Conference, Salt Lake City, UT, April 1995.

[Sisti94] Sisti F, Joseph S. Software Risk Evaluation Method. Version 1.0. Technical report CMU/SEI-94-TR-19. Pittsburgh, PA: Software Engineering Institute, Carnegie Mellon University, 1994.

5

Analyze Risk

Knowing our risks provides opportunities to manage and improve our chances of success.
—Roger VanScoy

The techniques of risk analysis are powerful tools to help people manage uncertainty. You can use risk analysis to make and obtain support for your decisions. Using automated tools for risk analysis, you can store, organize, and process data into meaningful knowledge. Any risky situation, from business to science and engineering, can be modeled. Risk analysis tools incorporate uncertainty in your estimates to generate results that show all possible outcomes. The result is a more intelligent decision.

In this chapter, I discuss the process definition steps for analyzing risk. I describe the **risk analysis** process, which defines the activities and methods to estimate and evaluate risk. **Estimation** is the appraisal of the risk probability and consequence. **Evaluation** is an assessment of the options using defined criteria. I explain the tools and techniques used to understand and prioritize software risk effectively.

This chapter answers the following questions:

- ❑ What are the activities of the risk analysis process?
- ❑ How can you estimate risk exposure?
- ❑ What automated analysis tools are available to evaluate risk?

5.1   Define the Risk Analysis Process

I define risk analysis success criteria in terms of the process goals, the results that we expect to achieve by using the process. We can view the risk analysis process from two perspectives: external and internal. The external view specifies the process controls, inputs, outputs, and mechanisms. The internal view specifies the process activities that transform inputs to outputs using the mechanisms.

5.1.1   Process Goals

The risk analysis process is sufficient when it satisfies these goals:

❏ Analyze risk in a cost-efficient manner.

❏ Refine the risk context.

❏ Determine the source of risk.

❏ Determine the risk exposure.

❏ Determine the time frame for action.

❏ Determine the highest-severity risks.

These goals can be used as a checklist to ensure the process quality.

5.1.2   Process Definition

The risk analysis process definition is shown as an IDEF0 diagram in Figure 5.1. IDEF0 is a standard process definition notation used to describe a reusable process component for predictable risk analysis. The diagram describes the top-level process by its controls, inputs, outputs, and mechanisms [AirForce81].

Process Controls.   Project resources, project requirements, and the risk management plan regulate the risk analysis process similar to the way they control the risk identification process (see Chapter 4).

Process Inputs.   A risk statement and its associated risk context are input to the risk analysis process.

A *risk statement* is a concise declaration of risk in a standard notation: Issue • probability • consequence. On input, the statement is a subjective and sometimes even vague description of the risk. Through risk analysis activities, you can improve the risk statement by clarifying the issue. Restate the risk by refining the context, and by merging or decomposing risk statements. You can also improve

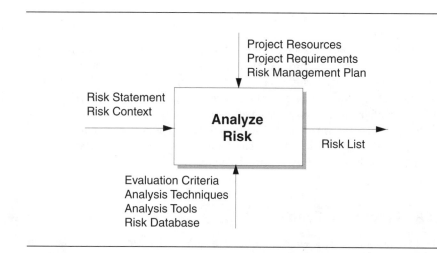

FIGURE 5.1   Risk analysis process definition. *Analyze Risk* encapsulates the activities of the process that transform inputs to outputs. Controls (at the top) regulate the process. Inputs (on the left) enter the process. Outputs (on the right) exit the process. Mechanisms (at the bottom) support the process.

the risk statement by stating the probability and consequence more quantitatively. The value of a quantitative risk exposure can be used to prioritize the risks. Risk communication is more powerful through the simplicity of using numbers (instead of words) to convey the risk exposure.

The *risk context* provides the collateral information surrounding the risk statement (events, conditions, constraints, assumptions, circumstances, contributing factors, and related issues). A cursory risk identification will not provide sufficient risk context. You can either modify or determine the risk category through risk analysis. Refining the risk context is part of the risk analysis process.

Process Outputs.   A prioritized risk list and refined risk context are output from the risk analysis process.

A prioritized **risk list** is an inventory of risks that contains the relative ranking of all identified risks. The risk context provides the collateral information surrounding the risk statement (events, conditions, constraints, assumptions, circumstances, contributing factors, and related issues). The refined risk context adds information obtained from risk analysis, such as the risk category and the source of risk, which is captured in the database.

Process Mechanisms.   Evaluation criteria, analysis techniques, analysis tools, and a risk database are mechanisms of the risk analysis process. Mechanisms can be methods, techniques, tools, or other instruments that provide structure to the process activities.

Evaluation criteria for probability, consequence, and time frame for action help to measure risk exposure and to rank risks relative to one another. *Analysis techniques* help in structuring decisions and determining the bounds for acceptable outcomes. Automated *analysis tools* help to organize information, show relationships graphically, and make calculations efficiently. A *risk database* contains the evaluated risk information and the refined risk context. Responsible individuals update the risk database with the current and previous priority. The risk database maintains the total number of weeks on the risk list.

5.1.3   Process Activities

The activities of the risk analysis process are the tasks necessary to transform statements of risk into a prioritized risk list. The activities of the risk analysis process are as follows:

1. Group similar and related risks.
2. Determine risk drivers.
3. Determine source of risk.
4. Use risk analysis techniques and tools.
5. Estimate the risk exposure.
6. Evaluate risk against criteria.
7. Rank risks relative to other risks.

I discuss the risk analysis process activities as sequential steps, but they can be iterative or parallel in execution.

Group Similar and Related Risks.   You can group similar risks by sorting the risk database based on risk category. A redundant risk should be tagged as a duplicate and closed. You should note the number of redundant risks that are closed as duplicates—the fact that the same risk was identified more than once may affect its perceived importance. Related risks can be combined when it makes sense to work the risks together. Dependent risks can be linked together when the outcome of one should be considered when prioritizing the other.

Determine Risk Drivers.   **Risk drivers** are the variables that cause the probability and consequence of software risk to fluctuate significantly. (Risk drivers for performance, support, cost, and schedule are described in [AirForce88].) Performance drivers can be found in technical specifications. Additional cost drivers are factors found in software cost-estimation models [Horowitz97]. Schedule drivers include the items on your critical path. Determining the risk drivers refines the risk context and helps to evaluate the risk.

Determine Source of Risk. Sources of risk are the root causes of the risk, determined by asking the same question—"Why?"—five times for each risk. Although the question remains the same, the response will differ until the root cause is determined. Here, for example, are the responses to why the vendor poses a schedule risk:

1. Why: Vendor cannot ensure delivery of the ABC subsystem to meet our integration schedule.
2. Why: The ABC subsystem is a development item for vendor.
3. Why: The ABC subsystem design requires component XYZ.
4. Why: Component XYZ requires the application of advanced technology.
5. Why: Vendor does not have engineers experienced in this technology.

Use Risk Analysis Techniques and Tools. Risk analysis techniques deal with conflicting cost and performance goals, uncertainty, and risk preference. They can be used to conduct trade studies, make decisions, decide whether to make or buy, and select system designs [Buede96]. We use risk analysis techniques to structure, analyze, evaluate, and communicate difficult problems:

- *Structure* states the decision, alternatives, uncertainties, and value of outcomes and specifies their relationships. Influence diagrams and decision trees are useful in structuring a decision model and describing possible scenarios. (An example of an influence diagram is found in section 5.2.)
- *Analyze* the decision model to determine the important variables and define their probabilistic relationships. (I describe several techniques for risk analysis in section 5.2.)
- *Evaluate* the decision model by calculating possible outcomes to determine risk profiles and the optimal decision policy. (I describe evaluation criteria for risk analysis in section 5.3.)
- *Communicate* risk analysis results by sharing understanding and insights to facilitate decision making. Results of risk analysis can be made accessible by storage in a centralized risk database.

Since the 1980s, techniques for risk analysis have become automated in risk analysis tools that range in both price and complexity [Horner97]. These tools use different decision algorithms and can arrive at different conclusions. Automated risk analysis tools can be grouped into the following categories [Buede96]:

- *Multiattribute utility*. To create a hierarchy of objectives and criteria for evaluating the options using a weighted score. Multiattribute utility models measure the performance of alternatives against competing objectives. These tools support sophisticated preference models to evaluate situations where the outcomes are difficult to compare (e.g., profit and customer satisfaction or costs and environmental considerations) [Saaty87].

❑ *Multicriteria optimization.* To provide a framework for finding an optimal solution by weighting or sorting multiple criteria.

❑ *Multicriteria partial ordering.* To accept limited weighting information to separate the dominated options from those that should remain candidates given the information provided.

❑ *Inference.* To support the probabilistic analysis of nested or sequential events.

❑ *Decision tree or influence diagram.* To evaluate risky decisions that incorporate both uncertainties and conflicting objectives.

❑ *Group process.* To support decision making in a group or team environment. Decision makers provide inputs and see the results as part of a group session.

Estimate the Risk Exposure.   Risk exposure is calculated by multiplying the probability and consequence if the risk occurred (the equation is shown in Figure 5.2) [Boehm89]. Probability is defined as greater than zero but less than 100. Consequence is typically determined in relation to cost, schedule, and technical goals. Quantifying risks by risk exposure provides a relative priority order to all the identified risks—for example:

❑ *Product*: Functionality XYZ will not likely be ready for the next release. (RE = .35 x Cost of missing functionality)

❑ *Time*: Very likely that testing will continue for three more months. (RE = .80 x Cost of 3 months testing)

❑ *Ballpark*: Independent verification and validation will likely cost about $15,000. (RE = .70 x $15,000)

❑ *Range*: Testing will likely cost between $10,000 and $20,000. (RE = (.70 x $10,000) to (.70 x $20,000))

❑ *Cost*: The regression test will almost certainly take one month with three senior engineers working on it. (RE = .95 x Cost of regression test)

Risk exposure (RE) = P x C

FIGURE 5.2   Risk exposure equation. Risk exposure is the product of the primary risk attributes of likelihood and loss. Likelihood *P* is the probability of an unsatisfactory outcome. Loss *C* is the consequence if an unsatisfactory outcome occurs.

Risk Exposure

	Low	Moderate	High
Short	5	2	1
Medium	7	4	3
Long	9	8	6

Time Frame

FIGURE 5.3 Risk severity. Risk exposure and the time frame for action determine the relative risk severity. Risk severity helps to distinguish the current risk priority. Over time, risk severity will change to help provide focus for the issues currently facing the project.

Evaluate Risk Against Criteria.   Predefined criteria for evaluating risk ensure that all risks will be judged against the same standard. **Risk severity** determines relative priority by mapping categories of risk exposure against the criteria of time. **Time frame** is how soon action is required to prevent the risk from occurring. Figure 5.3 shows how risk severity incorporates the time frame for action to arrive at a final, prioritized list of assessed risks. Risk severity groups risks such that the highest priority risks have a risk severity equal to 1.

Rank Risks Relative to Other Risks.   Risks can be sorted by evaluation criteria, so that the risks with the highest risk exposure and a short time frame for action are reviewed first. Rank the risks to focus project resources effectively and efficiently, and consider the time frame to arrive at a final, prioritized list of assessed risks. The prioritized risks are used to support the **Top-*N* Risk List**, a report of the most significant risks. A sample risk list is shown in Figure 5.4.

5.2   Define Risk Analysis Techniques

The risk statement and risk context can be refined through the use of risk analysis techniques. In this section, we look at several of these techniques.

Risk	Current Priority	Previous Priority	Weeks on Top 10	Action Plan Status	Risk Rating
High software productivity rate	1	1	2	Capturing requirements into requirements database tool. Ensuring availability of adequate personnel resources.	High
Off-site software development	2	9	2	Increasing the travel budget for additional site reviews. Setting up network access capability.	High
System weight	3	3	2	Established an action team to work this issue.	High
Algorithm validation	4	4	2	Acquiring algorithms. Generating output verification test plan.	High
Display projected image time line	5	5	2	Investigating incorporation of new development projection routines.	High
New user interface	6	7	2	Beginning the early prototyping of the user interfaces. Review with the end user being scheduled.	High
Demod/bit sync card delivery	7	6	2	Maintaining close monitoring/supervision of supplier's progress.	Moderate
Computer resource contention	8	8	2	Establishing a computer resource schedule sign-up list.	Moderate
Technical documentation	9	2	2	Training personnel on existing tools that facilitate the documentation process.	Moderate
Delivery schedule for hardware	10	N/A	1	Not yet assigned.	Moderate

FIGURE 5.4   Top-*N* Risk List.

5.2.1   Causal Analysis

Causal analysis shows the relation between an effect and its possible causes to get to the root cause of risk. Its purpose is to prevent problems by determining the problem's root cause. Among the techniques for causal analysis are the fishbone diagram and the five whys. The philosophy of causal analysis is that if an error has occurred, it will happen again unless something is done to stop it. Future errors are prevented by learning from past errors. Thus, people should evaluate their own errors as part of the process of producing software systems. Causal analysis is a simple three-step process:

1. Determine the cause of the error.

2. Determine the actions that will prevent the error in the future.

3. Implement these corrective actions.

Say that an error has been discovered: the control block field was not initialized, and four test errors were found. Some probing found that the cause was an oversight. Then a search tool was used to find additional occurrences. Finally, to prevent the error from occurring again, action was taken by enhancing the macro to set the field and adding the macro to the module checker tool.

5.2.2   Decision Analysis

Decision analysis is used to structure decisions and to represent real-world problems by models that can be analyzed to gain insight and understanding [Clemen91] [Baird89] [Raiffa68]. The elements of a decision model are the decisions, uncertain events, and values of outcomes. Once you have identified the elements of your decision, you can use two popular techniques for structuring your decision model: the influence diagram and the decision tree.

An **influence diagram** provides a graphical representation of the elements of a decision model. A common notation is used:

❏ Squares represent decisions nodes.

❏ Circles represent chance events.

❏ Rectangles with rounded corners represent values.

❏ Double circles represent outcomes known when the inputs are given.

Nodes are connected by arrows (called *arcs*) to show the relationship between the elements of a decision model. Arcs show precedence relationships; the node at the beginning of an arc is called a *predecessor*, and the node at the end is called a *successor*. There are two types of arrows: solid arrows pointing to chance and value nodes and dashed arrows pointing to decision nodes. (The influence diagram shown in Figure 5.5 illustrates the relationship of the elements of a

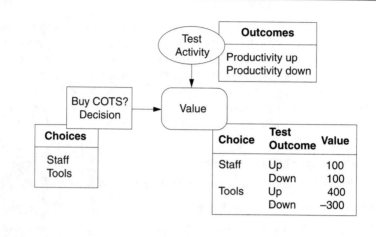

FIGURE 5.5   Influence diagram. The major components of a decision model are represented in this influence diagram: the decision to buy commercial off-the-shelf (COTS), the chance test activity outcome, and the value of the possible outcomes.

basic decision model.) Details can be added to a basic model until all relevant aspects of the decision are modeled. Influence diagrams form a *graph* without cycles. Cycles are not allowed to account for information (known or unknown) at each decision. Influence diagrams contain the same information as decision trees, but they have the additional capability to hide the details.

A decision tree provides a graphical representation of the elements of a decision model. (An example decision tree was shown in Chapter 2.) A common notation is used:

- ❑ Squares represent decisions.
- ❑ Branches emanating from a square represent choices.
- ❑ Circles represent chance events.
- ❑ Branches emanating from a circle represent possible outcomes.
- ❑ The ends of the branches specify values of outcomes.

5.2.3   Gap Analysis

Gap analysis determines the difference between two variables. The gap analysis in Figure 5.6 shows the difference between perceptions of importance and performance of risk management practices [Hall95]. The practices have been sorted by magnitude of the difference. The large gap for risk control illustrates the

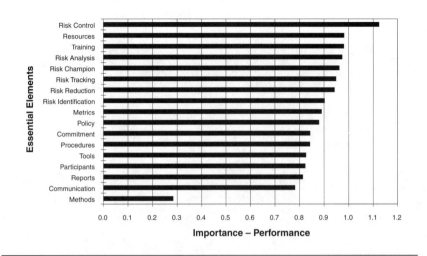

FIGURE 5.6   Gap analysis. In a risk management practices survey, gap analysis is used to determine the need for improvement of risk management practices. For each practice, survey respondents rated their perceived importance and performance. The difference between these two variables shows the need for improvement in risk management practices.

deficiency in this area. The smaller gap in risk identification shows that survey respondents believed they were performing risk identification better than risk control. Gap analysis shows that the organization is not performing at the level of importance in all areas.

Radar charts show gaps among a number of current and ideal performance areas [Brassard94]. The chart displays the important categories of performance (typically four to eight on a chart) and defines full performance in each category. Figure 5.7 shows process goals and current performance, and the progress made since the previous survey. Strengths and weaknesses are visible in the size of the gaps among current and ideal performance areas. This gap score can be added to each category by subtracting the team rating score from the highest number on the rating scale. For example, on a scale of 1 to 10, a team rating of 4 produces a gap score of 6 in categories B and E.

5.2.4   Pareto Analysis

Pareto analysis determines the order to address the issues. The basis of it is the 80/20 rule, or the Pareto principle: 20 percent of the sources cause 80 percent of

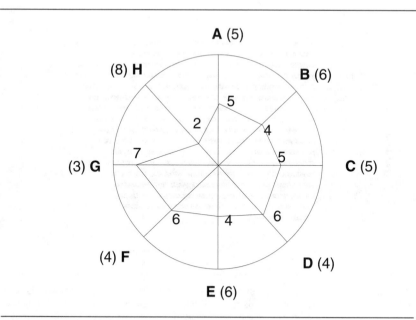

FIGURE 5.7   Radar chart. Progress in performance over time is easy to visualize using a radar chart. Prioritize the rating categories and write them clockwise on the chart. Zero at the center denotes no performance; the highest number on the scale denotes full performance. The goal for performance should be clearly marked. Work on the largest gap in the most critical category.

the problems. Pareto analysis is used to focus on the risks that have the greatest potential for reducing problems.

A Pareto chart displays the relative importance of the risks in a quickly interpreted visual format. A Pareto chart can display the number of identified risks (frequency) or the risk exposure (cost). In Figure 5.8, a Pareto chart is used to display the distribution of identified risks by SEI taxonomy element [Hall95]. The frequency of each risk category shows the highest number of risks identified. Knowing the most frequent risks and the greatest cost helps you to determine the most important issues with respect to your goals.

5.2.5   Sensitivity Analysis

Sensitivity analysis helps to determine the sensitivity of the model to variations in input variables by setting each variable to its extreme points (holding all other

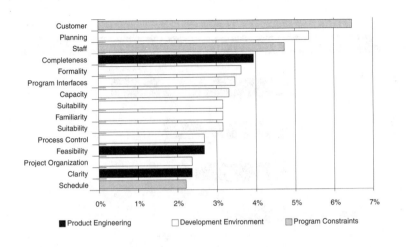

FIGURE 5.8   Pareto chart. The relative frequency of risks identified during risk assessments shows the top 20 percent that offer the greatest potential for improvement.

variables at nominal values). Variables with the ability to affect the decision are important; the others are relatively less important. Variables that are not sensitive to variation can be set to their nominal values and treated as known variables rather than uncertain variables. Sensitivity analysis focuses attention on the variables that have the greatest significance and helps to prioritize data collection. Two useful techniques for sensitivity analysis are tornado diagrams and utility functions.

Tornado diagrams allow you to see the most sensitive variables first. As shown in Figure 5.9, the graphic created by plotting a range for each variable does indeed resemble a tornado. The most sensitive variable is found at the top, and the least sensitive variable is at the bottom. The data required to plot a tornado diagram are a list of variables and their range of possible values. The high and low values of each variable determine how much effect the variable might have. The length of the bar for any given variable represents the extent to which (in this diagram) profit is sensitive to this variable.

Utility functions incorporate the decision maker's risk attitude to maximize expected utility rather than expected value. Utility functions represent an individual's feelings about risk. Different people have different risk attitudes and are willing to accept different levels of risk. Some are more prone to taking risks, while others are more conservative and avoid risk.

An exponential utility function uses a parameter known as the **risk tolerance** that determines how risk averse the utility function is. Larger values of risk

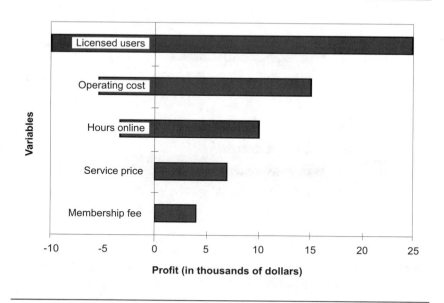

FIGURE 5.9   Tornado diagram. The profit of an Internet service provider is largely determined by the number of licensed users.

tolerance mean that an individual is less risk averse. To perform sensitivity analysis to understand risk preference, you can vary risk tolerance to determine at
what point the decision changes.

5.3   Define Risk Evaluation Criteria

Evaluation criteria serve as a first cut at ordering risks according to their importance. Evaluation criteria are defined to measure each risk against a known yard-
stick. Criteria to measure are probability, consequence, and time frame for action.

5.3.1   Probability

The likelihood of risk occurrence can be evaluated qualitatively or quantitatively.
As shown in Table 5.1, probability can be defined as a percentage, a phrase, or a
relative number.

TABLE 5.1 PROBABILITY EVALUATION CRITERIA

Probability	Uncertainty Statement	Evaluation
> 80%	Almost certainly, highly likely	5
61–80%	Probable, likely, probably, we believe	4
41–60%	We doubt, improbable, better than even	3
21–40%	Unlikely, probably not	2
1–20%	Highly unlikely, chances are slight	1

5.3.2 Consequence

The effect of a risk occurrence should be tailored to a specific project. Project goals can help to refine the evaluation criteria. Table 5.2 shows sample consequence criteria for cost, schedule, and technical goals.

TABLE 5.2 CONSEQUENCE EVALUATION CRITERIA

Criterion	Cost	Schedule	Technical
Low	Less than 1%	Slip 1 week	Slight effect on performance
Moderate	Less than 5%	Slip 2 weeks	Moderate effect on performance
High	Less than 10%	Slip 1 month	Severe effect on performance
Critical	10% or more	Slip over 1 month	Mission cannot be accomplished

5.3.3 Time Frame

The time frame for action to prevent risk occurrence should be tailored to a specific project. As shown in Table 5.3, the time frame for action can be short, medium, or long.

TABLE 5.3 TIME FRAME EVALUATION CRITERIA

Time Frame	Evaluation
1 Month	Short
2 Months	Medium
3 Months	Long

5.4   Establish the Risk Prioritization Scheme

Prioritization is necessary to provide focus for important risks. The nominal group technique and weighted multivoting are generally useful in planning, quality management, and process improvement [Brassard94].

5.4.1   Nominal Group Technique

Nominal group technique is a prioritization scheme that allows a team to come to a consensus quickly on the relative importance of risks by combining individual priorities into team priorities. Individuals rank the risks from one to the total number of risks. The summation of all rankings is the risk score. The lowest score is the most important risk.

5.4.2   Weighted Multivoting

Weighted multivoting is a consensus-based prioritization scheme used to *rate* risks. Team members rate (not rank) the relative importance of risks. Each team member is given the same number of tokens to distribute among the risks. Tokens may be a value (e.g., 100 points) or a number of stickers (e.g., 10 stars). Team members distribute the tokens among as many or as few risks as they desire.

5.5   Summary

In this chapter, I described the process definition steps for analyzing risk:

1. Define the risk analysis process.
2. Define risk analysis techniques.
3. Define risk evaluation criteria.
4. Establish the risk prioritization scheme.

I described the risk analysis process, which defines the activities and methods to estimate and evaluate risk. The activities of the risk analysis process are as follows:

1. Group similar and related risks.
2. Determine risk drivers.
3. Determine source of risk.

4. Use risk analysis techniques and tools.

5. Estimate the risk exposure.

6. Evaluate risk against criteria.

7. Rank risks relative to other risks.

I described several ways to describe an estimate of risk exposure:

- Product: Missing functionality in a software system.
- Time: Delay of days, weeks, months, or years.
- Ballpark: A rough estimate that includes a margin for error.
- Range: Two estimates spread to include the uncertainty.
- Cost: Quantification of resources over time.

I described several techniques for risk analysis:

- Causal analysis
- Decision analysis
- Gap analysis
- Pareto analysis
- Sensitivity analysis

I described the categories of automated analysis tools that are available to evaluate risk:

- Multiattribute utility
- Multicriteria optimization
- Multicriteria partial ordering
- Inference
- Influence diagram or decision tree
- Group process

5.6   Questions for Discussion

1. Describe the risk analysis process goals. Why is each goal important? Define quantitative success criteria for each goal.

2. List five ways that a risk database can assist the risk analysis process. How would you ensure that the risk database is maintained?

3. What are risk drivers? Describe the known software project risk drivers for both cost and schedule. Develop a matrix to show how these risk drivers relate to each other.

4. Why is it important to determine the source of risk? Describe the techniques that are available to understand the root cause of risk.

5. Unrealistic schedule and budget has been identified as a risk. Perform a causal analysis to prevent this problem on your next assignment. What are the chances that your corrective actions will be implemented successfully? Why do you think so?

6. You are the technical leader of a project that is on the cutting edge of wireless communication technology. Time to market is critical to your project's success, but there is a shortage of people with domain expertise. Use the risk analysis technique of your choice to structure, analyze, evaluate, and communicate this risk.

7. How can you define time frame for action to help prioritize risks? What is the value of using time to evaluate risk? Give an example that uses time to evaluate risk.

8. When should risk analysis be qualitative? When should risk analysis be quantitative? Explain your answer.

9. Many risks are interrelated. Analyze the following compound risk: Unstable requirements with a tight budget will likely cancel the project. Discuss the dependencies that exist between the two risks.

10. Why are consensus-based prioritization schemes useful on software projects? In general, would you expect individuals to agree on risk priorities? Discuss why you would or would not expect agreement.

5.7   References

[AirForce88] Air Force. *Software Risk Abatement*. AFSC/AFLC pamphlet 800-45. Wright-Patterson Air Force Base, OH: Air Force Systems Command, Air Force Logistics Command, 1988.

[AirForce81] *Integrated Computer Aided Manufacturing Architecture*, Part II, Vol. IV: *Function Modeling Manual (IDEF0)*. AFWAL-TR-81-4023, Wright-Patterson Air Force Base, OH: Air Force Systems Command, June 1981.

[Baird89] Baird B. *Managerial Decisions Under Uncertainty: An Introduction to the Analysis of Decision Making*. New York: Wiley, 1989.

[Boehm89] Boehm B. *IEEE Tutorial on Software Risk Management*. New York: IEEE Computer Society Press, 1989.

[Brassard94] Brassard M, Ritter D. *The Memory Jogger II*. Methuen, MA: GOAL/QPC, 1994.

[Buede96] Buede D. Decision/risk analysis software: Survey for trade studies. *Proc.* 7th INCOSE Symposium, Boston, July 1996.

[Clemen91] Clemen R. *Making Hard Decisions: An Introduction to Decision Analysis*. Boston: Wadsworth, 1991.

[Hall95] Hall E, Natwick G, Ulrich F, Engle C. Streamlining the risk assessment process. *Proc*. Seventh Software Technology Conference, Salt Lake City, UT, April 1995.

[Horner97] Horner P. (editor) Spreadsheet Add-Ins Survey. *ORMS Today*, Vol. 24, pp. 46–48, Atlanta: Institute for Operations Research and the Management Sciences (INFORMS), February 1997. [Note: This is a bimonthly journal]

[Horowitz97] Horowitz E, et al. *USC COCOMOII.1997 Reference Manual*. Los Angeles: University of Southern California, 1997.

[Raiffa68] Raiffa H. *Decision Analysis: Introductory Lectures on Choices Under Uncertainty*. New York: Random House, 1968.

[Saaty87] Saaty R. The analytical hierarchy process: What it is and how it is used. *Mathematical Modelling*, 9 (3–5): 161–176, 1987.

[VanScoy92] VanScoy R. Software development risk: Problem or opportunity. Technical report CMU/SEI-92-TR-30. Pittsburgh, PA: Software Engineering Institute, Carnegie Mellon University, 1992.

6

Plan Risk

All you need is the plan—the road map—and the courage to press on to your destination.
—Earl Nightingale

At all organizational levels, plans precede the accomplishment of work. Although management is responsible for high-level project planning, everyone plans with respect to accomplishing their assigned work. Planning for risk management includes the activity of developing risk management policy and procedures. A risk management plan is documented to respond to the goals established for the risk management initiative. Technical staff and integrated product teams develop more detailed action plans to resolve technical risk. These plans are needed to delegate responsibility and authority for managing risk to the lowest possible levels within the organization.

In this chapter, I discuss the process definition steps for risk resolution planning. I describe the **risk planning** process, which defines the activities and methods to develop alternatives for risk resolution. I explain how to establish thresholds that help you determine when to execute the risk action plan.

This chapter answers the following questions:

❏ What are the activities of the risk planning process?

❏ When should you use each of the strategies for risk resolution?

❏ How do risk scenarios help to monitor risk?

6.1   Define the Risk Planning Process

I define risk planning success criteria in terms of the process goals, the results that we expect to achieve by using the process. We can view the risk planning process from two perspectives: external and internal. The external view specifies the process controls, inputs, outputs, and mechanisms. The internal view specifies the process activities that transform inputs to outputs using the mechanisms.

6.1.1   Process Goals

The risk planning process is sufficient when it satisfies these goals:

- ❏ Provide visibility for key events and conditions.
- ❏ Reuse successful risk resolution strategies.
- ❏ Optimize selection criteria (e.g., risk leverage or risk diversification).
- ❏ Understand the next action for each high-severity risk.
- ❏ Establish automatic triggering mechanisms.

These goals can be used as a checklist to ensure the process quality.

6.1.2   Process Definition

The risk planning process definition is shown as an IDEF0 diagram in Figure 6.1. IDEF0 is a standard process definition notation used to describe a reusable process component for predictable risk action planning. The diagram describes the top-level process by its controls, inputs, outputs, and mechanisms [AirForce81].

Process Controls.   Project resources, project requirements, and the risk management plan regulate the risk planning process similar to the way they control the risk identification process (see Chapter 4).

Process Inputs.   A risk list, refined risk context, measures, metrics, and triggers are input to the risk planning process:

- ❏ *Risk list*—a list containing the priority order of all identified risks.
- ❏ *Refined risk context*—the collateral information surrounding the risk statement (events, conditions, constraints, assumptions, circumstances, contributing factors, and related issues) accessed via the risk database.

FIGURE 6.1   Risk planning process definition. *Plan Risk* encapsulates the activities of the process that transform inputs to outputs. Controls (at the top) regulate the process. Inputs (on the left) enter the process. Outputs (on the right) exit the process. Mechanisms (at the bottom) support the process.

- *Measures*—a unit to determine the dimensions, quantity, or capacity (e.g., lines of code are a measure of software size). Measures are usually input from the project tracking system.

- *Metrics*—a quantitative result of a measure (e.g., the software productivity metric was 20 lines of code per day). Metrics are guidelines or rules of thumb that are useful in planning. Metrics are often input from the project tracking system.

- *Triggers*—a device to activate, deactivate, or suspend a risk action plan. Triggers can be set by the project tracking system.

Process Outputs.   Scenarios, thresholds, and a risk action plan are output from the risk planning process.

A **risk scenario** is the projection of events and conditions that can lead to an unsatisfactory outcome. An **event** describes what must happen for the risk to occur. A **condition** describes the circumstance that enables a future event.

A **threshold** value defines the inception of risk occurrence. Predefined thresholds act as a warning level to indicate the need to execute the risk action plan.

The **risk action plan** documents the selected approach, resources required, and approval authority for risk resolution.

Process Mechanisms.   Mechanisms can be methods, techniques, tools, or other instruments that provide structure to the process activities. Quantitative targets, resolution strategies, selection criteria, and a risk database are mechanisms of the risk planning process.

Quantitative targets express the goals and objectives quantitatively. *Resolution strategies* (acceptance, avoidance, protection, reduction, research, reserves, and transfer) help to determine alternative ways to resolve a risk. **Selection criteria** formulate guidelines to help decide on a course of action. A *risk database* contains the risk action plan, associated scenarios, and threshold values.

6.1.3   Process Activities

The activities of the risk planning process are the tasks necessary to transform a prioritized risk list into a plan for risk resolution. The activities of the risk planning process are as follows:

1. Develop risk scenarios for high-severity risks.
2. Develop risk resolution alternatives.
3. Select the risk resolution approach.
4. Develop a risk action plan.
5. Establish thresholds for early warning.

I discuss the risk planning process activities as sequential steps, but they can be iterative or parallel in execution.

Develop Risk Scenarios for High-Severity Risks.   A risk scenario is the projection of events and conditions that can lead to risk occurrence. Risk scenarios should be developed for all risks that are critical to project success. These high-severity risks are found on the Top-*N* Risk List. There are three steps to develop a risk scenario:

1. Think about the risk as if it had occurred.
2. State the risk scenario as if the risk had already happened.
3. List the events and conditions that would precede the risk occurrence.

For example, the risk scenario "Code is produced without traceability to requirements" has not yet occurred. For this risk to be realized, several events might occur:

❏ Design reviews focus on data flow diagrams.

❏ Code produced is not backed up by requirements.

❏ Software tests cannot be traced to design specifications.

The following conditions increase the likelihood that the events will occur:

❏ The process is not documented or repeatable.

❏ There is no automated tool for requirements analysis.

❏ Design reviews are informal and ad hoc.

❏ The award fee is based on lines of code produced.

Develop Risk Resolution Alternatives.   Risk resolution alternatives are the set of options that may resolve risk if implemented. A risk resolution strategy uses acceptance, avoidance, protection, reduction, research, reserves, and transfer to develop alternatives for risk resolution. Each strategy should contain objectives, constraints, and alternatives. Risk resolution strategies are defined with examples in section 6.2.

Select the Risk Resolution Approach.   The risk resolution approach narrows the set of options to focus on the best alternative to resolve risk. You may want to combine several risk resolution strategies into one hybrid approach. For example, you may decide to perform market research to obtain demographics. Depending on the results of the research, you will either transfer the risk to a third party, or use risk reserves and develop a new technology in-house. Selection criteria help you determine the best alternative to resolve a risk. Selection criteria are defined in section 6.3 to help you determine your risk resolution approach.

Develop a Risk Action Plan.   The risk action plan details the selected approach to risk resolution. It documents the approach, resources required, and approval authority and contains the following elements:

❏ Approval authority.

❏ Responsible person.

❏ Resources required.

❏ Start date.

❏ Activities.

❏ Due date.

❏ Actions taken.

❏ Results achieved.

Establish Thresholds for Early Warning.   The risk action plan need not be implemented immediately. Early in the project, risk assessments tend to identify important risks that are not yet urgent. Because their time frame is not immediate, these important issues tend to be overlooked in planning and forgotten in tracking. Unless you put a triggering mechanism in place, you might not remember to address the issue until it is too late. For early warning, you can use triggering devices based on quantitative targets and thresholds.

Quantitative targets are the goals expressed quantitatively. They provide best-in-class objectives that can be determined by benchmarks and metrics. Every measurement should have a full-performance value that defines the quantitative goal, or target. A minimum performance value defines the warning level, or threshold. Understanding the range of acceptable values provides meaning to measurement data. Table 6.1 shows the quantitative targets for DoD-contracted software projects [Brown95]. Both management (e.g., voluntary staff turnover) and technical (e.g., system response time) goals for performance should be defined.

A threshold is a warning level associated with a quantitative target. Thresholds establish the minimum acceptable value with respect to the quantitative target. Values over threshold define the inception of risk occurrence. Predefined thresholds act as an early warning system to indicate the need for action.

TABLE 6.1 QUANTITATIVE TARGETS FOR A SOFTWARE PRODUCT

Measurement	Target	Threshold
Defect removal efficiency	>95%	<85%
Schedule slip or cost in excess of risk reserve	0%	10%
Total requirements growth	≤1% per month	≥50% per year
Total software program documentation	<1,000 words per function point	<2,000 words per function point
Voluntary staff turnover per year	1–3%	10%

6.2   Define Risk Resolution Strategies

In this section, I define several strategies for risk resolution.

6.2.1   Risk Acceptance

Risk acceptance is a strategy for risk resolution of consciously choosing to live with the risk consequence. It is a strategy to use when you can live with the loss.

For example, managers expect a low percentage of voluntary staff turnover. The expense of replacing an entry-level engineer might be the same as trying to keep the person by increasing his or her benefits. The strategy is to accept the risk that trained personnel will leave the project. The cost of hiring their replacement is the price that is paid as a consequence.

6.2.2   Risk Avoidance

Risk avoidance is a strategy for risk resolution to eliminate the risk altogether. Avoidance is a strategy to use when a lose-lose situation is likely. For example, you may choose not to bid a proposal for a fixed-cost project. In this example, the project is a semiautonomous robotic vehicle for a NASA mission to Mars [Shishko96]. You review the risk to determine if a lose-lose situation is likely:

- *Cost risk*. There is a fixed budget of $25 million over its entire life cycle.
- *Schedule risk*. The robotic vehicle must be integrated into the spacecraft.
- *Performance risk*. There are design constraints on vehicle volume, mass, and power. The vehicle has an interface with the spacecraft and makes use of commercial and government specified parts.
- *Operability risk*. There is an unknown landed configuration for the space-craft lander; new approaches to command, control, and communication; and uncertain environmental conditions.

You determine that the stakes are high for each identified risk. If the cost risk is realized, your organization cannot afford to continue the project, resulting in major customer dissatisfaction. If the schedule or performance risk is realized, the vehicle will not be integrated into the spacecraft and the technical mission will be compromised. If the operability risk is realized, the vehicle will not perform in operation, and the technical mission will be compromised. Use a risk scenario to determine if you have the organizational support, staff experience, and risk management expertise to win on the project, *not* just the proposal.

6.2.3   Risk Protection

Risk protection is a strategy to employ redundancy to mitigate (reduce the probability and/or consequence of a risk). For example, the Federal Aviation Administration (FAA) procured a voice switching and control system in the early 1990s at a cost of over $1 billion. The winning proposal specified Tandem computers as the hardware. The extra cost for fault-tolerant computers was like buying reliability insurance. If one processor failed, the Tandem would switch over to the other processor.

6.2.4   Risk Reduction

Risk reduction is a strategy to decrease risk through mitigation, prevention, or anticipation. Risk is reduced by decreasing either the probability of the risk occurrence or the consequence when the risk is realized. Reduction is a strategy to use when risk leverage exists. For example, peer reviews reduce the likelihood of defects in work products. The use of peer reviews is proved to reduce rework, the consequence of defects. Peer reviews cost money, but they save more than they cost.

6.2.5   Risk Research

Risk research is a strategy to obtain more information through investigation. Research is a strategy to use when more information is needed. For example, prototyping is a technique for eliciting information from users to define system interfaces. In market research, knowledge is gained through consumer questionnaires. Trade studies are another type of strategy for buying information to make a better decision.

6.2.6   Risk Reserves

Risk reserves is a strategy to use contingency funds and built-in schedule slack. Reserves is a strategy to use when uncertainty exists in cost or time. For example, instead of padding estimates across the board, you could identify the high-risk subsystems. By specifying where the risk is in the system, you can associate your reserves with the risk. When dealing with risk, having a margin for error makes sense.

6.2.7   Risk Transfer

Risk transfer is a strategy to shift the risk to another person, group, or organization. Transfer is a strategy to use when another group has control. For example, outsourcing is used to combat wage differentials between engineers in different countries. The risk of high-cost software is transferred to a group with more competitive wages. Within the United States, the risk of high employee overhead rates is transferred by using subcontractors to develop software.

6.3   Define Selection Criteria

Selection criteria help determine the best alternative to resolve a risk. Defined selection criteria provide a common basis to understand the characteristics of a good alternative. Agreement on the priority of selection criteria helps to make necessary trade-offs. Conflicting objectives that maximize (e.g., profit, sales, control, quality) or minimize (e.g., cost, defects, uncertainty, loss) can be sorted. Two policies often used as selection criteria are leverage and diversification.

6.3.1   Risk Leverage

Risk leverage is a measure of the relative cost-benefit of performing various candidate risk resolution activities. The equation for risk leverage is shown in Figure 6.2. Leverage is a rule for risk resolution that reduces risk by decreasing the risk exposure (RE). **Risk resolution cost** is the cost of implementing the risk action plan. The concept of leverage helps determine actions with the highest payback. Major risk leverage exists in the early phases of software development. Early detection of risks reduces rework costs [Boehm89].

In fact, major risk leverage does exist in later phases of software development. Risk management can be used to recover allowable cost in contract performance when a request for equitable adjustment fails. From my experience working with large aerospace corporations, a reasonable damage claim returns 75 cents on the dollar. The risk exposure before the claim activity is the probability of a cost overrun times the consequence of the overrun. At project completion, 100 percent of the cost overrun is the prior risk exposure (see Figure 6.3). Assuming 75 cents on the dollar for a reasonable claim, only 25 percent of the cost overrun remains at risk after the damage claim activity. If the cost to

$$\text{Risk leverage} = \frac{RE_{(before)} - RE_{(after)}}{\text{Risk resolution cost}}$$

FIGURE 6.2   Risk leverage. Risk leverage is a measure of the relative cost-benefit of performing various candidate risk resolution activities. $RE_{(before)}$ is the risk exposure before risk resolution. $RE_{(after)}$ is the risk exposure after risk resolution.

prepare the entitlement (the legal basis for the claim) and quantum (the value of the claim) takes $100,000 (roughly three experts for six months), the risk leverage would be 7.5 to 1 for a 1 million overrun, and 75 to 1 for a 10 million overrun.

$$\text{Risk leverage} = \frac{(100 \text{ percent} \times \text{cost overrun}) - (25 \text{ percent} \times \text{cost overrun})}{\text{Cost of claim}}$$

FIGURE 6.3   Risk leverage at project completion. Major risk leverage exists for direct and indirect (delay and disruption) changes that cause a software project to overrun.

6.3.2   Risk Diversification

Diversification is a rule for risk resolution that reduces risk by distribution. (In the financial world, mutual funds provide diversification in stock market investment.) In software systems, we know there are no silver bullets, no single solutions. Diversification tells us not to put all our eggs in one basket. In other words, do not rely heavily on one customer, vendor, method, tool, or person to fulfill project needs. For example, General Electric (GE) has successfully broadened its customer base by the application of government defense technology to the commercial (auto) industry [Schine96]. Another way to diversify is to cross-train individuals so there is no single point of failure on the team. Diversification builds a balanced approach that stresses mastery of software project fundamentals.

6.4   Develop the Risk Action Plan Template

A risk action plan template is used to capture the risk resolution strategy in a standard format. The template provides room to add the events and conditions of the risk scenario. The template contains the following fields:

- ❏ Risk resolution strategy.
- ❏ Objectives.
- ❏ Alternatives.
- ❏ Approach.
- ❏ Approval authority.

- ❑ Responsible person.
- ❑ Resources required
- ❑ Start date.
- ❑ Activities.
- ❑ Due date.
- ❑ Actions taken.
- ❑ Results achieved.

6.5   Summary

In this chapter, I described the process definition steps for risk resolution planning:

1. Define the risk planning process.
2. Define risk resolution strategies.
3. Define selection criteria.
4. Develop the risk action plan template.

I described the risk planning process, which defines the activities and methods to develop alternative strategies for risk resolution. The activities of the risk planning process are as follows:

1. Develop risk scenarios for high-severity risks.
2. Develop risk resolution alternatives.
3. Select the risk resolution approach.
4. Develop a risk action plan.
5. Establish thresholds for early warning.

I described when to use each of the strategies for risk resolution:

- ❑ Acceptance—when you can live with the loss.
- ❑ Avoidance—when a lose-lose situation is likely.
- ❑ Protection—when redundancy will mitigate the risk.
- ❑ Reduction—when risk leverage exists.
- ❑ Research—when more information is needed.
- ❑ Reserves—when uncertainty exists in cost or time.
- ❑ Transfer—when another group has control.

I described how risk scenarios help to monitor risk. The events and conditions of the risk scenario serve as a checklist to determine whether progress in risk resolution is being made. If progress is not made, events occur and conditions still exist that increase the probability of risk occurrence. There are three steps to develop a risk scenario:

1. Think about the risk as if it had occurred.
2. State the risk scenario as if the risk already happened.
3. List the events and conditions that would precede the risk occurrence.

6.6   Questions for Discussion

1. Describe the risk planning process goals. Why is each goal important? Define quantitative success criteria for each goal.
2. Do you agree that risk scenarios should be developed for significant risks only? Justify your answer.
3. Describe the events and conditions in the following risk scenario: The development process has been ignored, and product defects are increasing.
4. Discuss how you might use risk protection and risk transfer to combat a system reliability risk. Discuss the similarities and differences between these risk resolution strategies.
5. Many individuals within your organization have trouble keeping up with new technology. The learning curve for integrating new technology into your organization has been identified as a risk. Develop a risk resolution strategy to address this risk. Include your organization's objectives, constraints, and alternatives.
6. A significant integration risk has been identified. The cause is determined to be a lack of thorough software testing due to insufficient time allocated to the integration and test phase. You have been assigned to investigate this risk and make recommendations to reduce the risk. Project management wants to maximize software quality and minimize total cost. How would you trade off these conflicting objectives? What are your recommendations to project management regarding this risk?
7. Discuss the risk leverage that exists in the operations and maintenance phase of the life cycle.
8. How can a threshold be used as part of an early warning system?
9. As a system engineer, you are responsible for requirements management. Develop a graph of expected software requirements volatility over the project life cycle. Define the quantitative target and associated warning level for software requirements volatility at each stage of development.

10. Discuss the following human traits that are useful in coping with uncertainty: attitude, belief, confidence, courage, faith, and imagination. Which trait do you think is the most important? Explain your answer.

6.7 References

[AirForce81] *Integrated Computer Aided Manufacturing Architecture*, Part II, Vol. IV: *Function Modeling Manual (IDEF0)*. AFWAL-TR-81-4023. Wright-Patterson Air Force Base, OH: Air Force Systems Command, June 1981.

[Boehm89] Boehm B. *IEEE Tutorial on Software Risk Management*. New York: IEEE Computer Society Press, 1989.

[Brown95] Brown N. *The Program Manager's Guide to Software Acquisition Best Practices*. Arlington, VA: Software Program Managers Network, 1995.

[Nightingale86] Nightingale E. *Lead the Field*. Audiocassette, Chicago: Nightingale-Conant, 1986.

[Schine96] Schine E., et al. Liftoff: Michael Armstrong has made Hughes an electronics and telecom contender. *Business Week*, 136–147, April 22, 1996.

[Shishko96] Shishko R. Evaluation of risk management strategies for a low-cost, high-risk project. *Proc.* Sixth International Symposium of the International Council on Systems Engineering, Boston, July 1996.

7

Track Risk

The greatest potential for control tends to exist at the point where action takes place.

—Louis A. Allen

Monitoring risk may seem like a passive activity, but that is far from the truth. Risk tracking activities include measuring risk and observing project indicators for valuable information regarding when it is time to execute the risk action plan. An **indicator** implies a value without specifying the quantity directly (e.g., the number of function points is a size measure that indicates software complexity). Groups of indicators provide visibility into project status (e.g., planned versus actual cost). A **leading indicator** is one that has a predictive capability (e.g., requirements growth may be a leading indicator for software size). Indicators help us to know when to take action to avoid the consequences of risk. Knowing when to take action is key to effective risk control.

In this chapter, I discuss the process definition steps for tracking risk. I describe the **risk tracking** process, which defines the activities and methods to monitor risk status. I explain techniques and tools to compare risk status with planned thresholds in order to determine when to trigger risk action plan execution.

This chapter answers the following questions:

❑ What are the activities of the risk tracking process?

❑ How can static measures indicate dynamic risks?

❑ What types of triggers provide notification of unacceptable risk?

7.1   Define the Risk Tracking Process

I define risk tracking success criteria in terms of the process goals, the results that we expect to achieve by using the process. We can view the risk tracking process from two perspectives: external and internal. The external view specifies the process controls, inputs, outputs, and mechanisms. The internal view specifies the process activities that transform inputs to outputs using the mechanisms.

7.1.1   Process Goals

The risk tracking process is sufficient when it satisfies these goals:

- ❏ Monitor the events and conditions of risk scenarios.
- ❏ Track risk indicators for early warning.
- ❏ Provide notification for triggering mechanisms.
- ❏ Capture results of risk resolution efforts.
- ❏ Report risk measures and metrics regularly.
- ❏ Provide visibility into risk status.

These goals can be used as a checklist to ensure the process quality.

7.1.2   Process Definition

The risk tracking process definition is shown as an IDEF0 diagram in Figure 7.1. IDEF0 is a standard process definition notation used to describe a reusable process component for predictable risk tracking. The diagram describes the top-level process by its controls, inputs, outputs, and mechanisms [AirForce81].

Process Controls.   Project resources, project requirements, and the risk management plan regulate the risk tracking process similar to the way they control the risk identification process (see Chapter 4).

Process Inputs.   Scenarios, thresholds, and risk status are input to the risk tracking process:

- ❏ *Scenarios* monitor the events and conditions that can lead to an unsatisfactory outcome to determine whether the probability of risk occurrence is increasing.

❏ *Thresholds* define the inception of risk occurrence. Predefined thresholds act as a warning to indicate the need to send notification to execute the action plan.

❏ *Risk status* captures the results of implementing the risk action plan in the risk database.

Process Outputs.   Measures, metrics, and triggers are output from the risk tracking process.

Measures determine the dimensions, quantity, or capacity (e.g., lines of code measure the software size). *Metrics* are a composite measure (e.g., the software productivity metric was 20 lines of code per day) that serves as a guideline or rule of thumb and is useful in planning. *Triggers* are devices to activate, deactivate, or suspend activity (e.g., the trigger activated the risk action plan).

Process Mechanisms.   Mechanisms can be methods, techniques, tools, or other instruments that provide structure to the process activities. Risk tracking techniques, risk tracking tools, and a risk database are mechanisms of the risk tracking process.

Risk tracking techniques are measures and metrics that help to monitor risk status over time. *Risk tracking tools* automate the tracking process. The *risk database* contains the measures, metrics, and triggers.

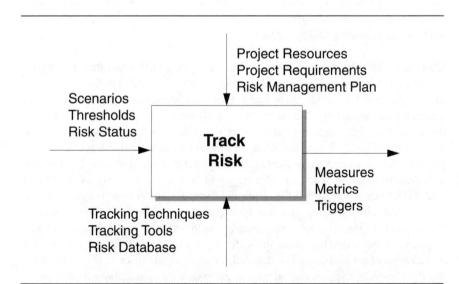

FIGURE 7.1   Risk tracking process definition. *Track Risk* encapsulates the activities of the process that transform inputs to outputs. Controls (at the top) regulate the process. Inputs (on the left) enter the process. Outputs (on the right) exit the process. Mechanisms (at the bottom) support the process.

7.1.3   Process Activities

The activities of the risk tracking process are the tasks necessary to monitor risk status and provide notification to trigger risk resolution. The activities of the risk tracking process are as follows:

1. Monitor risk scenarios.
2. Compare thresholds to status.
3. Provide notification for triggers.
4. Report risk measures and metrics.

I discuss the risk tracking process activities as sequential steps, but they can be iterative or parallel in execution.

Monitor Risk Scenarios.   The time required to monitor risk scenarios is an investment that we make for high-severity risks. Risk scenarios are like threads that string a risk to a problem. The events and conditions in it are the checkpoints along the road to a problem. Risk scenarios are monitored to determine if the probability of risk occurrence is increasing. When it is difficult to see the big picture, risk scenarios can provide evidence that attention is required because the risk is materializing. Events and conditions of a risk scenario are tracked to decide whether the increase in risk exposure justifies immediate action. Changes in events and conditions can also indicate successful risk resolution. Tracking risk scenarios over time increases the level of confidence that risk probability is decreasing, indicating that progress is being made.

Compare Thresholds to Status.   Work activity yields status that is captured in a project tracking tool. When status is input, individual indicators are compared to their planned thresholds. Indicator values outside their accepted norms detect unacceptable conditions and serve as an early-warning system. A *trigger* is a device to control the implementation of a risk action plan. It can be set through the monitoring of status indicators, planned thresholds, quantitative targets, and the project schedule. The variance between planned thresholds and actual status provides information on when to set a trigger. For risk that is within the planned threshold, triggers can signal the closure of the risk resolution activity.

The anticipated value of a threshold can change at predetermined points in the life cycle. For example, an iterative build strategy can allocate memory requirements such that the threshold is 75 percent capacity at build one completion and 25 percent at build three. For thresholds that change at discrete points throughout the life cycle, triggers can be used to put risk resolution activity on hold.

Provide Notification for Triggers.   When a trigger is set, notification is sent to the appropriate personnel through established communication channels. Four types of triggers (described in section 7.4) can provide notification of unacceptable risk:

- ❏ *Periodic event*—notification for project-scheduled activities.
- ❏ *Elapsed time*—notification for dates based on a calendar.
- ❏ *Relative variance*—notification outside a range of acceptable values.
- ❏ *Threshold value*—notification for values that cross a predetermined threshold.

Report Risk Measures and Metrics.   A measure is a standard unit of measurement to determine dimensions, quantity, or capacity. For example, the number of logged risks is a measure of identified risk captured in the risk database. A more complex measure is risk exposure, which is a measure of risk magnitude calculated by multiplying risk probability and consequence. A metric uses historical measures to provide guidelines that can help manage the future. It is determined from a composite of measurement data taken over time. For example, the **risk management index** (RMI), a percentage of total risk exposure to project cost, is a risk metric that provides a rule of thumb for acceptable risk. Through historical data, the RMI can be used to indicate whether a project is high, moderate, or low risk. (Measures and metrics that help determine effectiveness of risk management are defined in section 7.3.)

7.2   Define Risk Tracking Techniques

Project tracking techniques are often driven by the availability of tools. A project's level of automation depends on the tool set used. Simple spreadsheet applications can be used to chart progress and report trends. A **trend** is a time series of metrics data (e.g., the trend in productivity is up from last quarter). Sophisticated scheduling tools can be used to track activities and resources over time. Whatever your level of automation, tracking a minimum set of programmatic and technical performance measures is essential to monitoring risk. **Technical performance measures** (TPM) describe the quantitative targets (i.e., goals) for system performance.

One risk tracking technique uses static measures to indicate dynamic risks. A range of acceptable status is defined; then status is tracked to determine trends. When measures fall below acceptable values, action plans are triggered. The three steps to monitor risk using static measures are as follows:

1. Define warning levels of unacceptable status as thresholds.

2. Monitor status indicators in terms of measures and metrics.

3. Regulate the risk action plan execution using triggers.

In this section, I describe a project control panel used as a tool for project management and the software measures that are used as key project indicators.

7.2.1   Project Control Panel

A project control panel is a visualization of key project indicators that serves as the status display for management and technical metrics. Figure 7.2 depicts the top layer of a project control panel [Brown95]. The control panel is both a communication tool and an operational tool. A project is on course when the gauges of the control panel are kept within accepted ranges. A **gauge** is a graphic display of a status indicator, a quantitative target, and a threshold warning level. Several commercial companies, including Lockheed Martin and Texas Instruments, have implemented the control panel as an automated project tracking tool. There are several features of an automated control panel:

❏ Monitor project health by a core set of metrics.

❏ Group metrics into gauge clusters.

❏ Convey dissimilar metrics using different formats.

❏ Highlight safe operating areas and warning levels.

❏ Update display based on real-time work flow.

❏ Display lower-level and trend data.

Software measures such as earned value are leading risk indicators. By setting thresholds for each indicator, you ensure that you will be alerted to any danger. However, the accumulation of several indicators that are each 10 percent off target will drastically affect your project with no prior warning. To handle this situation, accumulate these indicators in your project cost model throughout the life cycle. (This concept is implemented in the Living Lifecycle Model, described by example in Chapter 22.) Trust your updated cost model, and it will warn you of impending danger, even when others are clueless. Following are key indicators of the project control panel:

❏ *Progress*. Earned value measures the amount of work remaining by comparing planned and actual milestone completion. Cumulative months measure the schedule remaining by comparing planned and actual time used. Cumulative dollars measure the budget remaining by comparing the estimated completion cost with the actual dollars spent.

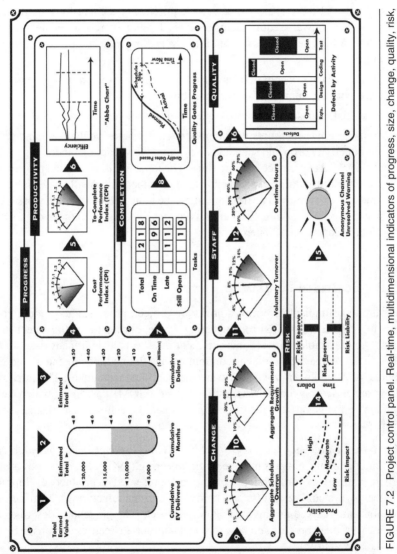

FIGURE 7.2   Project control panel. Real-time, multidimensional indicators of progress, size, change, quality, risk, and staff are embodied in a project control panel [Brown95].

❏ *Size*. Lines of code measure the software size by counting physical or logical source statements.

❏ *Change*. Volatility measures the number of requirements that are added, deleted, or modified. You should expect some requirements growth early in the life cycle. For example, derived requirements account for requirements growth in software requirements analysis. Eventually requirements must stabilize. A high percentage of volatility is a leading indicator of instability and failure.

❏ *Quality*. The number of defects closed and open measure the errors found and fixed with the number of errors remaining.

❏ *Risk*. Risk exposure measures the level of unresolved risk.

❏ *Staff*. Turnover measures the number of staff who leave the team and cause a productivity drop and schedule disruption. New team members, regardless of skills and experience, require time to become familiar with the project and processes. In addition, a productive team member will usually have to devote time to the new hire. Overtime measures the hours over a standard work week that the staff is working. Staff effectiveness decreases when the overtime percentage approaches 20 percent.

7.2.2   Software Measures

Software measurement determines how well project, process, and product goals are being met. It is essential for indicating where a project is with respect to its goals. (An unreliable software measurement process is a significant risk.) In the past five years, the measurement community has defined, documented, and distributed guidebooks on proved software measurement techniques. The three that follow are based on the Goal/Question Metric (GQM) paradigm, which helps maintain a focus on the measures appropriate to achieve established goals [Basili84]:

1. *Metrics Guidebook for Integrated Systems and Product Development*, by the International Council on Systems Engineering (INCOSE), describes a metrics framework for functions commonly represented on product development teams (systems, test, software, hardware, and manufacturing). Management goals are derived through the GQM approach. The guidebook describes the measurement process and how to select appropriate metrics to manage by the data [Wilbur95].

2. *Practical Software Measurement* (PSM), by the DoD's Joint Logistics Commanders Joint Group on Systems Engineering, is a guidebook for project managers, written by measurement analysts. It uses measurement indicators

to deal with issues (and risks) that cannot be measured directly. PSM recommends using multiple indicators to analyze a software issue [PSM96].

3. *Software Measures and the Capability Maturity Model*, from SEI, applies the GQM paradigm to the goals of each CMM key process area. Indicators are grouped into categories that provide visibility for status and insight into process effectiveness. Indicators change depending on the maturity level of the organization [Baumert92].

7.3   Define Risk Measures and Metrics

The following measures can be used to determine risk management metrics:

- *Number of risks*—the count of risks currently being managed.
- *Number of logged risks*—the cumulative total of identified issues logged in the risk database.
- *Risk category*—a count of the number of risks identified in each risk category, an indication of the extent to which risks in a specific category might affect the project.
- *Risk exposure*—defined by the relationship [Risk exposure $(RE) = P \times C$], where RE is the risk exposure, P is the probability of an unsatisfactory outcome, and C is the consequence if the outcome is unsatisfactory.
- *Risk severity*—a level of relative risk that includes the dimension of time (e.g., a risk severity category of 1 on a scale of 1 to 9 indicates the highest risk prioritized by risk exposure and time frame for action).
- *Risk leverage*—defined as [$(RE_{before} - RE_{after})$/Risk resolution cost] where RE_{before} is the RE before initiating the risk resolution effort and RE_{after} is the RE after resolution. Thus, risk leverage is a measure of the relative cost-benefit of performing various candidate risk resolution activities.
- *Risk threshold*—determined based on a quantitative goal. Risk threshold is a value that triggers a risk action plan. A notification is sent for variance above the threshold value.
- *Risk indicator*—the current value of project, process, and product measures monitored for risk (e.g., cost, schedule, progress, productivity, completion, change, staff turnover, quality, and risk).
- *Risk management index*—a summation of the risk exposure in quantifiable terms for all risks as a percentage of total project cost.
- *Return on investment*—a summation of the savings for all risks divided by the cost of risk management, which I call $ROI_{(RM)}$.

7.4   Define Triggering Devices

Triggers provide three basic control functions. To *activate*, triggers provide a wake-up call for revisiting a risk action plan (or the progress made against the plan). To *deactivate*, triggers can be used to signal the closure of the risk resolution activity. To *suspend*, triggers can be used to put the execution of risk action plans on hold. Four types of triggers provide notification of unacceptable risk levels:

❏ *Periodic event*—notification for activities. Project-scheduled events (e.g., monthly management reports, project reviews, and technical design reviews) are the basis for periodic event triggers.

❏ *Elapsed time*—notification for dates. A calendar (e.g., thirty days from today, end of the quarter, and beginning of the fiscal year) is the basis for elapsed-time triggers. You can also use specific dates as time-based triggers.

❏ *Relative variance*—notification outside a range of acceptable values. In Figure 7.3 relative variance is the difference between a predetermined quantitative target and the actual value. A deviation of a specified percentage, either above or below a planned quantitative target, will set a trigger to raise a flag. The relative variance trigger device is useful when monitoring to a requirement window. You may want to know when the actual value is above or

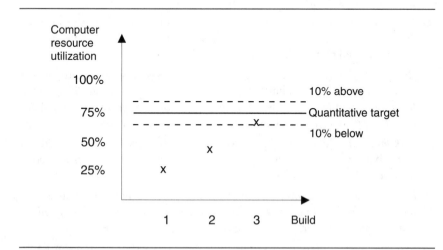

FIGURE 7.3   Relative variance. A trigger based on relative variance provides notification outside a range of acceptable values. A threshold is set at 10 percent above and below the quantitative target.

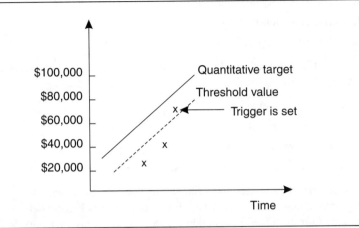

FIGURE 7.4   Threshold value. A trigger based on threshold value provides notification for values that cross a predetermined threshold.

below a range of acceptable values relative to your target. A positive variance can indicate a system that is engineered beyond specification. The advantage is that exceeding the specification in this area may leave response time in another area. The disadvantage is that overbuilt systems can be more costly than planned. A negative variance can indicate unmet requirements. In this example, threshold value is the percentage above and below the quantitative target that determines the size of the monitoring window. The more risk averse you are, the larger the monitoring window should be.

❏ *Threshold value*—notification for values that cross a predetermined threshold. In Figure 7.4, a comparison of a status indicator to a threshold value is the basis for threshold value triggers. A trigger is set when a status indicator crosses a threshold value. In this example, a study has a not-to-exceed budget of $100,000. A cost indicator of $80,000 will wake up the primary investigator in time to conclude the experiments and report the results within the fixed-cost budget.

7.5 Summary

In this chapter, I described the process definition steps for tracking risk:

1. Define the risk tracking process.

2. Define risk tracking techniques.

3. Define risk measures and metrics.

4. Define triggering devices.

I described the risk tracking process, which defines the activities and methods to monitor risk status:

1. Monitor risk scenarios.

2. Compare thresholds to status.

3. Provide notification for triggers.

4. Report risk measures and metrics.

I described how static measures can indicate dynamic risks. A range of acceptable status is defined. Over time, status is tracked to determine trends. When measures fall below acceptable values, action plans are triggered. The three steps to monitor risk using static measures are as follows:

1. Define warning levels of unacceptable status as thresholds.

2. Monitor status indicators in terms of measures and metrics.

3. Regulate the risk action plan execution using triggers.

I described techniques and tools to compare risk status with planned thresholds in order to determine when to trigger action plan execution. A project control panel is a tool that displays the status of key project indicators. A project is on course when the gauges of the control panel are kept within accepted ranges. Gauges are defined for performance measures in the areas of progress, size, change, quality, risk, and staff.

I described four types of triggers that provide notification of unacceptable risk:

❑ *Periodic event*—notification for activities on the schedule.

❑ *Elapsed time*—notification for dates based on a calendar.

❑ *Relative variance*—notification for values outside an acceptable range.

❑ *Threshold value*—notification for values that cross a predetermined threshold.

7.6   Questions for Discussion

1. Describe the risk tracking process goals. Why is each goal important? Define quantitative success criteria for each goal.

2. Do you think tracking risk scenarios can indicate success or failure of the risk resolution activity? Explain how monitoring risk scenarios increases your certainty over time.

3. Your project tracking tool has been updated to include the latest software modules completed through unit test. The cumulative earned value indicator fell below the planned threshold. Explain how your risk tracking process will react to this event.

4. Explain how triggers can be used to regulate risk action plan execution.

5. List two types of triggers that can be used to provide notification of unacceptable risk. Give an example of how each trigger can activate a risk action plan. Describe who will be notified, and how they will be notified.

6. Discuss the relationship among the key indicators of a software project: progress, size, change, quality, risk, and staff.

7. No single metric can provide wisdom. Describe the minimum set of metrics that you would recommend to ensure project success.

8. Discuss the consequences of reporting risk metrics that are not timely, validated, economical, or understandable.

9. What measures and metrics should be tracked to ensure a cost-effective risk management process?

10. How do you think risk management reserve should be monitored? Explain your answer.

11. Do you agree that the greatest potential for control tends to exist at the point where action takes place? Discuss why you do or do not agree.

7.7   References

[AirForce81] *Integrated Computer Aided Manufacturing Architecture*, Part II, Vol. IV: *Function Modeling Manual (IDEF0)*. AFWAL-TR-81-4023. Wright-Patterson Air Force Base, OH: Air Force Systems Command, June 1981.

[Basili84] Basili V, Weiss D. A methodology for collecting valid software engineering data. *IEEE Transactions on Software Engineering*, 10 (6):728–738, 1984.

[Baumert92] Baumert J, McWhinney M. Software measures and the Capability Maturity Model. Technical report CMU/SEI-92-TR-25. Pittsburgh, PA: Software Engineering Institute, Carnegie Mellon University, 1992.

[Brown95] Brown N. *The Program Manager's Guide to Software Acquisition Best Practices*. Arlington, VA: Software Program Managers Network, 1995.

[PSM96] *Practical Software Measurement: A Guide to Objective Program Insight*. Newport, RI: Naval Undersea Warfare Center, 1996.

[Wilbur95] Wilbur A, et al. *Metrics Guidebook for Integrated Systems and Product Development*. Seattle: International Council on Systems Engineering, 1995.

8

Resolve Risk

The mastery of risk is the foundation of modern life, from insurance to the stock market to engineering, science, and medicine. We cannot see the future, but by calculating probabilities, we can do the next best thing: make intelligent decisions— and take control of our lives—on the basis of scientific forecasts.
—Peter L. Bernstein

When you think of techniques for risk resolution, you might think of prototyping and simulation. **Prototyping** is a technique for reducing risk by buying information. Knowledge is gained through creating a physical model without adding the implementation details. Prototyping validates mental models and provides an effective means for communicating with the user community. **Simulation** is an analytic model of system behavior used to determine performance capabilities and limitations. Computer simulations help us evaluate large and complex systems that require numerous trade-offs. Prototyping and simulation are techniques under the class of risk resolution strategy that we defined as risk research. As we know from Chapter 6, there are several other strategies for risk resolution. The danger in describing specific approaches to risk resolution is that you might develop tunnel vision to the possibilities.

In this chapter, I discuss the process definition steps for resolving risk. I describe the **risk resolution** process, which defines the activities and methods to reduce risk to an acceptable level.

This chapter answers the following questions:

❏ What are the activities of the risk resolution process?

❏ How can you creatively resolve risk?

❏ When is the level of risk acceptable?

8.1   Define the Risk Resolution Process

I define risk resolution success criteria in terms of the process goals, the results that we expect to achieve by using the process. We can view the risk resolution process from two perspectives: external and internal. The external view specifies the process controls, inputs, outputs, and mechanisms. The internal view specifies the process activities that transform inputs to outputs using the mechanisms.

8.1.1   Process Goals

The risk resolution process is sufficient when it satisfies these goals:

- ❑ Assign responsibility and authority to the lowest possible level.
- ❑ Follow a documented risk action plan.
- ❑ Report results of risk resolution efforts.
- ❑ Provide for risk aware decision making.
- ❑ Determine the cost-effectiveness of risk management.
- ❑ Is prepared to adapt to changing circumstances.
- ❑ Take corrective actions when necessary.
- ❑ Improve communication within the team.
- ❑ Systematically control software risk.

These goals can be used as a checklist to ensure the process quality.

8.1.2   Process Definition

The risk resolution process definition is shown as an IDEF0 diagram in Figure 8.1. IDEF0 is a standard process definition notation used to describe a reusable process component for predictable risk resolution. The diagram describes the top-level process by its controls, inputs, outputs, and mechanisms [AirForce81].

Process Controls.   Project resources, project requirements, and the risk management plan regulate the risk resolution process similar to the way they control the risk identification process (see Chapter 4).

Process Inputs.   The risk action plan is input to the risk resolution process. It contains the objectives, constraints, and strategy for risk resolution and documents

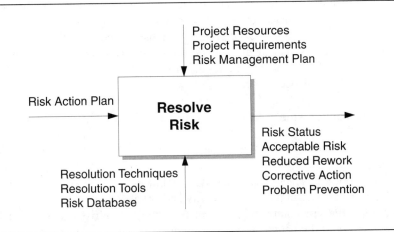

FIGURE 8.1   Risk resolution process definition. *Resolve Risk* encapsulates the activities of the process that transform inputs to outputs. Controls (at the top) regulate the process. Inputs (on the left) enter the process. Outputs (on the right) exit the process. Mechanisms (at the bottom) support the process.

the selected approach, resources required, and approval authority. The plan provides top-level guidance and allows for flexibility in achieving the objectives.

Process Outputs.   Risk status, acceptable risk, reduced rework, corrective action, and problem prevention are output from the risk resolution process.

Risk status is the progress (or lack of it) made against a risk action plan. By reporting risk status, you report the results of implementing the plan.

Acceptable risk means you can live with the risk consequence, possibly the worst-case outcome. When you make sufficient progress in risk resolution, project status indicators will improve. Status indicators within acceptable ranges trigger the deactivation or suspension of risk resolution activity.

Rework is the cost of not doing something right the first time. By *reducing rework*, you do not have to do work over because you did it right the first time. You do not waste your time. Calculate reduced rework in terms of cost savings by doubling the cost of work, then adding an overhead factor.

Corrective action is an activity required to solve a problem. You assume that there is a known solution to a problem that can be found using corrective action. Use these procedures to find the solution that is generally acceptable to everyone. Then perform the activities to solve the problem.

Problem prevention occurs when you avoid problems, thereby eliminating their result: problem detection cost, rework cost, and opportunity cost. Because we define a problem as a risk occurrence, we must also consider the consequence of risk occurrence. Calculate problem prevention in terms of cost savings by summing the cost of detecting and fixing the problem, rework, opportunity cost, and consequence of risk occurrence.

Process Mechanisms.   Mechanisms can be methods, techniques, tools, or other instruments that provide structure to the process activities. Risk resolution techniques and tools and a risk database are mechanisms of the risk resolution process.

Risk resolution techniques are ways to help with the details of risk resolution. (I describe basic techniques for creativity and collaboration in section 8.2.) *Risk resolution tools* use computers to automate techniques for risk resolution such as prototyping and simulation. The *risk database* contains the name of the responsible person and the results of risk resolution activities. The database also contains a completion date for significant results.

8.1.3   Process Activities

The activities of the risk resolution process are the tasks necessary to execute the risk action plan to reduce risk to an acceptable level:

1. Respond to notification of triggering event.
2. Execute the risk action plan.
3. Report progress against the plan.
4. Correct for deviation from the plan.

I discuss these process activities as sequential steps, but they can be iterative or parallel in execution.

Respond to Notification of Triggering Event.   Triggers provide notification to appropriate personnel. An individual with authority must respond to the triggering event. This does not mean dropping other important work. Rather, triggers should provide a reasonable time for response and should not constitute a crisis situation. An appropriate response includes a review of the current reality and an updated determination of the time frame for action. The decision to set another trigger or to assign the risk action plan is made.

A responsible person must be identified if the risk action plan will be assigned. Even if the plan is assigned to a group, there should be a group leader with clear authority to proceed. Factors such as availability and skill level help to determine who should be responsible for executing the risk action plan. The individual who identified or analyzed the risk need not be the one responsible for resolving it. The idea that the person who finds it fixes it does not properly motivate risk identification, because (unlike corrective action) the fix is rarely easy. The risk action plan should be delegated to the lowest level possible, the most cost-effective approach in terms of labor rates. It also provides individuals the experience that they need to increase their ability to manage risk.

Execute the Risk Action Plan.   You should follow a written risk action plan to resolve risk. If the plan is not documented, chances are there is a miscommunication already. Remember that a documented plan merely provides top-level guidance. To guide you through the details, I recommend using the engineering model of requirements, design, implement, and test.[1] The phases may be very short in duration (e.g., one hour for requirements definition, one hour for design, four hours for implementation, and two hours for testing). The main idea is that you understand what it is that you are supposed to do: create a mental model prior to developing a physical model and then check the results.

You are responsible for mapping the objectives of the risk action plan to specific actions that you will take to reduce uncertainty and increase control. For example, the action matrix shown in Figure 8.2 supports a decision to add a new feature to an existing product. It maps actions to planned objectives to ensure complete coverage. If an objective is not completely satisfied, another action should be added to the matrix. There are many actions that could be taken to meet planned objectives. The key is to list the actions that are requisite to making a decision, *and no more*.

Any two individuals assigned to execute a risk action plan will likely list different actions for risk resolution. Nevertheless, there are a few principles to follow that will serve you as you resolve any risk:

❏ *Think about working smarter.* When you find yourself saying, "I am too busy," you are working hard. The question is, "Are you working as *smart* as you could be?" What would help you to become more efficient in your work? Think about it.

❏ *Challenge yourself to find a better way.* Sometimes we get complacent and think that we are already doing enough. Pretend that your competition has found a better, faster, or cheaper way. How will you respond to this challenge? What could you do?

---

[1] As an engineer, I am comfortable with the iterative steps of the engineering model and find that it is a useful paradigm—even in writing this book.

Objectives
1. Understand the existing competition.
2. Determine the feature's cost benefits.
3. Determine the market demand.

Actions
A. Assess competing software applications.
B. Perform survey of customer needs.
C. Estimate the development cost.
D. Poll users on price.

Objective/Action Map	A	B	C	D
Objective 1	●			
Objective 2		●	●	
Objective 3		●		●

FIGURE 8.2   Action matrix. A decision on adding a new product feature to an existing product has several unknowns. The action matrix maps the objectives as stated in the risk action plan to risk resolution actions.

❑ *Exploit opportunities.* Take advantage of opportunities (but *not* of other people). Opportunities exist in the middle of difficulty and uncertainty. I have often found that when difficulty and uncertainty are gone, so are opportunities. Know when you have sufficient certainty to make a risk aware decision.

❑ *Be prepared to adapt.* Circumstances change. Be prepared to adapt to them. Take notice of your outcomes. If your results are not what you expected, determine why not. Try again, using a different approach.

❑ *Use common sense.* Let your common sense prevail in reasoning about difficult issues. Sometimes compromise and concession are the only way to reach a settlement. Many little steps add up to giant strides forward.

Report Progress Against the Plan.   You must report the results of risk resolution efforts. Determine and communicate progress made against the plan. Report risk status on a regular basis to improve communication within the team. Simply reporting risk status is not sufficient to manage risk. The team must review risk status, measures, and metrics regularly to provide for risk aware decision making.

Correct for Deviation from the Plan.   There are times when your results are not satisfactory and you must use another approach. You should take corrective actions when necessary. Determine the action required by using the corrective action procedure described in section 8.4.

8.2   Define Risk Resolution Techniques

Rather than describing techniques to deal with specific risks, it is more important to understand the two fundamental components of risk resolution: creativity and collaboration. You will repeatedly use these two fundamental components to resolve risk.

8.2.1   Creativity

Creativity is inventiveness in originating ideas [Miller87]. Implementing the risk action plan may require generating new and innovative ideas. We can use techniques for innovation to resolve risk creatively. The **creative process**—how we generate new ideas—is based on our preferences for thinking of new ideas. An **innovation style** is an approach to the creative process. Each of us has a unique innovation style profile that determines how we like to create. We can learn techniques to apply innovation styles to generate new ideas. Whether we want to improve on an existing product, think of a new feature, or develop a completely new process, there are four innovation styles that help us to use the creative process methodically:

❑ *Envisioning*. This style focuses on the end result. You can imagine an ideal outcome, and then let your goals guide you to realize your dream. Envisioning provides teams with direction, inspiration, and momentum. An example of the envisioning style is John F. Kennedy's vision of putting a man on the moon and returning him safely to earth.

❑ *Experimenting*. This style uses the scientific method of trial and error: following a known process to obtain repeatable and practical results. Experimenting emphasizes fact finding and information gathering, and then tests new combinations of ideas. An example of the experimenting style to help a major aerospace company find qualified software engineers is shown in Figure 8.3.

❑ *Exploring*. This style adds a sense of adventure by its unpredictable nature. You use analogies and metaphors to generate new ideas. Exploring provides

Technology	Incentives	Lifestyle	Media
Engineering	Salary	Location	Journal
Software	Benefits	Schools	Internet
Aerospace	Bonus	Casual	Newspaper
Radar	Stock options	Flying	Radio

FIGURE 8.3 Experimenting innovation style. The experimenting innovation style generates and tests different combinations of ideas for advertising and hiring software engineers.

a team with the potential for dramatic breakthroughs by approaching problems from new angles. An example of the exploring style is General Electric's application of defense technology to the automobile industry [Schine96].

❑ *Modifying.* This style moves forward one step at a time, building on what is true and proved by applying known methods and using experience. Modifying provides a team with stability and incremental improvements. An example of the modifying style is the SEI Capability Maturity Model.

When we use all four innovation styles, we identify a complete set of options.

8.2.2   Collaboration

In his book *Shared Minds*, Michael Schrage says **collaboration** is "two or more individuals with complementary skills, interacting to create a shared understanding that none had previously possessed or could have come to on their own" [Schrage90]. There are barriers to collaboration, as Edward Hall describes in his book *Beyond Culture*: "There is positive reinforcement for not collaborating. Where talent is centered on making a personal reputation, collaboration will get the back of the hand" [Hall76].

Risks are rarely resolved in isolation. More often, it is the lack of understanding among people that causes risk. One of the best ways to reduce uncertainty, gain knowledge, and increase chances for success is through other people. "Two heads are better than one" is the old adage for involving other people to help you reduce risk. Team collaboration, dialogue in working with others on your team, is essential in risk resolution. Successful collaboration is based on your ability to communicate. As you work with others, there are three problems that are possible in communication:

- ❏ *Sending the wrong message.* You can send the wrong message when written communication is ambiguous and when spoken communication is vague. Team communication is best when you check to verify the interpretation of the reader or listener.

- ❏ *Receiving the wrong message.* When you read between the lines or do not listen to body language, you can receive the wrong message. Team communication can be improved if you repeat back what you thought you heard. The time spent clarifying written documents and verbal questions will be small compared to the rework they might have otherwise caused.

- ❏ *A break in the communication link.* When you leave a voice-mail message, you cannot be sure that the other party received it. Team communication should ensure that what one group sent, the other received and understood.

8.3   Define Risk Management Return on Investment

Risk management ROI is the savings for all managed risks divided by the total cost of risk management activities, which is expressed in the following equation:

$$\text{ROI}_{(RM)} = \frac{\sum \text{Savings}}{\text{Cost}}$$

Cost of risk management is the total investment in resources—time spent in risk management meetings, the cost of reporting risk information, and the staff to develop a risk action plan—for risk assessment and risk control. **Savings** is the return for each managed risk. There are two types of savings: avoidance and reduction.

Cost avoidance is the difference between possible cost without risk resolution and the actual cost with risk resolution. An example of cost avoidance is any resolution strategy that successfully contains cost growth to maintain the budget. Table 8.1 describes the calculation for cost avoidance, which depends on four possible risk outcomes.

Cost reduction is the difference between planned and actual costs. Through cost reduction, it is possible to underrun the budget. Risk management practices can also lead to opportunities for a project to do better than the baseline plan. Unless an

TABLE 8.1 COST AVOIDANCE CALCULATION

Outcome	Cost Avoidance	Rationale
Risk did not occur because of successful risk resolution.	Max (RE_t)	Cost avoidance is based on the maximum estimate of risk exposure. Using the Max function promotes periodic updates of the risk action plan to reflect more accurate estimates of probability and consequence.
Risk did not occur because of good fortune.	0	Cost avoidance is zero if no risk management efforts were initiated.
Risk occurred; the consequence is less than the initial estimate.	Max $(C_t) - C_{t=1}$	Cost avoidance is the difference between how bad it could have been and how bad it was when the consequence was realized.
Risk occurred; the consequence is equal to (or greater than) the initial estimate.	0	Risk resolution strategies were ineffective. Investment in risk management has a zero return. No cost was avoided. (Negative returns are not used because they promote use of worst-case estimates.)

Note: RE_t: the interim expectation of risk exposure. C_t: the interim expectation of risk consequence. $C_{t=0}$: the initial expectation of risk consequence. $C_{t=1}$: the measured actual risk consequence.

alternate course of action is taken, planned resources will be used. When the alternate course of action was the result of risk management activities, savings are captured as a reduction in cost.

8.4   Develop a Corrective Action Procedure

A corrective action procedure helps to correct for variations in the process or the product. For example, the risk management process may require corrective action in terms of process improvement. The risk action plan is an intermediate product that may require corrective action in terms of modifying an approach that has not produced satisfactory results.

The corrective action procedure has four steps:

1. *Identify the problem.* Find the problem in the process or the product. The product can be an intermediate work product, such as the risk action plan.

2. *Assess the problem.* Perform an analysis to understand and evaluate the documented problem.

3. *Plan action.* Approve a plan for action to solve the problem.

4. *Monitor progress.* Track progress until the problem is solved. Record lessons learned for future reference.

8.5 Summary

In this chapter, I described the process definition steps for resolving risk:

1. Define the risk resolution process.
2. Define risk resolution techniques.
3. Define risk management return on investment.
4. Develop a corrective action procedure.

I described the risk resolution process, which defines the activities and methods to reduce risk to an acceptable level. The activities of the risk resolution process are as follows:

1. Respond to notification of triggering event.
2. Execute the risk action plan.
3. Report progress against the plan.
4. Correct for deviation from the plan.

I described four innovation styles for creatively resolving risk:

❏ Envisioning.
❏ Experimenting.
❏ Exploring.
❏ Modifying.

I described when the level of risk is acceptable. When there is sufficient progress in risk resolution, project status indicators will improve. Status indicators within acceptable ranges trigger the deactivation or suspension of risk resolution activity. You make a risk-aware decision to live with the risk consequence.

8.6   Questions for Discussion

1. Describe the risk resolution process goals. Why is each goal important? Define quantitative success criteria for each goal.

2. Your requirements specification contains 100 requirements. The design phase began even though 20 percent of the requirements had TBDs (to be determined shall statements). The best-case outcome is that all your assumptions will be correct. Your training in risk management leads you to believe that about half of the TBDs are at risk. Calculate the cost of rework based on the assumption that half of the TBDs are at risk. What is the most likely outcome?

3. You identified an external system interface risk at a design review, and a technical interchange meeting was scheduled to resolve it. Ten people met for two hours before deciding on an agreeable resolution. Calculate the cost savings for preventing this problem, assuming that it would have been detected during system integration.

4. What is the rationale for assigning a risk action plan to the lowest possible level? What do you think would happen if the project manager was personally responsible for all the risks and their resolution?

5. What are the two fundamental components of risk resolution? Why are they fundamental?

6. List five difficulties and five uncertainties that you have in your current assignment. Describe an opportunity that exists in each difficulty and uncertainty that you face. How could you exploit these opportunities?

7. Reporting risk status on a regular basis improves communication within the team. What are the problems that are possible in communication among team members?

8. What is your plan to sustain the risk management process once it is in place? Quantify the resources your plan will require. What mechanisms will provide a check and balance to perpetuate an effective process?

9. How do you generate new ideas? What are the advantages of using the creative process to generate new ideas?

10. Do you agree that the mastery of risk is the foundation of modern life? Discuss why you do or do not agree.

8.7   References

[AirForce81] *Integrated Computer Aided Manufacturing Architecture*, Part II, Vol. IV: *Function Modeling Manual (IDEF0)*. AFWAL-TR-81-4023. Wright-Patterson Air Force Base, OH: Air Force Systems Command, June 1981.

[Bernstein96] Bernstein P. *Against the Gods: The Remarkable Story of Risk*. New York: Wiley, 1996.

[Hall76] Hall Edward. *Beyond Culture*. New York: Doubleday, 1976.

[Miller87] Miller W. *The Creative Edge*. Reading, MA: Addison-Wesley, 1987.

[Schine96] Schine E., et al. Liftoff: Michael Armstrong has made Hughes an electronics and telecom contender. *Business Week*, April 22:136–147, 1996.

[Schrage90] Schrage M. *Shared Minds*. New York: Random House, 1990.

PART III

Risk Management
Infrastructure

Here is a basic rule for winning success. Let us mark it in the mind and remember it. The rule is: Success depends on the support of other people. The only hurdle between you and what you want to be is the support of others.
—David Joseph Schwartz

Part III provides the methods to establish the infrastructure for a risk aware culture. Organizational building blocks include establishing risk management policy, conducting training, verifying compliance, and improving the process.

Chapter 9, "Develop the Policy," describes a policy for risk management performance. Read Chapter 9 to learn how to develop a risk ethic within your organization.

Chapter 10, "Define Standard Process," describes how to establish an action team to define a standard risk management process. Read Chapter 10 to understand how to leverage a reusable process across your organization.

Chapter 11, "Train Risk Technology," defines risk management training topics to provide instruction in progressive increments. Read Chapter 11 to be able to raise your organization's awareness and understanding of risk management technology through training.

Chapter 12, "Verify Compliance," describes the method to verify compliance of risk management activities through an independent audit. Read Chapter 12 to learn how to ensure that project practices adhere to a documented risk management plan.

Chapter 13, "Improve Practice," provides a method to ensure incremental improvement of risk management practices. Read Chapter 13 to understand how to appraise and improve risk management practices using a systematic approach.

With the knowledge of the infrastructure required to support risk management provided in Part III, you will be ready to establish an environment that will support the implementation of risk management on your project.

Reference

[Davis88] Davis W. *The Best of Success*. Lombard, IL: Great Quotations, 1988.

9

Develop the Policy

Sometimes if you want to see a change for the better, you have to take things into your own hands.
—Clint Eastwood

It is easier to turn the wheel of a car when it is in motion. An organization is no different from a car when it comes to changing directions. The key to a faster response to change lies in the ability of the organization to have forward momentum.

Software organizations have had (and will continue to have) many changes—for example, new distribution channels over the Internet, relaxed government software standards, and increased competition due to globalization of the workforce. We cannot react easily and swiftly if we have not established the direction for our organization. To set an organization in motion requires the development of policy, an administrative order that sets the direction for the organization. It is policy, not process, that starts an organization on the path to institutionalizing a behavior. Policy is determined at the highest level in the organization. A top-down approach ensures that policy is important enough to allocate resources to it. It is what the administration expects the organization to follow.

In this chapter, I provide a risk management policy, which is designed to help you develop a risk ethic within your organization. I describe how to establish a firm foundation for managing risk by developing a strategic plan to institutionalize risk management.

In this chapter, I answer the following questions:

❑ Why is a risk ethic important to an organization?

❑ What does a risk management policy contain?

❑ How does policy set expectations for project behavior?

9.1   Obtain Commitment

To obtain the commitment required for organizational change to risk management, the need for and benefit of a risk ethic must be communicated.[1] A **risk ethic** is the rules of conduct that characterize a proper risk management philosophy. The central theme of the philosophy is the notion that risk is the organization's responsibility. A risk ethic follows from this philosophy as a set of behaviors appropriate for handling risk at work. The doctrine of the risk ethic supports the following rules:

❑ Take responsibility for risk.

❑ Do not blame people for risk.

❑ Communicate risk to the right people.

❑ Be proactive in managing risk.

❑ Learn from unexpected outcomes.

The need for a risk ethic can be substantiated by the challenges facing the entire software industry. The general problems the organization faces also support the need to manage risk. Instances of missed opportunities, such as proposals that were lost to the competition, can point to a need to strengthen risk management practices. Specific surprises on projects that could have been avoided also show the need for increasing the ability to manage risk. Communicating the needs is a matter of documenting and sharing both general and specific areas where risk management can help people work better.

The benefits of nurturing a risk ethic are demonstrated by organizations that have achieved success through diversification and individual responsibility. The open communication of risk helps an organization to resolve risk, avoid problems, reduce rework, and provide focus.

Obtaining commitment is the first step in developing a policy for risk management. Commitment is demonstrated top-down when the administration allocates resources to a task and bottom-up from the employees who support the task. Change

---

[1] SEI describes a risk ethic as involving everyone in a continuous process of identifying, communicating, and resolving risks in an open and nonthreatening environment [VanScoy92].

occurs when there is *both* top-down and bottom-up commitment; one without the other will not suffice. As shown in Figure 9.1, institutionalization depends on the level of commitment over time [Fowler93]. Commitment, not interest, is what it takes for long-term success in changing or developing an organizational culture. When we are interested in something, it can hold our attention for a time until we find something else to take its place. When we are committed, we understand that it is our duty to see the task through to completion. Interest will wane over time; commitment strengthens as progress is made toward goals. Early on, commitment is based on trust and faith that the goal is worth the effort. Closer to the goal, our commitment is based on knowledge and understanding that we did the right thing.

9.2   Allocate Resources

To set a car in motion, fuel and a driver are required. Leaders of the organization are the drivers of policy. To be a leader, you do not have to be on the senior management team. If you see a need within the organization, you can enlist the support of key opinion leaders and influence those at the top. Sign petitions, make telephone calls, and send letters to make your concerns known. Anyone, at any level of the organization, can be a leader. If you are not currently in a position of

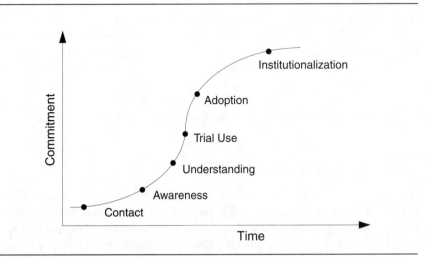

FIGURE 9.1 Phases of the learning process. Institutionalization is the result of a learning process that requires increasing levels of commitment over time. (Source: [Fowler92])

influence, you need to know that the senior management team would probably welcome your ideas and energy.

Resources are the organizational fuel that is needed to develop policy that sets the organization in motion. Personnel resources—needed to survey the existing practices, obtain the commitment for the policy, define the policy, and communicate it to the organization—must be budgeted and scheduled. People accomplish little without time and money. When the administration allocates resources to develop policy, it demonstrates the importance of it to the organization.

I once went to my organizational management and asked for $3,000 to establish a policy and procedure for human factors in software systems. My ideas for the problem, objectives, and team to carry this out were hand-written on one piece of paper. Because I am not trained in human factors, I was not qualified to serve as a member of the team. My leadership was in recognizing a need and asking for the resources to make it happen. My point is that anyone can influence policy, but policy influences everyone.

9.2.1   Apportion the Budget

If you are going to influence everyone through policy, you need money from a budget. Budgets are planned before they are allocated. To find a sponsor for your idea— that is, someone who controls budgets, and therefore money—think about who would benefit from the policy. Engineering managers may support several project managers and understand the needs of their projects. Directors may support use of their budget to help several projects and proposals in their business area. General managers may have an entire division that would benefit from a policy on risk management. Once a source of money is found, you must sell your idea to the sponsor. Briefly state the cost and benefits to the sponsor. Justify your statements using a few facts with your enthusiasm for the task of developing policy and ensuring its success into implementation to serve the organization better. Close by asking for a specific amount over a specific time period. If money cannot be allocated from the current budget, ask the sponsor to place a line item for this task in the next budget.

9.2.2   Apportion the Schedule

The schedule bounds the time for each activity required to achieve the objectives. The schedule will be dependent on the amount of money received from the sponsor. Funding may be incremental, and activities should be scheduled to show progress at each increment. Figure 9.2 shows the dependencies of the activities and the relative time for each activity. The activities should have deliverables such as the documented policy, a standard process definition, training material,

Action Team Name	Duration	Cost	Work
Software Risk Management	16 weeks	$12,000	8 weeks
– Policy Recommendation	8 weeks	$6,000	4 weeks
– Initial Media Updates	4 weeks	$3,000	2 weeks
– Final Media Updates	4 weeks	$3,000	2 weeks

FIGURE 9.2   Chart of scheduled activities. The plan for developing a policy and process for software risk management includes allocating resources in terms of budget and schedule.

and a method to verify and improve the practice. The schedule may show how the process will be piloted on either a small project or a small part of a large project. Time for feedback from the pilot program and incorporating improvements should be scheduled prior to requiring the organization to follow the documented policy.

9.2.3   Assign the Personnel

When it comes to initiatives at the organizational level, it is best to recruit a volunteer team. Talk with people to get an indication of their interest and ability to commit their time to the task. Set the proper expectations of what is required of individuals before they sign up. For example, check that the schedule and meeting time fit the expectations of the individuals. Ask that they discuss the possibility of signing up with their supervisor, to be sure that each team member is fully supported in his or her efforts. Let these people know what they will receive in return: the personal benefits in learning new skills and taking a leadership role within the organization, and celebrating when the objectives are met, such as having lunch with the sponsor. Remember that there is strength in diversity, so be sure to recruit a cross-functional team.

9.3   Survey Existing Practice

The first task of the team in establishing a firm foundation for managing risk is to survey the existing organizational practices. If you are from the software development side of the organization, you will need to check the practices in new business, proposals, other projects, and internal studies. The policy must consider that the practices of implementation will vary depending on the application. As such, the policy is a general statement of the commonality for all applications.

9.3.1   New Business Practices

There is risk in new business, often due to uncertainty in customer demand and the ability to deliver on promises made to customers. Those who work in the marketing department might ask the following questions:

- ❑ Will sales prices have to be changed to reflect unanticipated demand levels for the product?
- ❑ Will organizational downsizing affect time to market?
- ❑ Can the software engineers be trusted to deliver a quality product?
- ❑ Is project management easier than this job in marketing?[2]

Chances are that the marketers have methods for dealing with these risky situations. To develop a policy that accommodates new business practices in software risk management, ask several people in marketing how they accomplish their work. Do they run business models on spreadsheets? Do they use customer surveys? How do they track product features of the competition? How do they manage their uncertainty and make decisions with incomplete information? Gather any procedures, forms, tips, guidelines, or tools that they use.

9.3.2   Proposal Practices

There is significant risk in writing proposals. There must be a balance between the resources invested in a proposal and the likelihood of contract award. The bid–no bid decision is probably the decision with the greatest risk that is made during the proposal phase. What could prevent success in winning the contract? Having a risk philosophy enables proposal teams to quantify their chances for success. One proposal team could have saved $3 million and years of effort in preparing a demonstration, if the prime contractor had only assessed their risk early in the proposal. Evidently they thought software capability could be bought by subcontracting the software development to an SEI Level 3 company. The risk that was recognized by the customer (but not the prime, until too late) was the doubt that an SEI Level 1 prime contractor could manage an SEI Level 3 subcontractor.

Risk management can be used as a discriminator throughout the proposal document. Your plan to handle risk intelligently, from using uncertainty to improve the cost model to simulating system performance, will win points. Chances are that the proposal writers have methods for dealing with these risks. To develop a policy that accommodates proposal practices in risk management,

---

[2] Changing jobs is a career decision that requires careful risk analysis.

ask several people working on proposals how they accomplish their work. Gather any customer-driven requirements for risk management and prior proposal write-ups, especially those from winning proposals. From proposals that were lost, ask the people on the proposal team for lessons learned.

9.3.3   Project Practices

Projects are more likely to have persistent problems than managed risks. Chances are that there are some risk management activities going on. When you survey people who are working on projects, try to capture their terminology. They may discuss risk in terms of potential problems or issues. Do they write down potential problems in weekly status reports? Are issues reviewed at technical staff meetings? Does someone coordinate issues that affect several integrated product teams? When are technical interchange meetings scheduled? Does system engineering track technical performance measures at the software level? How does software engineering prevent problems in meeting specifications, cost, and schedule? By surveying people at all project levels, you will have a general sense of attitudes toward risk. Does the organization push technical capabilities, develop complex systems, or maintain safety-critical systems? Knowing the extent of project risks helps to establish the rigor of the risk management policy needed. Knowing the level of risk management practice helps to provide the training material needed to implement the policy. Gather any documented processes, templates, completed forms, or needs to implement risk management practices successfully. Note too what is missing. For example, people in the organization may need to become aware of tools that support risk analysis.

9.3.4   Research and Development Practices

Internal research and development (R&D) often has different risk management practices from either proposals or projects. All innovation involves a degree of uncertainty [Souder87]. Only by taking a risk can we move forward to learn new things. Ideas by themselves will not make a difference. Experimentation gives ideas the reality required to be practical and useful. By experimentation, we test out new ideas and handle unexpected outcomes. When you have a successful outcome, you have improved something. When you have an unexpected outcome, you have learned something. Treating each unexpected outcome as a mistake is a destructive practice that reduces confidence and inhibits risk taking.[3]

---

[3] I learned this concept from a videotape titled *Risk Taking for Higher Performance*, produced by Synectics Corporation in Cambridge, MA.

To develop a policy that accommodates risk management for small studies and laboratory environments, ask several people in R&D how they accomplish their work. Do they have the courage to take a risk when they do not know the outcome? Do they understand that the risk of not taking risks is being left behind? Are they able to embrace their mistakes? Do they own the mistake, examine it, and learn from it? Knowing the attitudes toward risk in the part of the organization responsible for future growth helps you understand the need for education. Gather innovation techniques, experimentation methods, and benefits they have found by managing uncertainty. For example, people in R&D may have benefited by increasing the number of experiments, which actually lowers risk by increasing knowledge and the ability to adapt through trial and error.

9.4   Define Draft Policy

The purpose of a draft policy is to enroll the opinion leaders in the change process. Before a new approach can be embraced, people must let go of the old ways that are no longer effective. People can contribute to shaping the policy by a top-level review of the policy description. They can own a piece of it through their comments and suggestions. Through ownership, people will be more likely to accept the policy and less resistant to it.

9.4.1   Involve the Opinion Leaders

Through involvement, opinion leaders are made aware of a draft policy for risk management. Opinion leaders influence others because they are vocal about their beliefs. Involving them late in the policy definition process is a mistake. It shows that you did not depend on their input but are now asking for their support. It is important to spend individual time with opinion leaders to understand their concerns and prepare to address them. A kickoff meeting can then be held to generate ideas with the rest of the organization.

9.4.2   Outline the Policy Contents

Although the entire policy is subject to negotiation by team members, here is an outline to start with:

- ❏ *Subject*: Software Risk Management.
- ❏ *Reference*: Standard procedure SP-050-SRM.

❑ *Purpose*: To establish a proactive approach to managing risk by routinely assessing and controlling project, process, and product risk.

❑ *Policy*: It is the policy of the XYZ organization that risks will be managed by each employee.

❑ *Scope*: New business, proposals, projects, and internal research and development.

❑ *Objectives*: Maximize profit and minimize risk.

❑ *Responsibility*: Individuals are accountable for identifying risk to their team leaders. Team leaders are responsible for communicating issues that cannot be resolved at the team level to their manager. Managers are responsible for ensuring coordination with affected third parties. The project manager is responsible for ensuring coordination with affected external parties.

❑ *Authority*: The project manager delegates authority as required to manage risk.

❑ *Procedure*:

1. Document a risk management plan.
2. Perform a baseline risk assessment early in the project.
3. Report risks at weekly status meetings.
4. Review risks at monthly project reviews.
5. Maintain a risk database, and deliver it at project completion.[4]

9.5 Review Draft Policy

Circulate the draft with plenty of time for busy people to review the policy and prepare their comments. Host a meeting where people bring changes, and discuss the issues. The policy review should promote understanding of the risk management practices expected within the organization and result in incorporating the feedback of the people who will be practicing risk management to obtain their concurrence. Use a consensus process to ensure that everyone can live with the draft policy.

---

[4] Maintaining a corporate risk database allows reuse of successful risk resolution strategies and a knowledge base of lessons learned.

9.5.1 Promote Understanding

Limit the policy to one page. The advantage of a single page is that more people will read it, the intent will be clearer, and the direction will be limited to allow for a flexible implementation. Standard terminology should be used in the draft policy. For example, if the term *shall* is too formal for your organization, do not use it. If the project manager is called *principal investigator* on internal research and development, then incorporate that language so that the policy will speak to all affected individuals. Be sure to define and agree on all the terminology. *Establishing a common vocabulary within the organization is the most important aspect of the policy.*

9.5.2 Incorporate the Feedback

The personnel assigned to develop the policy are responsible for incorporating changes. All changes should be consistent with respect to the intent and vocabulary of the policy. It is appropriate to thank those who contributed comments and perhaps provide an explanation to anyone whose suggestion was not incorporated. After changes are made, you may want to post the draft policy on a bulletin board to show work in progress.

9.6 Document Policy

The policy should be documented in a standard format and incorporated in a manual of operating procedures. A hard copy should be available at a specific location, such as the personnel department. It is also helpful to have this in soft copy for employees to browse on-line.

NASA policy objectives with regard to project risks are expressed in the *NASA Systems Engineering Handbook* [NASA95]. Section 4.6 of the handbook references the following risk management policy (NMI 8070.4A):

- Provide a disciplined and documented approach to risk management throughout the project life cycle.

- Support management decision making by providing integrated risk assessments (i.e., taking into account cost, schedule, performance, and safety concerns).

- Communicate to NASA management the significance of assessed risk levels and the decisions made with respect to them.

9.7   Approve Policy

The policy should be approved at the highest levels to ensure that senior management agrees with the changes from the policy review. This approval should include the signature of a senior manager who represents the management team. *Commitment from the top sets expectations for project behavior.*

9.8   Communicate Policy

The policy should be communicated to the organization in a memo that states when it will take effect. Senior management can take this opportunity to communicate their support for the policy.

9.9   Summary

In this chapter, I provided a risk management policy for developing a risk ethic within an organization. The activities to develop a policy follow:

1. Obtain commitment.
2. Allocate resources.
3. Survey existing practice.
4. Define draft policy.
5. Review draft policy.
6. Document policy.
7. Approve policy.
8. Communicate policy.

A risk ethic is important to an organization because it establishes the rules of conduct for managing risk. A risk ethic has five such rules:

- ❏ Take responsibility for risk.
- ❏ Do not blame people for risk.
- ❏ Communicate risk to the right people.

❑ Be proactive in managing risk.

❑ Learn from unexpected outcomes.

A risk management policy includes a statement of purpose and responsibility. As a minimum, your policy should contain the following requirements:

1. A risk management plan shall be documented.
2. A baseline risk assessment shall be performed early in the project.
3. Risks shall be reported at weekly status meetings.
4. Risks shall be reviewed at monthly project reviews.
5. A risk database shall be maintained and delivered at project completion.

I described how to establish a firm foundation for managing risk by developing a risk management policy to institutionalize risk management. Because policy directs the way we conduct business, it sets the expectations for organizational behavior. A risk management policy controls behavior by requiring people to manage risk.

9.10   Questions for Discussion

1. Describe how the risk management policy is a strategic plan to institutionalize risk management. Identify the risks of documenting a policy that will be supported by the entire organization. What is your mitigation strategy to combat these risks?

2. Do you agree that anyone can influence policy but policy influences everyone? Discuss why you do or do not agree.

3. Develop a survey that you can give to people that will determine the current risk management practices. Would the survey be different for new business, proposals, projects, and internal research and development teams? Explain your answer.

4. Discuss the concept of commitment. Why is commitment important for long-term success? Give three ways that commitment is demonstrated in an organization from the top down and three ways that commitment is demonstrated from the bottom up.

5. What is a risk ethic? What do you think is the significance of fostering a risk aware culture?

6. What is the point of involving opinion leaders in organizational change? Identify five risks of dictating an organizational policy on software risk management. Discuss the probability and consequence for each of the identified risks.

7. Write a risk management policy for NASA. Write another risk management policy, this time for Microsoft. Compare and contrast the two policies.

8. Write a risk management policy for your organization. Discuss how the terminology reflects your environment.

9. People communicate through vocabulary. Underline and define the important terms used in a risk management policy.

10. You are an engineer working on a large software development. The project schedule is slipping due to technical problems. Management does not appear to know how to change this situation. You have been inspired to make a difference for your project. What will you do? Explain the difference your actions can make for your project.

9.11   References

[Fowler93] Fowler P, Levine L. A conceptual framework for software technology transition. Technical report CMU/SEI-93-TR-31. Pittsburgh, PA: Software Engineering Institute, Carnegie Mellon University, 1993.

[Fowler92] Fowler P, Levine L. Toward a Designed Process of Software Technology Transition. *American Programmer*, Vol. 5, Issue 3, page 6, 1992.

[NASA95] National Aeronautics and Space Administration. *NASA Systems Engineering Handbook*. SP–6105. June 1995.

[Souder87] Souder W. *Managing New Product Innovations*. Lexington, MA: Lexington Books, 1987.

[VanScoy92] VanScoy R. Software development risk: Problem or opportunity. Technical report CMU/SEI-92-TR-30. Pittsburgh, PA: Software Engineering Institute, Carnegie Mellon University, 1992.

10

Define Standard Process

We gain the advantage by doing things before they need to be done—positioning ourselves ahead of time in the best place. Those who think ahead of the approaching action will have the advantage. They will be the winners.
—Wynn Davis

An organization that is expending resources to ensure product quality knows that its product is only as good as its process. A **standard process** is a minimum set of procedures defined and approved for use by an organization. It is like the script in a drama class because it synchronizes the sequence of activities. Each person is given the same script, but everyone has a different role to play. A role may be assumed by one or more individuals. Having a defined process allows us to follow a written script and organize into clearly defined roles. As we execute the defined process, we know who is playing each role, and we can work together more efficiently. In software development, there are no dress rehearsals.

A software engineering process group (SEPG) should have a defined process for process improvement [Fowler90]. An SEI Level 1 SEPG cannot guide an organization to SEI Level 2 and beyond because its methods will be ad hoc. An SEPG needs a script for process definition. The SEPG is itself an action team that can help to structure the improvement organization, develop top-level action plans, and define the process of process improvement. Then other action teams can be established to achieve action plan goals. Each team established to improve a process needs the process definition script to be successful in meeting its objectives. Following this script, the output of all the actions teams will be in harmony, because the detailed work flows from one master design.

In this chapter, I explain the process of process definition. I describe how to establish an action team to define a reusable risk management process for your organization.

This chapter answers the following questions:

❑ What are the activities of the process definition process?

❑ What does a high-performance team have that other teams do not?

❑ Why is a process definition notation important?

10.1   Establish an Action Team

The risk management process action team should have cross-functional membership because the diversity of various engineering and management disciplines provides a wealth of experience the team can draw on. Individuals should represent both large and small projects and various product lines. Organization members who want to participate should be recruited and given a charge number to track effort.

The key to establishing an effective team is understanding three important team concepts:

❑ *A team is not a group.* Groups communicate; teams collaborate. Communication is the exchange of thoughts or information. Collaboration occurs when two or more individuals with complementary skills interact to create a shared understanding that none had previously possessed or could have come to on their own [Schrage90]. Team members must collaborate to solve problems under constraints.

❑ *A team is task oriented.* A team is brought together to achieve specific goals. An effective team commits itself to achieving those objectives. Team members have a sense of shared purpose. When the objectives have been met, the team celebrates their accomplishment and disbands.

❑ *A team matures over time.* As the task evolves, the team roles also evolve. **Consensus** is the decision-making process of a mature team. It ensures that everyone can live with the decision. In spite of obstacles, growth and progress are made. The process for working together is refined over time.

Task orientation demands the assignment of team roles. Team members may be assigned one of four roles on a rotating basis:

❑ *Leader.* The leader ensures the clarity of the task requirements; sees to it that the team has adequate resources to complete the task; guarantees deadlines and the quality of deliverables; clarifies team roles and responsibilities; coordinates meeting time, location, and agenda; and is responsible for improving the team's performance. The leader's team notebook is the master copy and is maintained in the organization's technical library.

❑ *Facilitator*. The facilitator manages the decision-making process, encourages participation of all team members, keeps the team discussion focused, keeps track of the time and the meeting agenda, and can remind the team of constraints, such as the time remaining. The facilitator may also be a participant, and all team members may act as secondary facilitators.

❑ *Recorder*. The recorder provides a team memory. He or she keeps notes of ideas, decisions, and working procedures; generates and distributes meeting minutes in a timely fashion; and documents essential facts and synopsis without editorializing.

❑ *Participants*. Participants become fully involved in discussions. They contribute ideas, seek clarification to avoid misunderstanding, and help the facilitator keep the team on track.

As the task evolves, so will team roles [Scholtes88]. A team matures over time in four stages:

1. *Forming*. The team sets the ground rules for operation. They define their mission, task, and requirements and determine what behavior is acceptable and how much they are expected to do. Relationships for working within the team are established.

2. *Storming*. Some team members value their individuality over the identity of the team. They may ignore goals set by the leader and resist the requirements of the given task. When individuals do not conform to team rules, their behavior results in conflict and struggle.

3. *Norming*. As team members develop closer relationships with each other, new standards of conduct for operation of the team develop, and members adopt new roles within the team. The team is now capable of using consensus as a method of making decisions. A consensus process requires team members to share information and openly discuss their views. Issues are ranked to focus the discussion on possible decisions for dealing with the issues.

4. *Performing*. When the team is performing, issues are resolved, progress is made, and goals are achieved.

10.1.1   Build a High-Performance Team

High-performance teams have been created by beginning with an innovative workshop that trains in the basics of teamwork, problem-solving methods, and using data to achieve a goal [Janson95]. There are other important factors as well:

❑ *A shared compelling vision.* A high-performance team is results oriented. The members share a common vision and have positive expectations of achieving success. Have your team brainstorm a vision statement, such as "No surprises." Take several photographs of what that means to use risk management to prevent project disasters: a smiling customer, a clean lab environment, or an impressive demonstration at a trade show.[1]

❑ *Individual accountability.* Each person contributes through clearly defined roles and responsibilities. There is a sense of pride in belonging to the team. There is ownership and accountability for the product. Commitment is a by-product of accountability.

❑ *Synergy in collaboration.* Team members are open to new ideas. They appreciate the diversity that the team is more than the sum of the individual members. Conflict and disagreement is a natural process that is handled with mutual trust and respect for each person. The team decides by consensus. Although decisions using the consensus process initially take longer to reach, once the decision is made, less time is spent resisting it, and real progress is made.

A high-performance team has the following characteristics:

❑ Working on the team is fun.

❑ More is accomplished than thought possible.

❑ Ego and blame are replaced with commitment.

❑ Conflict results in breakthroughs.

❑ The team shares a sense of empowerment.

How will you know if you manage a high-performance team? The view from outside a high-performance team has the following characteristics:

❑ Seamless operation as a team.

❑ Accomplishment without visible effort.

❑ Unwavering commitment.

❑ Accountability for action as a norm.

❑ Little or no direction required.

Your team can evaluate itself on the following characteristics of team excellence, rating itself on a scale of 1 to 5:

❑ A clear, elevating goal.

❑ Principled leadership.

---

[1] A picture is worth a thousand words. We process a picture using our nonverbal right brain, which stimulates both emotion and imagination.

- ❑ Competent team members.
- ❑ Unified commitment.
- ❑ Collaborative climate.
- ❑ Results-driven structure.
- ❑ Standards of excellence.
- ❑ Reward and recognition.

10.1.2 Organize the Team for Success

The team leader should be responsible for creating team notebooks to be given to each team member at the first organizational meeting. There are several advantages for each person's maintaining a notebook:

- ❑ Team members stay on track better when they know the path to completion.
- ❑ Process definition is reinforced through notebook tabs that serve as placeholders for the remaining work.
- ❑ If an individual leaves the team, his or her notebook is passed on to the new team member.
- ❑ Notebooks serve later as a handy reference that can be checked out from a technical library and used to educate others.
- ❑ Notebooks can be used in process assessments to verify work in progress.

  The team notebook includes the following sections:

- ❑ *Action plan*—the task requirements, budget, and schedule given to the team leader by the organization, and team goals and products to be delivered.
- ❑ *Action team interfaces*—a diagram that illustrates how the action team operates within the context of the organization defined for software process improvement (see Figure 10.1).
- ❑ *Member directory*—the names and contact information for all team members.
- ❑ *Activity log*—a one-page journal for team members to capture the date, time, and activity they performed using the action team charge number.
- ❑ *Meeting rules*—the team operating principles. An example of guidelines for team meetings is shown in Figure 10.2.

  The agenda for the first meeting of a risk management process action team should include the following activities:

1. *Introduce team members.* Once a cross-functional team is gathered, personal introductions can be made. Getting to know individual strengths is the first step to understanding the talent represented in the group, the action team's

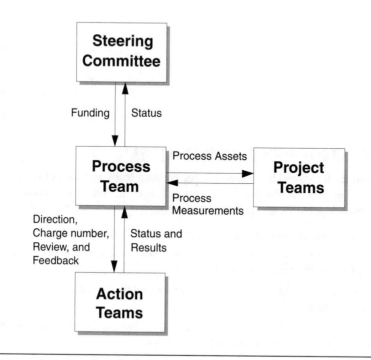

FIGURE 10.1   Improvement organization. The action team operates within the context of the organization defined for software process improvement.

Do	Do Not
Start and end meetings on time	Hold side meetings
Have an agenda and objectives	Interrupt others
Stick to the point and be concise	Criticize others
Listen and be sensitive to others	Take phone calls during meetings
Distribute and document meeting results	
Keep things in perspective	
Get information to the right people	
Commit and follow through	
Be a positive team player	

FIGURE 10.2   Team ground rules. Teams establish rules of order to ensure productive team meetings.

greatest resource. Introductions should be interactive. Take the time to get acquainted by pairing up, interviewing, and introducing one another. Another way to introduce team members is for groups of three to discuss themselves (e.g., name, background, current position, and special interests). Stage introductions of individuals to the entire team using two people who dramatize meeting the third.

2. *Clarify team goals.* The purpose of the team's existence is to define the standard risk management process for the organization. The deliverables are the process definition and supporting mechanisms. The team should agree on a clear statement of purpose of what is to be accomplished. In order to agree on the team's success criteria, have each team member finish the following sentence: "Our team will be successful if . . ." Arrange the responses in a purpose hierarchy, from general to specific. Achieve consensus on which statement best describes the scope of the action team.

3. *Review the action plan.* Develop an understanding of what has to be done and when.

4. *Agree on operating principles.* The ground rules for working together can be a brainstorming exercise by the team members. Ten rules are sufficient, and they can be prioritized in order of importance to the team.

10.1.3   Level the Playing Field

After the team is organized for success, there should be an educational meeting to level the playing field. This is important to ensure that everyone begins work with a common understanding of the vocabulary that will be used. Basic knowledge required to execute the action plan is established. Skills required include consensus, process definition, and risk management concepts. The team can be trained using videotapes, audiotapes, or a guest lecture. The team members can review a portion of the material and then present it to the team. To educate the risk management action team that I led, I invited the team to a risk management movie [Charette91], complete with popcorn and sodas. I also presented a risk analysis tutorial given by the Air Force Institute of Technology as part of an introduction to software engineering [AFIT92].

10.2   Develop the Draft Standard Process

A draft standard process is an important product for the action team. The draft is a brief overview of the final product, which is reviewed for understanding and

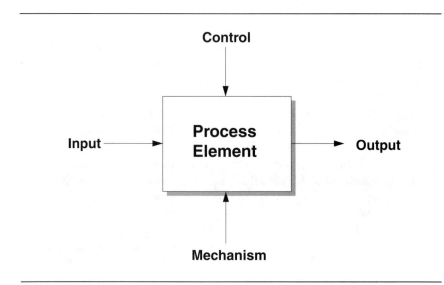

FIGURE 10.3   IDEF0 process design notation. Process elements are described by IDEF0 using inputs, outputs, control, and mechanisms.

consistency. It provides a sense of accomplishment early on that can serve as a catalyst for completion. There are four steps to develop the draft standard process:

1. Select a process design method.
2. Gather the risk practices data.
3. Scope the effort and products.
4. Define the draft standard process.

10.2.1   Select a Process Design Method

There are several process design methods that can be used as is or with modifications. If your organization does not already have a methodology, you may want to combine features to create your own process notation hybrid. There are three good process design methods:

- ❑ *IDEF0.* The basic building block of the IDEF0 process definition method [AirForce81] is shown in Figure 10.3.[2] Process elements are connected to

---

[2] IDEF0 is a function modeling standard established in 1981 for defining manufacturing processes. It has become the standard definition methodology for business process models.

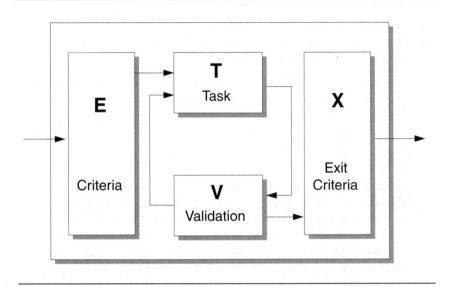

FIGURE 10.4   ETVX process design notation. Process elements are described by entry criteria, task, validation, and exit criteria (ETVX).

make a more complex process definition. Using IDEF0 is systematic and easily understood and implemented. (IDEF0 was used to define the risk management process in Part II.) There are extensions of IDEF0 that focus attention on the tools and information that support the processes. A parallel information modeling standard, IDEF1X [AirForce85], has been used to transform information requirements into physical database schemas [Hsiao95].

❑ *ETVX*. The ETVX method describes a process in terms of entry criteria, task, validation, and exit criteria. As shown in Figure 10.4, ETVX explicitly calls for the validation of activities prior to task completion [Tomayko91].

❑ *The 3 R's*. Role, responsibility, and resources are the 3 R's described by a business engineering approach developed by David Taylor [Taylor95]. As shown in Figure 10.5, customers and suppliers, both internal and external, are addressed. The approach is based on modeling roles that encapsulate responsibilities and resources associated with the role. Roles decompose hierarchically from general to specific. At each succeeding role level, responsibilities and resources are more specifically defined. Solutions are developed from recursive design, construction, and test of requirements mapped to responsibilities and resources.

10.2.2   Gather the Risk Practices Data

There are numerous sources of information on risk management practices. Your team should gather information and write a bibliography of the sources you will use. Three categories are especially useful:

- ❑ *Company practices*. Information on the current state of your practice. Policy, process guidebooks, process assessment findings, and project practices should be collected and catalogued in the team notebook.

- ❑ *Industry data*. Information on the current state of other organizations. Conferences, training seminars, books, tapes, and articles provide information on the state of the practice in other organizations.

- ❑ *Standards organizations*. The ideal model, considered "best practice." The IEEE standard for software project management plans identifies risk management as a managerial process [IEEE88]. The INCOSE Systems Engineering Capability Assessment Model (SECAM) contains a key focus area for risk management [INCOSE96]. Risk management practices are embedded in key process areas of the SEI CMM for Software [Paulk93].

10.2.3   Scope the Effort and Products

Understanding the difference between the action team's objectives and the organization's current practice will help the team to scope its effort and products. To properly scope its work, the team should consider the risk of defining scope incorrectly.

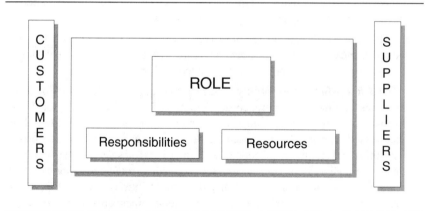

FIGURE 10.5   The 3 R's process design notation. Process elements are described by the 3 R's: role, responsibility, and resources.

A procedural change has a *narrow scope*. The degree of change may be an incremental improvement in an existing procedure. Small adjustments within existing functions are made. The philosophy may be, "We can do better." The risk is lower, but the percentage improvement may be small as well.

A change that is structural or cultural has a *broad scope*. The degree of change is radical. Sometimes there is a large degree of desired change from "as is" to "should be." We may start with a clean sheet of paper to define a new process. The philosophy may be, "We know what does not work." The risk is higher, but the reward may be greater.

How much change is acceptable within your organization? Depending on your constraints of budget and schedule, you can refine the action plan. Adjust the scope of team goals using the purpose hierarchy (developed in section 10.1.2) in order to meet your constraints and ensure success. Decompose the work into task assignments for the team members. Are the team members able to commit to their task assignments? If they cannot, that is another reason to de-scope. It is acceptable to challenge your team, but there is no reason to bite off more than you can chew.

Recognize that there is flexibility in the level of process detail the team will provide. For example, there may be phased upgrades planned, where version 1.0 addresses software projects and version 2.0 addresses system-level risk management. Reach consensus within the action team on product scope.

There are three intermediate work products that are produced to help bound the task. A product scope review checklist (see Figure 10.6) can be used to ensure the completeness of the following work products:

- ❏ *Draft outline*. Define the outline like a table of contents that contains the topics in the order that they will be covered. Describe the goal, objective, purpose, and context.

- ❏ *Product scope*. Define the process as a "black box," with input and outputs only. Define the process entry criteria and prerequisite conditions or products needed to start the process. Define the process exit criteria and verification criteria needed to end the process.

- ❏ *Process diagram*. Draw the process using the standard process notation.

10.2.4   Define the Draft Standard Process

When the task and work products are properly scoped, a draft process is written. There are several common improvement themes to consider in designing the process activities:

- ❏ *Reduce bureaucracy*. Remove unnecessary approval cycles and paperwork.

- ❏ *Eliminate duplication*. Remove steps that are repeated.

❑ *Add value.* Assess whether the activity serves the customer's requirements.

❑ *Minimize errors.* Make it difficult to introduce an error during the activity.

❑ *Standardize.* Select a single best way to do the activity.

❑ *Automate.* Use computers for routine or repetitive tasks.

The draft process is like a storyboard, with themes and figures that show both content and sequence of activity. There are three intermediate work products that are produced to generate the draft standard process:

❑ *Annotated outline.* Develop the structure of the document by writing one or two sentences under each heading that describe what the section will contain.

❑ *Process description.* Define the activities of each process element at a high level to describe the work flow.

❑ *Identify mechanisms.* List the methods and tools used by each process element.

Review Item	Compliance Criteria	Initials
Outline	Critical activities are identified. There are no missing process steps.	
Scope	The scope of the process is not too narrow or too broad. There is no overlap in charters between processes.	
Entry criteria	The inputs are identified. The readiness criteria for the inputs are defined. Inputs have been coordinated with the process generating them.	
Exit criteria	The outputs are identified. The completion criteria for the outputs are defined. Outputs have been coordinated with the process receiving them.	
Roles	Roles and responsibilities for the activities have been defined.	
Requirements	The process will satisfy the planned goals and objectives.	

FIGURE 10.6   Product scope review checklist. Items are reviewed according to compliance criteria using a product scope review checklist. The reviewer signifies acceptance of each review item by writing his or her initials in the space provided.

10.3   Review the Draft Standard Process

When the draft process is defined, the team members review the product in its entirety. A meeting is scheduled to discuss individual team members' comments and suggested changes. When the draft standard process is documented, it should be sent out to a large group of reviewers. Some reviewers may not have time to respond, but at least they will have the opportunity to do so.

10.3.1   Prepare the Review Package

The distribution list should be checked to ensure coverage to represent the organization projects and levels of hierarchy. The material should be packaged with a review form that identifies the product under review and the current level of completeness. A checklist should be included in the review package to guide reviewers. Distribute the review package at least one week prior to the review meeting.

10.3.2   Review the Draft Standard Process

The draft process is reviewed for content and focus. Major issues that reviewers wish to change or discuss at the review meeting are recorded on the review form. Corrections should be made in the review package.

At the review meeting, reviewers bring their comments and discuss their suggestions. Corrections are submitted to the action team with the completed review form. All major issues are discussed and resolved as action items. The team recorder captures specific decisions reached on key issues and documents action items of what to change. For each action item, a determination is made as to whether a re-review of the altered product is required. At the meeting, an individual is identified to serve as the review team leader. This person will closely evaluate all incremental action team work products to gain the insight necessary for future selection and leadership of the final product review team.

10.3.3   Incorporate the Recommended Changes

Reviewers' corrections will be incorporated into the product. The action team prioritizes the list of action items documented at the review meeting and determines which changes are feasible. When the team incorporates these changes, the action items are closed. Some suggestions will be good improvements but may need to be incorporated in future versions due to resource constraints. Action items in this category are carried forward.

10.4 Document the Standard Process

The standard process is an elaboration of the draft standard process, with examples added to increase understanding of the process. To assist process improvement, a change request form is part of the standard process documentation.

The action team may choose to use or reengineer the risk management process documented in Part II of this book. It may be easier to begin with a guide and suggest changes. When your work builds on existing work, be sure to cite your references. The purpose of defining a standard process for an organization is to own the process and thus avoid the "not-invented-here" syndrome. Spending three months (part time) defining a standard process is a small price to pay for the ability to leverage it on all projects.

10.4.1 Elaborate the Draft Standard Process

If the draft was properly decomposed, there should not be any new headings in the outline. After team members elaborate the draft standard process to the next level, they may uncover errors of omission in the draft outline. A process diagram will help to illustrate major process elements that can be described in the standard process definition. Document the detail in each section, and add examples as required.

10.4.2 Evaluate the Standard Process

The action team leader and the product[3] review team leader coordinate an evaluation of the standard process. A subset of reviewers (typically three or four) is selected based on their experience and position in representing the organization's business areas or product lines.

A comprehensive review of the product is guided by a review checklist. The documentation should be consistent with other standards governing process specification. The process is evaluated in the following areas:

- ❏ Implementation of approved organization policy.
- ❏ Compliance to action plan.
- ❏ Compliance to product standards.

---

[3] In this case, the process is a product.

❏ Closure of action items.

❏ Overall quality and usability.

The review team leader meets with the action team leader to discuss the evaluation findings. The actions necessary to resolve the issues are documented. As a guideline, if more than 25 percent of the product is changed, another evaluation is recommended.

10.4.3   Close the Action Items

Review team comments are incorporated into the final product. A brief response for each issue is prepared to indicate what specific changes were made. Action items not addressed are carried forward as open items.

10.5   Approve the Standard Process

The action team leader presents the standard process to the organization by sending the final document to those with signature authority. After the process is approved, the team should be recognized by management for their achievement. Recognition does not have to be expensive, but it must be timely to create a strong association between work and reward. Closure of an action team that collaborated on an approved standard process is cause for celebration.

10.6   Distribute the Standard Process

The action team leader is responsible for ensuring that the approved process is distributed within the organization. New processes should be pilot-tested and have a limited distribution until proved on projects. For a new process, associated training material should be given to the training department. For a modified process, updates to existing training material should be provided.

A summary process description may need to be written as a catalog entry in a higher-level guidebook that points to the process. Pointers, hot links, or icons need to be developed to locate the process definition. The leader's team notebook is catalogued and placed in the organization's technical library. The process repository may be on-line. Both hard copy and soft copy process definitions should be cross-referenced.

10.7   Summary

In this chapter, I explained the process of process definition. The activities of the process definition process are as follows:

1. Establish an action team.
2. Develop the draft standard process.
3. Review the draft standard process.
4. Document the standard process.
5. Approve the standard process.
6. Distribute the standard process.

I described how to establish an action team to define a reusable risk management process, and discussed what a high-performance team has that other teams do not have:

- A shared compelling vision.
- Individual accountability.
- Synergy in collaboration.

A process definition notation is important because it is a form of written communication that describes a process in shorthand. When the notation is understood, it may be used as a building block to define more complex processes. I showed three good process design methods: IDEF0, ETVX, and 3 R's.

A purpose hierarchy is used to describe the action team success criteria. I discussed how to adjust the scope of team goals in order to meet constraints and ensure success. While a procedural change has a narrow scope, a change that is structural or cultural has a broad scope. Teams must understand the risk and reward of defining too narrow or too broad a scope for their effort and products.

I listed several common improvement themes to consider in designing process activities:

- Reduce bureaucracy.
- Eliminate duplication.
- Add value.
- Minimize errors.
- Standardize.
- Automate.

10.8   Questions for Discussion

1. Symbolic metaphors help you gain different perspectives. Discuss how a defined standard process is like the script of a play. Explain how you would improvise the standard process "script" on a specific project.

2. Define the process of process improvement. Include an organization, action plan, and process notation. Explain how this process helps project teams.

3. Discuss the concept of diversity on process action teams. List the advantages and disadvantages of working in a cross-functional team environment.

4. What is the key to establishing an effective team? What is the difference between a group and a team? What is the difference between an effective team and a high-performance team? Do you think it is difficult to sustain a high-performance team? Discuss why you do or do not think so.

5. One way to clarify team goals is to ask team members to assess the risks of success. Identify and prioritize five risks of defining the organization's standard risk management process. Describe a mitigation strategy for each identified risk.

6. What does it mean to "level the playing field"? Do you think it is important for an action team to do so? Explain your answer.

7. Compare and contrast two process-design methods. You may select IDEF0, ETVX, the 3 R's, or another method. Discuss which process design method is best, and why. Can you design a hybrid method that would be better? If so, what improvement would your approach have over the current best method?

8. Discuss how scope relates to action team success. List five ways the scope of process definition can be adjusted to increase the chance of action team success.

9. Describe the not-invented-here syndrome. List three possible consequences of this syndrome with respect to a standard process definition. Explain how extensive review of the draft standard process helps to avoid the not-invented-here syndrome. Discuss other ways to prevent the not-invented-here syndrome.

10. What is the advantage to a project if its organization has a reusable risk management process? Estimate the cost savings to the project in terms of budget, schedule, and staff resources.

10.9   References

[AFIT92] Air Force Institute of Technology (AFIT). Introduction to software engineering: Risk analysis. *Proc.* Software Technology Conference, Salt Lake City, UT: 1992.

[AirForce85] *Integrated Computer Aided Manufacturing Architecture*, Part II, Vol. V: *Common Data Model Subsystem—Information Modeling Manual (IDEF1 Extended)*. AFWAL-TR-86-4006. Wright-Patterson Air Force Base, OH: Air Force Systems Command, November 1985.

[AirForce81] *Integrated Computer Aided Manufacturing Architecture*, Part II, Vol. IV: *Function Modeling Manual (IDEF0)*. AFWAL-TR-81-4023. Wright-Patterson Air Force Base, OH: Air Force Systems Command, June 1981.

[Charette91] Charette, R. Risk Management Seminar (video). *Software Productivity Consortium*. SPC-91138-MC. Herndon, VA, August, 1991.

[Davis88] Davis, W. *The Best of Success*. Lombard, IL: Great Quotations, 1988.

[Fowler90] Fowler, P, Rifkin S. Software engineering process group guide. Technical report CMU/SEI-90-TR-24. Pittsburgh, PA: Software Engineering Institute, Carnegie Mellon University, September 1990.

[Hsiao95] Hsiao D. Project management methodologies: Using IDEF to support a comprehensive business process. *Proc.* Seventh Software Engineering Process Group Conference, Boston, May 1995.

[IEEE88] ANSI/IEEE. *IEEE Standard for Software Project Management Plans*. ANSI/IEEE STD 1058.1-1987. October 1988.

[INCOSE96] International Council on Systems Engineering. *Systems Engineering Capability Assessment Model (SECAM), Version 1.50*, Seattle, June 1996.

[Janson95] Janson J, Piekos J, Warner A. The rise and fall of a high performance team. *Proc.* Seventh Software Engineering Process Group Conference, Boston, May 1995.

[Paulk93] Paulk M, et al. Capability maturity model for software. Version 1.1. Technical report CMU/SEI-93-TR-24. Pittsburgh, PA: Software Engineering Institute, Carnegie Mellon University, 1993.

[Scholtes88] Scholtes P. *The Team Handbook: How to Use Teams to Improve Quality*. Madison, WI: Joiner Associates, 1988.

[Schrage90] Schrage M. *Shared Minds*. New York: Random House, 1990.

[Taylor95] Taylor D. *Business Engineering with Object Technology*. New York: Wiley, 1995.

[Tomayko91] Tomayko J. *Software Project Management*. Academic Series (Lecture 19). Pittsburgh, PA: Software Engineering Institute, Carnegie Mellon University, Spring 1991.

11

Train Risk Technology

Talent alone won't make you a success. Neither will being in the right place at the right time, unless you are ready. The most important question is: "Are you ready?"
—Johnny Carson

Socrates said that you cannot teach anyone anything, you can only make them think. We should remember that people are more likely to retain information on a subject that they perceive as important. Training can help make students more receptive by providing the motivation for learning and help students understand why risk management is important.

Preparation is the key to implementing risk management successfully. I recommend starting at the beginning, with risk management concepts. Understanding the vocabulary of risk management is essential for communication of risk. Just-in-time training is most beneficial. Those who attend training should be able to apply immediately the knowledge learned to increase their skills in managing risk. For example, risk management metrics should not be trained until the project team is serious about following through with quantitative risk management.

In this chapter, I define training metrics that help you provide instruction in risk management. I describe how to increase your organization's knowledge of risk management technology through the learning process.

This chapter answers the following questions:

❏ What are the steps to train risk management technology?

❏ What training modules provide instruction in risk management?

❏ Why do people learn in stages?

11.1   Prepare for Training

Preparation is the key to successful training. Preparation includes all the logistics to obtain approval, determine location, and set the date for training. One of the most important steps to get ready for training is to determine the intended audience. To understand your audience, there are three major considerations:

❑ *Need*. Consider the need of the audience and tailor training illustrations to them. Ask in advance what their requirements are. For example, quality professionals need risk management to prevent problems; system engineers use it to meet technical requirements.

❑ *Level*. Consider the level of the audience. Executives require more of an overview; practitioners need more details. You need to know who your audience is to adjust the breadth or depth of the training material.

❑ *Size*. Consider the size of the audience. The training techniques and class exercises you use will vary depending on whether the number of students is 10 or 100.

11.2   Develop Training Material

Understanding the building blocks of fundamental knowledge in risk management will enable you to adapt to situations as they change and provide you the mental flexibility needed to respond to uncertainty. The following training modules provide risk management instruction:

❑ Session 1: Risk management concepts.

❑ Session 2: Risk assessment methods.

❑ Session 3: Risk management process.

❑ Session 4: Risk management measures.

❑ Session 5: Proactive risk management.

The intent of an introduction to risk management is to provide the breadth of knowledge for handling risk situations where there is no textbook answer. A certain amount of general knowledge is required to provide a foundation for reasoning about risk in these predicaments. Training should include the concepts of risk management such as definitions of risk management terminology. The vocabulary of risk management can be learned in a series of progressive steps. The terminology

TABLE 11.1 RISK MANAGEMENT TERMINOLOGY

Session 1	Session 2	Session 3	Session 4	Session 5
		Causal analysis		
		Corrective action		
		Diversification		
	Acceptable risk	Proactive	Cost-benefit analysis	
	Choice	Process	Measurement	
	Consequence	Risk action plan	Metrics	
	Decision	Risk analysis	Quantitative targets	
	Estimation	Risk category	Risk forecast	
	Evaluation	Risk context	Risk index*	
	Probability	Risk database	Risk leverage	
	Risk assessment	Risk drivers	Risk preference	
Crisis management	Risk checklist	Risk management plan	Risk scenario	Creativity
Loss	Risk exposure	Risk planning	$ROI_{(RM)}$	Opportunity
Rework	Risk identification	Risk resolution	Threshold	Opportunity cost
Risk	Risk list	Risk statement	Trigger	Problem prevention
Uncertainty	Risk management	Risk tracking	Utility function	Risk control

* Also known as the risk management index.

required to be mastered at each of five training sessions is shown in Table 11.1 Training provides the discussion of each of these terms using examples to illustrate the meaning of each. Various exercises should be incorporated into the training material to ensure that each student has a complete grasp of the concepts. Exercises should be performed during training to give students time to try techniques and have their questions answered. Students' skills in risk management increase from novice to expert as they comprehend the terminology of progressive training sessions. As shown in Figure 11.1 understanding more complex concepts

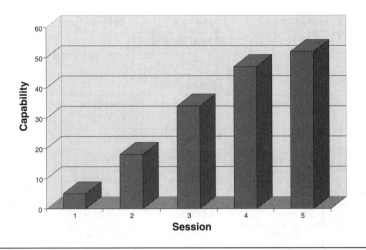

FIGURE 11.1   Increasing skills through training. Learning risk management terminology is an investment that builds vocabulary and increases your capability to manage risk. Each training session builds on knowledge learned in the previous session.

is an investment in increasing risk management capability. Over 50 words are learned in the process of mastering risk management concepts.

Using the Personal Software Process, individuals become competent in four stages of learning [Humphrey95]. Training material should help people through these stages of learning. The trainer should be sensitive to the current learning stage of the target audience. If people understand that the stages of learning are normal and universal, they will be able to articulate the stage they can associate with. Trainers should begin at that stage and progress through the learning stages. There are four stages of individual learning:

1. *Unconscious inability*. We are unaware of risk concepts and lack a vocabulary to reason about risk. In this stage, we are oblivious to the risks because we do not know how to verbalize them. We may feel frustration in a situation that appears beyond our control.

2. *Conscious inability*. We become aware of risk concepts but do not have the ability to manage risk. We may feel anxious and worry about risk consequences.

3. *Conscious ability*. We put risk concepts into practice, which increases our capability to manage risk. We see results in proportion to our persistence in managing risk.

4. *Unconscious ability.* Our brain can make associations based on new information and past experience. These associations exist in our mind, which can potentially identify and resolve risks even as we sleep.

As we develop training material, we must remember that people learn in different ways. Some people remember best by hearing, some by seeing, and some by doing.

Individual learning preferences require different types of instructional methods. As shown in Table 11.2 there are four categories of instructional techniques that are based on a person's primary reason for education [Keirsey84]. Be sure to use a variety of instructional techniques to reach your audience.

11.3   Apply Training Metrics

After you have determined the correct order of the training material, allocate time to each topic, bearing in mind that a relaxed pace is conducive to learning. You need to fit the training material to the time constraint, which undoubtedly will require a trade-off between breadth (covering more material at a higher level) and depth (covering less material in more detail). How can you be sure that you have planned the training material appropriately? The training metrics shown in Table 11.3 will help you refine your training plan by applying rules of thumb. These guidelines have been proved effective through historical data that I obtained from my one-day risk management training seminars. In this case, "effective" means covering all material on time at a relaxed pace.

TABLE 11.2 INSTRUCTIONAL TECHNIQUES

Primary Educational Purpose	Instructional Techniques
Growth of spontaneity and freedom	Contest, demonstration, game, project, show
Growth of responsibility and utility	Composition, demonstration, drill, quiz, recitation, test
Growth of knowledge and skills	Composition, lecture, project, report, test
Growth of identity and integrity	Discussion, game, group project, interaction, show, simulation

TABLE 11.3 TRAINING METRICS FOR A ONE-DAY PLAN

Question	Metric	Plan
How many slides?	3 minutes/slide	(5 hrs. × 60 min./hr.)/3 = 100 slides
How much time per section?	Spend 20% of time on the problem and 80% on the solution.	1 hour—Introduction and Top Risks 4 hours—Risk Management 　　　　　2 hours—Assessment 　　　　　2 hours—Control
When should each section begin?	Two 15-minute breaks Lunch, 1.5 hours	**9:00 Introduction and Top Risks** 10:15 Break **10:30 Risk Assessment** 12:00 Lunch **1:30 Case Study** 2:45 Break **3:00 Risk Control** 4:00 Adjourn
How many slides in each section?	3 minutes/slide	25—Introduction and Top Risks 30—Risk Assessment 25—Case Study 20—Risk Control

11.4 Deliver Training

There are numerous ways to deliver training, such as by cassette tape, video, and direct satellite broadcast. The method that is right for a project depends on the budget and the available technology. Training the old-fashioned way—in person—is preferable for the highest-quality interaction between instructor and student.

Regardless of the training method, the pace of the material should be relaxed to facilitate learning. Around 100 words per minute is a good metric to follow. Although risk management is a serious topic, it is not a somber one. Trainers should incorporate engaging illustrations that help students learn and understand how to moderate humor that opens the mind and makes students receptive to new ideas.

Here are some guidelines for effective communication [Rohn89] in risk management training:

- ❑ *Have something good to say.* There is no substitute for preparation and research of the training material. The knowledge of training risk management must come from real-world experience. Otherwise, risk management will seem superficial to the audience, and you will quickly run out of illustrations.

- ❑ *Say it well.* Practice the timing of the material so that you make each point with brevity and clarity. Use analogies and stories to illustrate your points.

❏ *Read your audience.* Notice the reaction of your audience to what you are saying. Are they nodding in agreement or falling asleep? Make adjustments as necessary.

❏ *Use words with emotion.* Inflection in your voice provides clues to your audience. Stories about risk management can be exciting as well as devastating. Teach your students with your own style. Use emotion to help students make associations that will enable them to remember. Repetition of phrases gives the clue that what you just said is worth remembering.

❏ *Identify with your audience.* Begin with the level of your audience. The reaction from the audience should be, "Me too," not, "So what?"

11.5   Obtain Training Feedback

When you begin training, ask the students what they hope to learn. Set appropriate expectations by reviewing this list and explaining what will and will not be covered. Periodically you can review these expectations to be sure that each topic will be covered by the end of the session. At the end of the session, review these expectations with your audience to show that each topic was addressed. Be sure to call for questions at the end of each training segment to encourage participation.[1] During a training session, it is important for you to review the checkpoints established in your plan. For example, you should note the actual time for each section. This information can be used to refine the timing of your current presentation, as well as future training sessions.

Training evaluations help you improve future training sessions. As an instructor, you should maintain metrics to improve your performance. Use the same five-point scale (1 = poor, 2 = fair, 3 = average, 4 = good, 5 = excellent) so that you can measure your progress over time. Be sure to specify the training title, instructor's name, and date on the evaluation form. A one-page form should be sufficient to gather feedback for improvement. Training evaluations should ask the students to rate and comment on their assessment of training in the following areas:

❏ Value of training content.

❏ Speaker presentation skills.

❏ Training facilities.

❏ The part of training I liked best.

---

[1] Many European cultures discourage the questioning of a lecturer. To overcome this, I use a slide containing three summary questions at the end of each section to stimulate discussion.

❏ The part of training I liked least.

❏ I still have a need for _____.

❏ Other comments.

By immediately using feedback from training, you will be better prepared for your next training session. Update the training material to reflect any errors found during the course of training, and develop new material to address the needs that students identified on the training evaluations. Make a mental note to research any questions the students had that you could not answer to their satisfaction. Instructors should maintain an appetite for learning, which will help them keep pace with software risk management technology.

11.6   Summary

In this chapter, I defined the steps to train risk management technology:

1. Prepare for training.
2. Develop training material.
3. Apply training metrics.
4. Deliver training.
5. Obtain training feedback.

I sequenced the training modules that provide risk management instruction:

1. Risk management concepts.
2. Risk assessment methods.
3. Risk management process.
4. Risk management measures.
5. Proactive risk management.

People learn in stages. At first, we are unaware of risk concepts and lack a vocabulary to reason about risk. We progress to the second stage when we become aware of risk concepts. In the third stage, we put risk concepts into practice, which increases our ability to manage risk. In the fourth stage, our brain makes associations based on new information and past experience. These associations exist in our mind, which can potentially identify and resolve risks even as we sleep. The four stages of individual learning are as follows:

1. Unconscious inability.
2. Conscious inability.

3. Conscious ability.

4. Unconscious ability.

11.7 Questions for Discussion

1. Do you think risk management is important? Explain your answer.

2. Explain the order of the risk management building blocks. Discuss what each training module provides as a foundation to prepare for the next building block.

3. Describe the five themes for the progressive increments of risk management vocabulary. Which term from each increment best represents this theme? Discuss how each group of terms supports this theme.

4. How can you determine the stage of learning your audience is in with respect to a given risk management training module? What is the likelihood that your students are in different stages of learning? How can you accommodate diverse abilities in a single classroom?

5. Which instructional techniques do you prefer? List the techniques you will use to ensure that all your students will learn.

6. Compare and contrast breadth and depth of training material. Give an example of each in risk management training.

7. Discuss the utility of training metrics. In your opinion, what is a good training metric for a high-quality instructor-to-student ratio?

8. List five ways that you can add emotion to your voice when you speak.

9. Do you think it is important to review students' expectations at the end of training? Discuss why you do or do not think so.

10. Are you ready to manage risk? If so, how have you prepared to manage risk? If not, what will you need to be prepared?

11.8 References

[Keirsey84] Keirsey D, Bates M. *Please Understand Me*. DelMar, CA: Prometheus Nemesis, 1984.

[Humphrey95] Humphrey W. *A Discipline for Software Engineering*. Reading, MA: Addison-Wesley, 1995.

[Rohn89] Rohn J. *Take Charge of Your Life*. Audiocassette. Chicago: Nightingale-Conant, 1989.

12

Verify Compliance

The goal of competitive industry is to provide a product and service into which quality is designed, built, marketed, and maintained at the most economical costs which allow for full customer satisfaction.
—A. V. Feigenbaum

W. Edwards Deming proved that improvement in quality starts a chain reaction that yields an increase in productivity. But as scientist Jonah told plant manager Alex Rogo, "Productivity is meaningless unless you know what your goal is" [Goldratt86]. The goal of managing risk has an intermediate objective of verifying compliance of project practices to the risk management plan, a way to engineer quality results. This intermediate objective is necessary to overcome the obstacle of a faulty plan or deficient practices. The objective of verifying compliance is to determine improvement potential of the plan and of the practice. The distinction between verifying compliance and improving process is the difference between short-term and long-term advantage. In the beginning of a project, "verify compliance" precedes "improve process." We cannot improve a process that has not been adequately planned or implemented correctly. In this chapter, we discuss improvement of the plan and the work, and *not* the process. Deming said, "It is not sufficient to improve processes. There must also be constant improvement of design of product and service" [Deming86].

Quality provides customers with products and services that fully satisfy their requirements. **Quality assurance** (QA) is the practice of ensuring that quality standards are met through **quality control**, which consists of the methods by which quality is measured, reported, and improved. The majority of quality assurance practices today are reactive, aimed at detecting and correcting problems that already exist [Kolarik95]. There is, however, a new quality philosophy, directed at problem prevention, which I call **proactive quality assurance**. Proactive QA takes a broad perspective and is not limited to reducing the number of software defects through inspection of source code. This strategy requires an emphasis on cause-effect knowledge, risk analysis, experience, and judgment to justify action. Proactive QA can lead to accelerated development cycles and avoidance of losses, advantages that contribute toward quality for the customer and thus yield a more productive environment. An important customer of proactive QA practices is project management.

In this chapter, I describe how to verify compliance of risk management activities through an independent audit. I describe how to ensure that project practices adhere to a documented risk management plan.

This chapter answers the following questions:

- What are the steps to verify compliance to a risk management plan?
- What are three major goals of quality assurance?
- Which standards provide guidance for quality assurance?

12.1   Review the Risk Management Plan

There is a cause-and-effect relationship between the quality of a plan and the quality of the results. For this reason, we begin an investigation into results by reviewing the plan of activities. The first step in verifying compliance to risk management practices is to review the risk management plan in order to understand the activities, agents, and artifacts of the plan to prepare for a compliance audit. *Activities* are the risk management practices expected to be performed by the project personnel. *Agents* are the project roles with responsibility for risk management activities. *Artifacts* are the expected outputs produced by performing risk management.

The plan should satisfy the following elements, established with the help of QA personnel through participation on process action teams:

- *Completeness*. Do the contents consider all aspects of risk management? Use an outline of a risk management plan as a checklist. Initial the checklist when the plan is complete with respect to the major sections of the outline.
- *Understandability*. Is the plan easy to read and comprehend? Perhaps a glossary is necessary so that new employees or subcontractors can interpret the plan as intended.
- *Level of detail*. Is the level of detail sufficient to execute the plan? A detailed plan specifies what will be done, when, by whom, and how much it will cost. If these aspects of the plan are not clear, the plan needs additional detail.

❑ *Consistency*. Is the plan ambiguous? Look for any contradictions that would confuse the implementation of the plan. For example, inconsistent terminology in the plan can cause people to have difficulty communicating about risks.

❑ *Realistic*. Is the perspective of the plan practical? Any plan that claims, "Everyone on the project will continuously perform risk management," is not realistic. Check for altruistic statements that lack common sense.

12.2   Audit Agents and Artifacts

When quality is vital, some independent checks are necessary—not because people are untrustworthy but because they are human [Humphrey89]. Quality assurance can be effective when competent professionals report through an independent chain of command and support the development of product quality. On large projects, managers need help performing the task of quality assurance. On projects that cannot afford to staff a quality organization, people can monitor each other's work. On small projects, managers can perform the role of quality assurance. On really small projects, quality assurance can be a part-time role. Quality assurance monitors its own organization to ensure that established standards and procedures are followed. Its prime benefit to management is the assurance it provides them that directions are actually implemented.

If you want a high-quality software system, you must ensure that each of its parts is of high quality [Humphrey95]. Auditing agents and artifacts will help to uncover potential problems. Quality assurance is responsible for auditing the quality actions of agents (e.g., project personnel) and alerting management to any deviations. Quality assurance audits the quality of artifacts (e.g., process evidence) to ensure management that the work is performed the way it is supposed to be. Table 12.1 contains a set of audit questions for agents, artifacts, and activities to investigate risk management practices, developed by twenty QA professionals from the Defense Logistics Agency (DLA) during software risk management training. (These questions are worth sharing, because they may help prepare you for a government audit of your risk practices.)

Three industry and government standards require quality audits: ISO 9001, MIL-STD-498, and SEI CMM.

The purpose of ISO 9001 is for external quality assurance [ASQC94]. Guidelines for the application of ISO 9001 to the development, supply, and maintenance of software are detailed in ISO 9000–3 [ISO91]. This standard is for use when you must ensure conformance to specified requirements during design, development, production, installation, or servicing. ISO 9001 requires a quality plan that implements a quality management system for a project. The quality plan is the basis for project

TABLE 12.1   DLA AUDIT QUESTIONS FOR AGENTS, ARTIFACTS, AND ACTIVITIES

Agents	Artifacts	Activities
Are you now or have you ever been involved in risk assessment?	Do you have, or have you read, the risk management plan?	How are risks prioritized?
Who has responsibility for your risk management plan?	Do you know where the risk database is?	What risk management training have you had?
What are your responsibilities related to risk?	Do you have any risks assigned to you for mitigation?	How often is the risk management plan updated?
Who briefs risk issues at staff meetings?	What is your mitigation/ action plan?	What regular risk meetings do you attend?
Who is responsible for analysis and risk management metrics?	What are the thresholds for your risks?	How do you formally submit a risk?
Who has received risk management training?	Do you have the risk management form and the risk management organization chart?	Do you have a risk watch list?
Project engineer: Is the PERT chart up to date?	Are there risk management meeting minutes or a list of meeting action items?	What methods are used to mitigate risk?
Risk manager: Is risk status up to date?	Are there closed risks?	How are risks tracked?
General manager: How do you support risk management?	How is risk management coordinated with the customer?	What kind of risk measures do you use?
QA manager: How do you track risks?	Can you show me metrics used in risk management or trend data used?	How is risk used for process improvement?

monitoring by reviews and audits. ISO 9001 emphasizes process management [Jenner95]. ISO 9001 describes Internal Quality Audits (clause 4.17) as an integral part of the input to management review activities. This clause requires an organization to establish and maintain documented procedures for planning and implementing internal quality audits. The procedures help to verify whether quality activities and related results comply with planned arrangements and determine the effectiveness of the quality system. Where you identify nonconformances to the quality management system, you should recommend corrective action. The results of audits are communicated to management, and any deficiencies found are corrected in a timely manner. Follow-up audit activities verify and record the implementation and effectiveness of the corrective action taken.

The purpose of DoD MIL-STD-498 is to establish uniform requirements for software development and documentation [DoD94]. This standard implements the development and documentation processes of ISO/IEC DIS 12207. It interprets all applicable clauses in MIL-Q-9858A (Quality Program Requirements) and ISO 9001 (Quality Systems) for software. MIL-STD-498 is the military standard for software development and documentation that supersedes DoD-STD-2167A, DoD-STD-7935A, and DoD-STD-1703. This standard requires software quality assurance (SQA) as ongoing evaluations of activities and resulting products to ensure that each activity is being performed according to the plan. It requires that the persons responsible for ensuring compliance with the contract shall have the resources, responsibility, authority, and organizational freedom to permit objective SQA evaluations and to initiate and verify corrective actions.

The purpose of SEI CMM for software is to describe the key elements of an effective software process [Paulk93]. The CMM describes an evolutionary improvement path from an ad hoc, immature process to a mature, disciplined process. The SEI CMM describes the auditing process of software quality assurance at Level 2. Software quality assurance involves reviewing and auditing the software products and activities. It verifies compliance with applicable procedures and standards and provides the software project and other appropriate managers with the results. The verifying implementation common feature in each key process area (KPA) describes the specified auditing practices to ensure compliance for that KPA. The software quality assurance KPA goals are as follows:

1. Software quality assurance activities are planned.

2. Adherence of software products and activities to the applicable standards, procedures, and requirements is verified objectively.

3. Affected groups and individuals are informed of quality assurance activities and results.

4. Noncompliance issues that cannot be resolved within the software project are addressed by senior management.

12.3   Generate an Audit Report

An audit report provides visibility into project risk management performance. It is generated to document the review and audit findings. The project audit findings summarize implementation performance and detail any discrepancies against the risk management plan. The report should show if requirements have been achieved and the nature of any nonconformance. The quality standards discussed in the previous section provide different views on the content of an audit report. The differences between the ISO and SEI standards are sufficient to preclude a rigid mapping, but the similarities provide a high degree of overlap [Paulk95]. Each standard supports a proactive quality assurance role on the project.

ISO 9001 recommends preventive action. In clause 4.14, Corrective and Preventive Action, ISO 9001 requires an organization to identify the causes of a nonconforming product. Corrective action attempts to eliminate the causes of actual deviations. British training literature interprets corrective action as addressing the noncompliance issues identified in an audit [UKBCS92]. Preventive action attempts to eliminate the causes of potential nonconformity's.

MIL-STD-498 requires analysis to detect trends in reported problems. MIL-STD-498 addresses the evaluation of corrective actions to determine whether problems have been resolved, adverse trends have been reversed, and changes have been correctly implemented without introducing additional problems.

SEI CMM requires SQA to review and audit activities and work products for defect prevention and report the results. The CMM's Software Quality Assurance KPA notes that compliance issues are first addressed within the software project and resolved there if possible. For issues not resolved within the project, the SQA group escalates the issue to an appropriate level of management for resolution.

12.4 Track Action Items

Quality assurance is responsible for tracking audit action items until closure. The quality system should require a timely response to action items. All quality standards require maintenance of records of each activity to verify compliance. Records may be in the form of any type of media, such as hard copy or electronic soft copy. In clause 4.16, Control of Quality Records, ISO 9001 requires identifying, collecting, cataloging, filing, and maintaining all records relating to the quality management system. These records need to be managed so that they can be easily retrieved to provide evidence that the quality management system is being used and that all its requirements are being satisfied. MIL-STD-498 requires preparation and maintenance of records for each SQA activity. These records are maintained for the life of the contract. In the SEI CMM, the practices defining the maintenance of quality records are distributed throughout several key process areas. The Software Project Tracking and Oversight KPA requires action items to be assigned, reviewed, and tracked to closure. This activity is reviewed with senior management on a periodic basis.

12.5   Summary

In this chapter, I described how to verify compliance of risk management activities through an independent audit. The steps to verify compliance to a risk management plan are as follows:

1. Review the risk management plan.
2. Audit agents and artifacts.
3. Generate an audit report.
4. Track action items.

I described three major goals of quality assurance:

❏ *Ensure compliance.* Conduct independent reviews and audits. Check the plans and work against established standards by auditing the evidence.

❏ *Report discrepancies.* Alert management to deviations from standards by reporting audit findings. Expose deviations from standards and procedures as soon as possible.

❏ *Monitor quality.* Improve quality by making recommendations to prevent problems and tracking action items to closure.

I described three standards that provide guidance for software quality assurance:

❏ ANSI/ISO/ASQC Q9001-1994, Quality Systems—Model for Quality Assurance in Design, Development, Production, Installation, and Servicing.

❏ DoD Military Standard MIL-STD-498.

❏ SEI Capability Maturity Model for Software.

12.6   Questions for Discussion

1. Compare and contrast reactive and proactive quality assurance.
2. Discuss why productivity is meaningless unless you know what your goal is.
3. Explain how verifying compliance of practices to plans is a way to engineer quality results.
4. Explain why you must verify risk management implementation before you improve the risk management process.
5. List five artifacts of performing risk management.
6. In your opinion, what are the attributes of a high-quality risk management plan?

7. Do you think that quality assurance professionals can be effective when they do not report through an independent chain of command? Discuss why you do or do not think so.

8. List five responsibilities for the project role of quality assurance.

9. Discuss how to ensure the compliance of quality assurance practices.

10. Do you agree that the goal of competitive industry is to provide quality products and services at the most economical costs? Discuss why you do or do not agree.

12.7 References

[ASQC94] American Society for Quality Control. *Quality Systems—Model for Quality Assurance in Design, Development, Production, Installation, and Servicing*. Milwaukee, WI: ANSI/ISO/ASQC Q9001–1994.

[Deming86] Deming W. *Out of the Crisis*. Cambridge, MA: MIT Center for Advanced Engineering Study, 1986.

[DoD94] Department of Defense (DoD). *Software Development and Documentation*. DoD Military Standard MIL-STD-498, AMSC NO. N7069, December 1994.

[Feigenbaum83] Feigenbaum A. *Total Quality Control*. Third ed., New York: McGraw-Hill, 1983.

[Goldratt86] Goldratt E. *The Goal: A Process of Ongoing Improvement*. Sarasota, FL: SMS, 1986.

[Humphrey95] Humphrey W. *A Discipline for Software Engineering*. Reading, MA: Addison-Wesley, 1995.

[Humphrey89] Humphrey W. *Managing the Software Process*. Reading, MA: Addison-Wesley, 1989.

[ISO91] ISO 9000–3. *Quality Management and Quality Assurance Standards—Part 3: Guidelines for the Application of ISO 9001 to the Development, Supply and Maintenance of Software*, 1991.

[Jenner95] Jenner M. *Software Quality Management and ISO 9001*. New York: Wiley, 1995.

[Kolarik95] Kolarik W. *Creating Quality: Concepts, Systems, Strategies, and Tools*. New York: McGraw-Hill, 1995.

[Paulk95] Paulk M. How ISO 9001 compares with the CMM. *IEEE Software*, January, pp. 74–83, 1995.

[Paulk93] Paulk M, et al. Key practices of the Capability Maturity Model, Version 1.1. Technical report CMU/SEI-93-TR-25. Pittsburgh, PA: Software Engineering Institute, Carnegie Mellon University, 1993.

[UKBCS92] United Kingdom. *TickIt: A Guide to Software Quality Management System Construction and Certification Using EN29001*. Issue 2.0. London: UK Department of Trade and Industry and the British Computer Society, 1992.

13

Improve Practice

The majority of men meet with failure because of their lack of persistence in creating new plans to take the place of those which fail.

—Napoleon Hill

We often rely on a system of checks and balances to maintain satisfactory process results. For example, we rely on the president, the Congress, and the Supreme Court to maintain democracy in our country. Laws are amended through a legal process designed to ensure liberty and justice. The U.S. Constitution has endured due to this system of checks and balances and the flexibility to create new laws to take the place of those that are outmoded. Similarly, a system for managing risk requires checks and balances to sustain the practice over time. We must periodically check our risk management practice for potential improvement. To obtain feedback for improvement, you can survey people's perception of their own practice. Collectively, the people should decide what needs improvement.

In this chapter, I provide an appraisal method to improve your risk management practice. I describe how to use a risk practices survey to measure your progress in managing risk quantitatively.

This chapter answers the following questions:

- ❏ What are the steps to improve your risk management practice?

- ❏ Why is importance the key to performance?

- ❏ Why is it necessary to improve quantitatively?

13.1   Develop an Appraisal Method

There are various reasons for assessing risk management practices. A structured appraisal method is used for the following reasons:

- ❏ To report risk management capability.
- ❏ To establish a baseline for improvement.
- ❏ To develop a plan for improvement.
- ❏ To measure progress against an improvement plan.
- ❏ To select a contractor or subcontractor.
- ❏ To monitor practice performance.

13.1.1   Design a Risk Practices Survey

The **risk practices survey** is an appraisal method to obtain perceptions of risk management practices. I developed it to provide a baseline for quantitative process improvement [Hall95b]. **Quantitative process improvement** (QPI) yields objective measures through statistical analysis of subjective perceptions. The risk practices survey shown in Figure 13.1 requires survey participants to identify their perceptions of the performance and importance of risk management practices. *Performance* is how well the practice is completed. *Importance* is how significant the practice is. A five-point scale is used to rate responses to each statement. Responses to five open-ended questions provide the supporting evidence for project strengths and weaknesses. The risk practices survey is inexpensive. The time to complete the survey is approximately 15 minutes. You can conduct the survey on a quarterly basis. It is also automated. After you enter survey responses into a spreadsheet, you can automatically generate a graph of strengths, weaknesses, and areas for improvement. And it is quantitative: people's perceptions translate into objective numbers that measure risk management practices. You can easily track progress by applying the survey periodically.

13.1.2   Categorize the Survey Participants

The survey is given to all those with responsibilities for risk management. Anyone who has used a project charge number can be considered a candidate survey participant. The survey includes categories for all possible roles, to ensure adequate project representation. As shown in Figure 13.2, risk practices survey participants are a mix of management and technical personnel. Survey results are the collective

Your title _____ Years of experience on software projects _____

Your primary role on the project is (check one):

Project management _____ Systems _____ Software _____ Test _____
Configuration management _____ Quality assurance _____ Customer _____ Other _____

This survey will be used to improve risk management practices on software-intensive projects. For each practice, give your perception of both performance (how well we do it) and importance (how significant it is) on the project. Characterize your level of agreement to each statement using the following five-point scale:

0 = Strongly disagree   1 = Disagree   2 = Undecided   3 = Agree   4 = Strongly agree

I. Risk Management Practices	Performance	Importance
0. Example: There is a policy to identify risks.	3	4
1. Risks are identified by individuals when asked directly.		
2. Risks are voluntarily identified by individuals.		
3. Risks are actively sought out.		
4. Opportunities for cost savings are identified.		
5. Risks are prioritized.		
6. Risks are analyzed for their root cause.		
7. Risks are analyzed quantitatively.		
8. Opportunities for cost savings are analyzed.		
9. Risk resolution alternatives are discussed.		
10. Risk resolution plans are documented.		
11. Thresholds are defined for quantitative targets.		
12. Risk scenarios are developed for high-severity risks.		
13. Critical risks are tracked.		
14. All identified risks are tracked.		
15. Notification is provided for triggering events.		
16. Risk scenarios are monitored.		
17. Status of efforts to resolve risk is reported.		
18. Risk resolution plan is executed to completion.		
19. Risk resolution plan is revised as required.		
20. The cost-benefit of resolving risk is cumulated.		

II. Risk Management Observations

1. Some effective risk management practices include _____
_____
_____

2. Some ineffective risk management practices include _____
_____
_____

3. One thing needed in my work group is _____
_____
_____

4. The risk management lessons learned include _____
_____
_____

5. Other comments regarding software risk management _____
_____
_____

FIGURE 13.1 Risk practices survey.

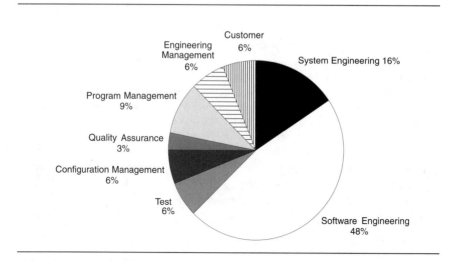

FIGURE 13.2 Risk practices survey participants. The survey participants' roles are shown as a percentage of the total surveyed.

knowledge and experience of the project team, organization management, and the customer. Responses are categorized by project and organization role, so that they may be compared. This particular mix of survey participants comes from data from three software-intensive projects in the early phase of development [Hall95a].

13.2   Assess Risk Practices

There are three steps to assess risk management practices using the risk practices survey: (1) Administer the survey to the participants. (2) Analyze the quantitative survey results using a spreadsheet. (3) Use the subjective survey feedback for the reasons discussed in section 13.1, such as "to establish a baseline for improvement."

13.2.1   Administer the Risk Practices Survey

Before administering the appraisal method, obtain permission from the responsi-ble manager. The manager can help you obtain timely data and can characterize the project in terms of size, structure, and application domain.

13.2.2   Analyze the Risk Practices Survey Results

To analyze the risk practices survey results, enter responses into a spreadsheet that you can use to graph the survey data. Survey responses from 0 to 4 provide an ordinal ranking, but this does not measure the distance between the data points. To normalize the data, scale the data to fit a normal distribution. Map the ordinal scale 0 to 4 to fit a standard normal curve with a mean of 0 and a standard deviation of 1. Count the total number of responses for each response (from 0 to 4) and divide that by the total number of responses to determine the percentage for each slice. Find the scaled value corresponding to each score from 0 to 4 by determining the mean for each slice. Table 13.1 shows the scaled values after the data were transformed. Substitute these adjusted scores for the raw scores in subsequent analysis. By normalizing the data, you enable metrics and statistical comparisons.

13.2.3   Establish a Baseline for Improvement

Plotting relative importance versus performance and the mean importance and performance provides four quadrants that categorize risk management practices. The quadrants show relative strengths and weaknesses and may be used to identify areas for improvement. In Figure 13.3, Identify Risk falls in the quadrant describing high importance and high performance, while Resolve Risk falls in the quadrant describing low importance and low performance. Importance is the key to performance because we prioritize activity based on importance. The consequence of improperly valuing importance is that performance will likely suffer in proportion. The gap between performance and importance shows the need for risk management practices.

13.3   Develop an Improvement Plan

An improvement plan should define specific areas to be improved. To develop a realistic improvement plan, you must understand the difference between "as is" and "should be." Determine your current "as is" practice by substantiating the

TABLE 13.1   DATA TRANSFORMATION FOR STATISTICAL ANALYSIS

Ordinal Scale	0	1	2	3	4
Scaled Values	0.2	1.2	2.0	3.0	4.3

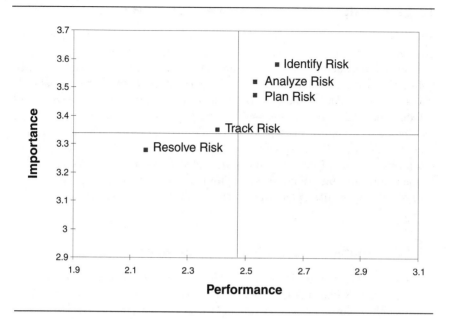

FIGURE 13.3   Perceived strengths and weaknesses of a risk management process.

objective[1] baseline using specific examples from the subjective[2] survey responses. The practice "should be" is detailed in the Risk Management Map (see Chapter 3). You can develop an improvement plan based on the difference between "as is" and "should be." Be sure to adjust the plan for your set of constraints.

13.4   Implement the Improvement Plan

Management should assign responsibility to implement the improvement plan. To execute the plan, involve people on projects as required to promote buy-in from the organization. Improvement plans should focus on the evolution of risk management technology that will be leveraged to satisfy the project's risk management needs.

---

[1] A statistical average is objective, assuming that the sample surveyed is representative of the project.

[2] Individual observations from the risk practices survey are subjective.

13.5   Summary

In this chapter, I described the steps to improve risk management practice:

1. Develop an appraisal method.
2. Assess risk practices.
3. Develop an improvement plan.
4. Implement the improvement plan.

Importance is the key to performance because we prioritize activity based on importance. To improve the performance of risk management practices, we must first understand the value of the practice.

It is necessary to improve quantitatively, because only then can we use metrics and statistical comparisons. Over time, quantitative results characterize progress and trends in performing risk management.

13.6   Questions for Discussion

1. Do you agree that the people who use a process should decide what needs improvement? Discuss why you do or do not agree.
2. What steps would you take to improve the risk management practice on your project?
3. List three reasons for using a structured appraisal method to assess risk management practices.
4. How could a person's job category be used to analyze a risk practices survey? In what way would comparisons of results by job category serve as a check and balance on the findings?
5. You are a process consultant hired to assess an organization's risk management capability. What could you do to ensure the integrity of the data from a risk practices survey?
6. Discuss the value of normalizing risk practices survey data.
7. You are a process group member responsible for improving risk management. The quantitative baseline of risk management practices shows that performance lags importance by at least a point. What does this tell you about the need for improvement?
8. You are a member of a process action team responsible for developing an improvement plan for risk management practices. Both performance and importance of risk management practices are consistently low. What is your strategy for improvement?
9. Explain how you would develop a realistic improvement plan. What constraints could cause you to adjust your plan?
10. How can you determine if a plan is failing? What would you do if your plan failed?

13.7   References

[Hall95a] Hall E. *Proactive Risk Management Methods for Software Engineering Excellence*. Doctoral dissertation, Computer Science Department, Florida Institute of Technology, Melbourne, FL, April 1995.

[Hall95b] Hall E, Natwick G, Ulrich F, Engle C. Streamlining the risk assessment process. *Proc.* Seventh Software Technology Conference, Salt Lake City, UT, April 1995.

[Hill96] Hill N. *Think and Grow Rich.* New York: Fawcett Crest, 1996.

PART IV

Risk Management
Implementation

Tornadoes are caused by trailer parks. Try to know in advance where the trailer parks in your business are located. They seem to attract trouble.

—Norman R. Augustine

Part IV provides an approach for planning and performing risk management on a project. Planning for risk management is described in Chapters 14 through 16. Performing risk management is described in Chapters 17 and 18. In each chapter I discuss who is responsible, where to find opportunities, when to take action, and why this is the recommended approach.

Chapter 14, "Establish the Initiative," contains a checklist of steps to establish risk management on your project. Read Chapter 14 to understand how to respond to project requirements for risk management.

Chapter 15, "Develop the Plan," defines the strategy used to perform risk management on a project. Read Chapter 15 to be able to develop an effective risk management plan.

Chapter 16, "Tailor the Standard Process," suggests some modifications to tailor the standard process to your project for a custom fit. Read Chapter 16 to learn how to recommend deviations from the standard process based on the unique aspects of a project.

Chapter 17, "Assess Risk," describes how to identify and analyze the possibilities in the project plan and remaining work. Read Chapter 17 to understand how to assess risk in a team environment and develop an awareness of the future.

Chapter 18, "Control Risk," describes how to plan, track, and resolve the risk in the plan and remaining work. Read Chapter 18 to understand how to control risk in a team environment using a creative process.

With the knowledge of how to develop a risk management plan provided in Part IV, you will be ready to implement risk management on your project to help achieve your team's goals.

Reference

[Augustine83] Augustine, N. Augustine's Laws, American Institute of Aeronautics and Astronautics, New York, 1983.

14

Establish the Initiative

Destiny is not a matter of chance; it is a matter of choice.
It is not something to be waited for; but, rather something to
be achieved.
—William Jennings Bryan

It takes initiative to respond to project requirements for risk management. I chose the word *initiative* because it has a circular definition that leads to risk. *Initiative* means to take the first step, as in a venture. Venture is synonymous with risk, because of the uncertainty in any new endeavor. An initiative is defined by the energy and enthusiasm that is associated with a new beginning. It is also defined by inventiveness and ingenuity, due to the creativity and resourcefulness required to build a new product.

The purpose of establishing a risk management initiative is to provide the context for performing risk management that is integrated within the project. Establishing an initiative involves reviewing requirements from the customer and organization and planning for risk management activities. The project manager, responsible for allocating resources for the risk management initiative, can delegate the task of coordinating training for project participants to encourage their involvement in risk management activities.

In this chapter, I provide a checklist to help you respond to project requirements for risk management.

This chapter answers the following questions:

❑ Why is risk management a derived requirement for all projects?

❑ How much does a risk management initiative cost?

❑ What is the recommended approach for risk management training?

14.1   Review Risk Management Requirements

In order to establish a risk management initiative, you should review where your project's risk management requirements come from because these requirements are the drivers for establishing this initiative. Project requirements are a combination of contractual, organizational, and derived requirements. Contractual requirements for risk management are often contained in a statement of work (SOW), which typically specifies planning risk management activities and implementing risk management on a project. Organizational standards for risk management start with a policy that sets expectations for project behavior. Some requirements are not explicitly stated but are derived from goals and objectives. Derived requirements for risk management can originate from the marketplace, competitive bids, the use of new technology, or system complexity. Risk management is a derived requirement from the need to nail the cost, schedule, or technical system performance. Another reason that risk management is a derived requirement for all software projects is the volatility of the software industry. Software has never been more complex or costly than in today's environment.

14.1.1   Review Contractual Requirements

A project SOW is likely to contain contractual requirements for risk management. The vocabulary that describes risk management in the SOW, however, is often different from the organizational standard terminology. Contractors as software producers and customers as software consumers often use different words to describe similar concepts. A lookup table like the one shown in Table 14.1 can be generated and used to translate customer requirements. It is best to use consistent terminology and avoid overloading words whenever possible.

TABLE 14.1   RISK MANAGEMENT TERMINOLOGY TRANSLATION

Contractor	Customer
risk management initiative	risk management program
risk assessment	risk analysis
probability	likelihood of occurrence
consequence	impact of risk
risk resolution	risk reduction
risk control	risk management

You may want to adapt the Glossary from this book to create your set of terms. Working on one particular proposal team, I generated a list of about 20 words to describe the contractor's risk management approach in the customer's terms. Risk was addressed consistently in the technical proposal by asking the proposal team members to use the words on the list. Note the consistent use of customer language in the following specification from a SOW [USCG94], which outlines the project management plan and the risk management program required by the contract:

Project management plan. Planning activities shall include risk management practices and mechanisms for controlling resources and schedule.

❑ *Project management review*: At each project management review, the contractor shall report progress and work status to the customer and shall address risk management areas and activities.

❑ *Risk management plan*: The contractor shall indicate plans for engineering specialties, such as risk management.

❑ *Risk management metrics*: The contractor shall describe the methods to be employed for software engineering planning and control, including the use of software management metrics for risk management.

❑ *Risk management status*: The contractor shall conduct a general session to report progress and work status on all active task orders to the customer and shall address risk management areas and activities.

Risk management program. The contractor shall plan and implement a risk management program that includes a continuing analysis of the risks associated with the cost, schedule, and technical parameters and describes the reduction of those risks to an acceptable level through effective management. The contractor shall address risk analysis, risk reduction, and risk management.

❑ *Risk analysis*: This analysis shall include identification and assessment of risk; the likelihood of occurrence, evaluation of the impact of risk on cost, schedule, and technical performance; and the identification of alternatives to avoid or minimize risk.

❑ *Risk reduction*: This activity shall involve the selection of risk reduction alternatives, definition of courses of action to implement risk reduction alternatives, commitment of staff, and financial resources to support risk reduction actions.

❑ *Risk management*: This activity shall establish a procedure to monitor progress of risk management activities, and report results of the risk management program to the customer.

❑ *Risk management progress*: The contractor shall document risk management activities and report progress to the customer in the monthly progress reports.

14.1.2   Review Organizational Standards

Organizational standard operating procedure should contain requirements for risk management. A draft company policy statement for risk management is defined in Chapter 9. Following is an example of a standard operating procedure for risk management that could serve as an organizational standard (note the consistent use of contractor language in this procedure):

> The purpose of risk management is to assess and control risks. Risk management involves identifying potential problems throughout the project. Identified risks are analyzed to determine their probability and consequence. Risk resolution plans are developed to resolve risk. Risks and risk resolution plans are then tracked to closure. Communication of risks and risk resolution plans to affected groups is emphasized.

> Risk management involves performing the tasks necessary to identify, analyze, plan, track, and resolve risks using a defined risk management process. The risk management process may be part of the project's defined management or engineering process.

> ❑ Goal 1: A risk management initiative is planned and implemented throughout the project (at all operational levels).

> ❑ Goal 2: Risks to the project are assessed and controlled according to a documented risk management process throughout the life cycle.

> ❑ Goal 3: Risk management activities are documented, reviewed, and reported.

> The project follows a written organizational policy for planning and implementing a risk management initiative. The policy specifies that:

> 1. The risk management plan is peer reviewed in order to promote commitment and understanding.
> 2. Risk management activities involve the project team, customer, end user, and suppliers as appropriate.
> 3. Risk management activities are reported and tracked.
> 4. A risk assessment is performed early in the project life cycle using a defined process.
> 5. Risk identification activities focus on the identification of risks, not placement of blame.
> 6. The results of risk identification activities are not used by management to evaluate the performance of individuals.
> 7. Each project routinely assesses and controls risk as part of project management tasks.

14.2   Plan Risk Management Activities

Once risk management requirements are understood, you can plan for risk management activities. Specific project requirements help to define the tasks to plan and implement risk management. The scope of the activities is based on the project attributes of size, budget, and complexity and is adjusted to fit project constraints. The project planning process [Paulk93] can be used to plan the risk management activities on the project. A sample project planning process is shown as an IDEF0 diagram [AirForce81] in Figure 14.1. The process elements Budget, Schedule, Staff, and Plan are the major tasks that transform requirements into cost estimates, a project schedule, an organization chart, and project plans. The risk management plan is an integral part of project plans [Thayer88]. (The details of the risk management plan are examined in Chapter 15.)

14.3   Budget Risk Management Activities

Phil Crosby [Crosby80] said that "quality is free," but risk is not free. Risk is a potential loss, and the only way to turn that around is risk management. Risk management is an investment in future payoff. We manage risk to gain[1] a return on investment. The old adage, "It takes money to make money," reminds us that life accumulates. For example, we expect each dollar that we invest to double in a certain amount of time. This payoff cannot be exactly known because of future uncertainty, such as inflation. But we do know that if we never invest the money, we will never have the opportunity for future payoff.

Budgeting for risk management activities is the initial investment required for future payoff. Later, mitigation costs are incurred when there is reason to believe that risk leverage exists. You should add a line item for each risk management activity on the project master schedule. Be sure to cost the baseline risk assessment using the assessment method that your project budget will support. How much does a risk management initiative cost? The answer to this question is the sum total of the budgeted line items.

14.4   Schedule Risk Management Activities

Schedule risk management activities—developing the risk management plan, training the people, baselining the risk, and verifying risk management practices—on the project master schedule. You may want to allocate more time on the schedule for a high-risk area to ensure a delivery date. If your budget is inflexible, schedule a lower level of effort over an extended period to provide the time needed

---

[1] It is not a good strategy to manage risk to the break-even point. Due to the uncertainty associated with risk, we should expect a return with a margin for error.

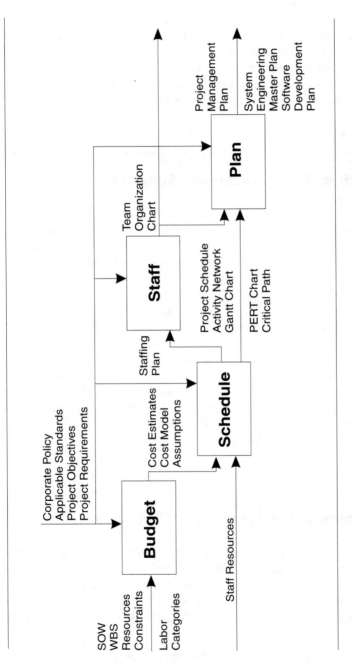

FIGURE 14.1   Project planning process diagram. The planning process is used to transform risk management requirements into a documented risk management plan. The plan may be contained within the project management plan, the system engineering master plan, or the software development plan.

to address a high-risk area. Consider schedule dependencies for high-risk areas, to schedule the correct order of activity. Activities that are not completely in your control, such as those with external interfaces, often take longer. You can specifically schedule technical interchange meetings to address risk and incorporate risk issues within project reviews and other meeting agendas.

14.5 Staff Risk Management Activities

Ultimately, the project manager is responsible for software risk, but the majority of the responsibility to manage risk must be delegated. People inherit responsibility for risk management by their assigned role on the project. For example, oversight for risk management verification can be delegated to quality assurance specialists. One way to coordinate risk management activities is to create a special assignment to the role of **risk manager**. This role is often filled by a senior technical person but is not required to be a full-time position. Staff risk management activities by involving the appropriate mix of people. Encourage participation from the customer, senior management, and the project team.

14.6 Coordinate Risk Management Training

Assigning responsibility for managing risk without the ability to execute the task is setting up people for failure. Coordinate risk management training for project staff to develop their ability to manage risk. With training, they will be prepared to perform risk management activities. Training should be specific to the project procedures that are used to implement the risk management plan. (Training for risk management is described in Chapter 11.)

Just-enough is a recommended approach for training material that builds on current knowledge. With just enough training, the people will not feel overwhelmed by the amount of information or feel they must become an expert overnight. They should understand there is a developmental path and know where they are on the path.

Just-in-time is another important concept. Train the project team so they can apply the concepts immediately. Lectures must be accompanied by exercises that provide practice in applying new methods. There should also be time for answering questions that arise when people practice new methods.

14.7   Summary

In this chapter, I provided a checklist to help you respond to project requirements for risk management. The checklist includes the following activities:

1. Review risk management requirements.
2. Plan risk management activities.
3. Budget risk management activities.
4. Schedule risk management activities.
5. Staff risk management activities.
6. Coordinate risk management training.

Risk management is a derived requirement for all projects because of the increasing rate of change in the software industry. The environment for software development is more complex and costly than ever before.

Risk is not free. It is a potential loss, and the only way to turn that around is risk management. *Risk management is an investment in future payoff.* This payoff cannot be exactly known, because we must consider future uncertainty, such as inflation. Budgeting for risk management activities is the initial investment required for future payoff. Later, mitigation costs are incurred when there is reason to believe that risk leverage exists. You should add a line item for each risk management activity on the project master schedule. A risk management initiative cost is the sum total of the budgeted line items.

The recommended approach for risk management training is to build on the team's current knowledge and have them apply the concepts immediately.

14.8   Questions for Discussion

1. List three risks in establishing a risk management initiative. Assess the probability and consequence of each risk.
2. Compare and contrast contractual and organizational requirements for risk management.
3. Explain why risk management is a derived requirement on most software development projects.
4. What would you do if your organizational standard terminology for risk management was different from your customer's vocabulary?
5. List three resources that you need to manage risk.
6. How could you add risk assessment as a line item cost to baseline software risk?

7. How could you add time for risk management to project meeting agendas?

8. How could you encourage participation from the customer, senior management, and the project team for managing software risk?

9. In what way is training for risk management specific to a project?

10. Do you agree that destiny is a matter of choice? Discuss why you do or do not agree.

14.9 References

[AirForce81] *Integrated Computer Aided Manufacturing Architecture*, Part II, Vol. IV: *Function Modeling Manual (IDEF0)*. AFWAL-TR-81-4023. Wright-Patterson Air Force Base, OH: Air Force Systems Command, June 1981.

[Crosby80] Crosby, Phil. *Quality Is Free*. New York: McGraw-Hill, 1980.

[Paulk93] Paulk M, et al. Capability Maturity Model for Software. Version 1.1. Technical report CMU/SEI-93-TR-24. Pittsburgh, PA: Software Engineering Institute, Carnegie Mellon University, 1993.

[Thayer88] Thayer R. *Software Engineering Project Management*. New York: IEEE Computer Society Press, 1988.

[USCG94] United States Coast Guard. Vessel Traffic Services (VTS2000) Statement of Work. Washington, DC, 1994.

15

Develop the Plan

Success or failure is often determined on the drawing board.
—Robert J. McKain

A risk management plan incorporates the documented goals, strategy, and methods for performing risk management on a project. The purpose of developing such a plan is to determine the approach for performing risk management cost-effectively on the project. The plan should be long enough to convey this information to project participants. For a small project, the risk management plan might be only 5 pages long. For a large project, the plan might grow to 20 pages. The plan may be a separate document or part of a larger plan (e.g., project management plan, system engineering master plan, or software development plan).

The risk management plan develops from a draft annotated outline that project leaders review to identify problems and promote understanding of the plan. Incorporating feedback from the reviewers helps to develop a better plan—better in the sense that people believe more in their own creations. The not-invented-here (NIH) syndrome is the resistance of people to execute plans that they did not invent. Involving others (as a minimum, the project leaders) in the development of the draft risk management plan is critical to removing the NIH roadblock.

The risk management plan should be documented in an easily understood format. It should be approved through the appropriate management to promote support and commitment, then be distributed to the project team to provide common goals, strategy, and methods for performing risk management. The plan should be maintained with a revision history that includes version number, date, and description of change.

In this chapter, I explain the contents of a comprehensive risk management plan. This chapter answers the following questions:

❑ What are the contents of a comprehensive risk management plan?

❑ How can you delegate responsibility and authority for risk management?

❑ What is the most effective approach for a risk management plan?

15.1   Outline the Risk Management Plan

The risk management plan maps human resources to project requirements for risk management. An outline for a risk management plan contained within a project management plan (PMP) is shown in Table 15.1. The PMP describes the budget, schedule, and staffing aspects of project planning for risk management requirements. Section 1.0, *Goals*, explains why the project needs risk management, what the project expects to gain from use of risk management, and how the risk management plan responds to risk management requirements. Section 2.0, *Strategy*, contains the philosophy and guiding principles of risk management, as well as how people will organize to manage risk. Section 3.0, *Process*, describes a tailored version of the standard risk management process. Section 4.0, *Verification*, shares the evaluation criteria for practice compliance. Section 5.0, *Mechanisms*, describes examples of the methods the project team will use to execute the risk management process.

15.2   Define Risk Management Goals

The risk management goals are the driving requirements for risk management on the project. Goals should provide direction and focus for the project team members. Purpose describes what you hope to achieve by following the risk management plan. The statement of purpose provides the motivation and expectation for risk management results. Objectives are specific actions that help achieve a goal. The objectives may be listed in order of priority and may be written as quantitative targets, such as "100 percent award fee" or "zero defects." Scope describes an overview for the major sections of the plan. A few sentences for each major section is sufficient to provide a synopsis of the risk management plan contents.

TABLE 15.1 RISK MANAGEMENT PLAN OUTLINE

1.0	GOALS
1.1	Purpose
1.2	Objectives
1.3	Scope
2.0	STRATEGY
2.1	Policy
2.2	Approach
2.3	Project Roles
3.0	PROCESS
3.1	Identify Risk
3.2	Analyze Risk
3.3	Plan Risk
3.4	Track Risk
3.5	Resolve Risk
4.0	VERIFICATION
4.1	Review Criteria
4.2	Audit Procedure
4.3	Audit Report
5.0	MECHANISMS
5.1	Risk Checklist
5.2	Risk Management Form
5.3	Risk Database Structure

15.3 Define the Risk Management Strategy

The risk management strategy is the manner in which the people will implement the plan. The risk management plan should comply with a written organizational risk management policy. You can reference the policy without duplicating the contents of the policy. Approach defines the principles by which people will manage risks. Projects may share a similar process but have a diverse approach, which yields different results. The recommended risk management approach is proactive, integrated, systematic, and disciplined.

Proactive risk management means actively attacking risks [Gilb88]. The proactive approach is favorably causing action or change. A proactive approach is for action, not reaction [Hall95]. The plan should describe a proactive approach for acting to assess and control risks. Your project plan can be proactive by establishing a system of rewards for early identification of risks.

Integrated risk management means incorporating awareness of risk into routine work activities. One way to integrate risk management into regular activities is to centralize a database for recording issues and actions associated with risk. We need routine risk management due to turnover and growth in staffing, an increase in awareness of project issues, and a different life cycle focus. Because risks are dynamic, risk management must be routine. Routine risk management is possible when it is integrated into regular project activities [Hall97].

Systematic risk management means establishing a set of checks and balances that perpetuate the process. A system of checks and balances, such as procedures for verification and improvement, helps to continue the process. Mechanisms that help address issues systematically are the risk checklist, risk management form, and risk database. One way to improve risk management systematically is to assign a risk manager and facilitator role on every project and import-export lessons learned.

Finally, disciplined risk management means growing in capability through knowledge and experience in six basic disciplines: Envision, Plan, Work, Measure, Improve, and Discover. The ability to manage risk has a developmental path from novice to expert for acquiring certain skills. We develop proficiency through the study and practice of risk management principles, methods, and tools [Hall94]. One technique that can help you develop a more disciplined risk management capability is root cause analysis.

A project role determines how to delegate responsibility and authority for managing risk. For each function on the project organization chart, clearly define the roles and responsibilities, as shown in Table 15.2. People inherit risk by assuming one of the project roles. Each role has internal and external interfaces where known risk must be communicated. When a role is filled by several people, individuals should designate a leader to coordinate the group. It is difficult to hold people or groups accountable for managing risk when there is ambiguity in their responsibilities. Authority should be granted explicitly to handle risk information among interpersonal interfaces, even though the hierarchical organization chart does not show the relationship.

TABLE 15.2   DELEGATE AUTHORITY FOR MANAGING RISK

Project Roles	Responsibilities	Interfaces
Project manager	Provide project leadership, maintain strategic plan	Sponsors, contractors, managers, system engineering
Administration support	Maintain office environment, time cards, travel, equipment	Project team, program office, contractor facilities
Finance manager	Budget execution and tracking, contract performance evaluation	Project manager, sponsor
Risk manager	Facilitate risk management, maintain risk database	Project manager, sponsor, project team, contractors, customers
Configuration manager	Perform data management, status accounting, change control	Project manager, project team
Quality manager	Enforce standards and procedures, conduct independent review	Project manager, engineering
Logistics manager	Oversee technical publications, site activation, inventory control	Project manager, field sites
Security manager	Determine hardware and software requirements for secure systems	Project manager, international program office
Document librarian	Provide list of documents, ensure latest documents are available	Program office, project team
System engineering	Develop concept of operations, requirements management	Project manager, engineering, contractors, quality manager
Hardware engineering	Oversee hardware cost estimation, procurement, integration	System engineering, quality manager, test engineering
Software engineering	Perform software requirements analysis, design, code, peer review	System engineering, quality manager, test engineering
Test engineering	Conduct internal verification and validation, integration of test schedules	System engineering, software, hardware, quality manager

15.4   Define the Risk Management Process

The risk management process is a systematic and structured way to manage risks that includes the activities and mechanisms used to transform project knowledge into decision-making information. The risk management plan can point to a documented risk management process. Whether by hard copy reference or soft copy linkage, the separation of process and plan enables the flexibility for change. You can define the risk management process by tailoring a standard risk management process. (A risk management process is provided in Part II. Chapter 16 describes how to tailor a standard process to the needs of a project.)

15.5   Define Risk Management Verification

Risk management verification is the method to ensure that project practices adhere to the documented risk management plan. Review criteria are specified to set expectations for compliance. The purpose of the review is to understand the activities, agents, and artifacts of the risk management plan to prepare for a compliance audit. An audit procedure verifies whether planned activities are conducted and participants are trained, and whether there is adherence to the risk management plan. The audit report is generated to summarize implementation performance and detail any discrepancies against the plan. The report should show if requirements have been achieved and the nature of any nonconformance. (Chapter 12 describes how to verify compliance of risk management activities through an independent audit.)

15.6   Define Risk Management Mechanisms

The risk management mechanisms are the techniques and tools used by a process to transform inputs to outputs. Mechanisms can be included in the risk management plan to help people visualize the organization of risk information. Three important mechanisms of risk management are the risk checklist, risk management form, and risk database structure.

❑ *Risk checklist.* A risk checklist organizes areas of concern into categories to understand the nature of the risk. Risk checklists help us to identify risks in a given area completely. For example, items on the critical path create a checklist of schedule risks that should be managed. (I describe several risk checklists in Chapter 4.)

Risk Management Form			
Log Number: 203	Date: 18 Oct. 97	Originator's Name: E. Hall	Risk Category: Product. Test
Risk Title: Test Growth	Probability: Likely	Consequence: High	Time Frame: Medium
Project: TEG-32	Phase: Code & Unit Test	Function: System Test	WBS Element: 01-05-03

Risk Assessment

Risk statement:
Growth in the number of object classes · will probably · increase the system test hours beyond plan.

Risk context: The number of object classes has grown over 20 percent beyond estimate used in test planning. Test is 10 months of 3 year program. Test is $10 million of $100 million total cost.

Risk analysis: 33 percent of system test is software integration test times 20 percent growth in software = 6.6 percent growth in overall system test schedule.

Risk exposure = probability between 61 to 80% times
consequence of 6.6% test growth
= 3.6 to 4.8%.

Cost impact = 660 K   Schedule slip = 3 weeks.

Risk Planning

Strategy:	Risk action plan:
☐ Avoidance	1. Use reserve to purchase COTS automated test tool and training.
☐ Protection	2. Use tool to increase productivity of test engineers and decrease likelihood of
☑ Reduction	schedule slip.
☐ Research	
☑ Reserves	
☐ Transfer	

Risk Tracking

Quantitative target: 2,000 object classes.	Comments: Per original estimate.
Indicator: Object class count.	
Threshold: 2,400 object classes.	Anticipated software growth.
Trigger: At each unit test.	Update actual object class count.

Risk Resolution

Software Engineer:	System Engineer:	Quality Assurance:	Project Manager:
Date:	Date:	Date:	Date:

FIGURE 15.1   Risk management form. This form captures essential risk information in a standard format.

❏ *Risk management form.* The risk management form documents risk information essential for managing risk. One way to record risk information systematically and track it to closure is a risk management form. Anyone can use the form at any time to identify an issue—and may use it anonymously. Figure 15.1 shows a sample risk management form for an active risk.

❏ *Risk database structure.* The risk database structure shows the organization of identified risks and associated information. It organizes risk information to support queries, status tracking, and report generation. A simple spread-sheet tool can implement the risk database, useful for its ability to sort and report automatically. Actual contents of the risk database are not part of the plan because risks are dynamic[1] and change over time.

15.7 Summary

In this chapter, I explained the contents of a comprehensive risk management plan:

- ❏ Goals.
- ❏ Strategy.
- ❏ Process.
- ❏ Verification.
- ❏ Mechanisms.

You can delegate responsibility and authority for risk management by clearly defining project roles. People can be held accountable for managing risk only when there is no ambiguity in their responsibilities. Project organization charts are not sufficient to convey people's responsibilities or their interpersonal interfaces, which are known sources of risk. Risk is a function of a project role, not an individual person. People inherit risk when they are assigned a project role.

The most effective approach for a risk management plan is proactive, integrated, systematic, and disciplined.

15.8 Questions for Discussion

1. In what ways can the risk management plan provide an approach for performing risk management cost-effectively?

2. Discuss the advantages and disadvantages of a proactive approach to managing risk.

3. List five responsibilities associated with the role of project manager. For each responsibility, provide a risk that might occur. Identify the associated interfaces for communication regarding each risk.

---

[1] The half-life of a risk may be six months or less.

4. List five responsibilities associated with the role of quality manager. For each responsibility, provide a risk that might occur. Identify the associated interfaces for communication regarding each risk.

5. List five responsibilities associated with the role of system engineer. For each responsibility, provide a risk that might occur. Identify the associated interfaces for communication regarding each risk.

6. List five responsibilities associated with the role of software engineer. For each responsibility, provide a risk that might occur. Identify the associated interfaces for communication regarding each risk.

7. Do you think the separation of process and plan enables flexibility for change? Discuss why you do or do not think so.

8. Discuss the advantages and disadvantages of an independent quality audit of the risk management practices to ensure adherence to the risk management plan.

9. Discuss the difference between the goal of minimizing risk and the goal of maximizing opportunity.

10. Do you agree that success or failure is often determined on the drawing board? Discuss why you do or do not agree.

15.9 References

[Gilb88] Gilb T. *Principles of Software Engineering Management*. Reading, MA: Addison-Wesley, 1988.

[Hall97] Hall E, Gorsuch T. A sixth discipline for future awareness. *Proc.* Seventh International Symposium of the International Council on Systems Engineering, Los Angeles, August 1997.

[Hall95] Hall E. *Proactive Risk Management Methods for Software Engineering Excellence*. Doctoral dissertation, Computer Science Department, Florida Institute of Technology, Melbourne, FL, April 1995.

[Hall94] Hall E. Evolution of essential risk management technology. *Proc.* 3rd SEI Conference on Software Risk, Pittsburgh, PA, April 1994.

16

Tailor the Standard Process

A defined software process provides organizations with a consistent process framework while permitting adjustment to unique needs.
—Watts Humphrey

In the automobile industry, standard vehicles are produced and then sold to individuals with added features known as options. Options, in other words, provide adjustment to individual preferences. Together, standard vehicles and options reduce the risk of producing cars and selling them to different people. Standard vehicles promote the economies of scale necessary for mass production; options provide the features that increase sales and customer satisfaction. Options are paid for by those who desire them.

Similarly, in the software industry, standard processes are defined and then used by projects with minor modifications. We refer to these modifications as tailoring options. **Tailoring** provides the flexibility required to modify a standard process to adjust for differences among projects. Together, a standard process and tailoring options reduce the risk of developing software that must satisfy different requirements. The standard process provides a common understanding of processes, roles, and responsibilities; tailoring provides the advantage of flexibility for disparate projects.

The purpose of tailoring the standard process is to define the risk management process for a specific project. Unique aspects of a project are addressed, such as size, budget, and organizational structure. Tailoring the standard process involves reviewing the organization's standard process and recommending changes to fit a cost-effective process for a particular project. Deviations from the organization's standard process are documented as waivers. The defined risk management process is peer reviewed, documented, approved, and distributed to the project team.

In this chapter, I provide suggestions for tailoring the standard process to custom-fit a particular project. I list the ways in which a project could be considered unique and provide a form for recommending deviations from the standard process based on the unique aspects of the project.

This chapter answers the following questions:

❏ What are the steps to tailor the standard process?

❏ Why is there a minimum standard risk management process?

❏ What factors can you use to differentiate risk management on projects?

16.1   Review the Standard Process

A defined software process should provide a minimum standard process and tailoring suggestions [Humphrey89]. A minimum standard risk management process provides a common set of metrics that enable project comparisons. At the organizational level, project comparisons provide visibility into progress so that intelligent decisions can be made. Allocation of staff resources among projects is one such decision made at the organizational level. The minimum standard process can be visualized as a process kernel, with the kernel defining the areas that need to be standardized to leverage knowledge between projects. The activities performed within each process can vary between projects if standardization occurs at the process output. The following risk management process outputs should be standardized:

❏ *Risk statement*. The standardization of how to communicate a risk can promote understanding between the project team and the rest of the organization.

❏ *Risk list*. The format of a risk list that shows the key issues facing a project can help management see common themes to address on all projects.

❏ *Risk action plan*. The attributes of an action plan should be consistent, to promote completeness and reuse of successful plans across the organization.

❏ *Risk measures*. The standard definitions of risk measures enable organizational risk metrics and consistent communication to senior management.

❏ *Risk database*. The project risk database should easily merge into an organizational database to retain lessons learned in corporate memory.

16.2   Examine Tailoring Options

After you determine the minimum standard part of the process that cannot be compromised, examine your tailoring options. Recommendations for tailoring are often defined in the standard process. Several tailoring suggestions are made for each process element in Table 16.1. Examine the options listed for each process element to understand some possible process modifications.

TABLE 16.1   PROCESS TAILORING OPTIONS

Process Element	Tailoring Options
Identify risk	When to use the risk assessment method When to use the risk appraisal survey How often the project team will meet to identify risk Modification of the identification section of the risk management form Addition of fields in the risk database to support risk identification Implementation of the risk database Who maintains and updates the risk database How to collect risk measures for risk identification
Analyze risk	How to delegate the responsibility for identified risk Who has the authority for identified risk How to prioritize the risks Modification of the analysis section of the risk management form Addition of fields in the risk database to support risk analysis How to collect risk measures for risk analysis Additional techniques and tools for risk analysis
Plan risk	How to generate risk action plans Modification of the planning section of the risk management form Addition of fields in the risk database to support risk action planning How to collect risk measures for risk action planning Additional techniques and tools for risk action planning
Track risk	How to track risk action plans Modification of the tracking section of the risk management form Addition of fields in the risk database to support risk tracking How to collect risk measures for risk tracking Additional techniques and tools for risk tracking
Resolve risk	How to implement risk action plans Additional techniques and tools for risk resolution Modification of the resolution section of the risk management form

16.3   List Unique Project Factors

How will you decide among all the options for customizing the risk management process? Base your decision on an understanding of the unique aspects of your project. In general, high-risk projects need a more rigorous process.

Three factors used to differentiate risk management on projects are most important:

❑ *Size.* Your risk is low if your project size is small (fewer than ten people).

❑ *Budget.* Your risk is high if your budget is tight or your contract is fixed price.

❑ *Structure.* Risk increases as a function of the number of interfaces within the project organization structure. Your risk is high if your project has no organization chart that defines the channels of communication.

There are other factors as well that can be used to differentiate risk management on projects:

❑ *Life cycle model.* If your project life cycle model is the *Grand Design* (a do-each-step-once strategy), your risk is high that you may not understand requirements well enough to deliver all capabilities at once. If the model is *Incremental* (a strategy that adds functionality to the existing system), your risk is high if your requirements are unclear or you expect rapid changes in mission technology. If the model is *Evolutionary* (a strategy that iteratively refines the total system), your risk is moderate if your user prefers all capabilities at the first delivery [DoD95].

❑ *Software development process.* If your project does not follow a documented software development process or is a new process, your risk is high.

❑ *Level of automation.* Your risk is high if your development tool set is new or not integrated throughout the life cycle. A lack of automation on large systems is also high risk.

16.4   Recommend Process Changes

Project personnel can optimize their risk management process by recommending process changes that provide the following enhancements:

❑ A *better process* is preferred because it is more suitable to the project needs. For example, a method may be preferred because it is familiar and will not require time for training.

❑ A *faster process* takes less time to implement. For example, an automated tool might expedite the process.

❑ A *cheaper process* is reduced in cost. When a process is economical, the return increases.

If your project has a subcontract, it is to your advantage to share your project's risk management process. Help your subcontractor understand what aspects of the process are standard and what may be tailored. Your partnership in managing risk will ultimately reduce project risk.

16.5   Document Standard Process Deviations

You should obtain a waiver for deviations from the standard risk management process. A *waiver form*—one is shown in Figure 16.1—is a mechanism to help projects customize standard processes. The time spent in negotiation and compromise up front is better than implementing a time-consuming process that is not suited to your needs. It is easier to refine a plan than it is to implement a bad plan. Approved waiver

---

Standard Process Waiver Request

Project XYZ requests the following changes to the standard risk management process:

_____
_____
_____

The justification for the change is:

_____
_____
_____

Name: _____   Phone number: _____
Date: _____   Fax number: _____
E-mail:_____   Mail stop: _____

Organization management response:

_____
_____
_____

Name: _____   Phone number: _____
Date: _____   Fax number: _____
E-mail:_____   Mail stop: _____

FIGURE 16.1   Waiver form. Deviations from the standard process are approved by project management using a standard process waiver request form.

forms help to promote support and commitment from the organization management. For example, a tailored risk management plan should be reviewed by quality assurance and approved by the project manager and functional manager. Highlighting changes from the standard process on a waiver form will assist these activities.

16.6   Summary

In this chapter, I provided suggestions to tailor the standard process to custom-fit a project. The steps to tailor the standard process are as follows:

1. Review the standard process.
2. Examine tailoring options.
3. List unique project factors.
4. Recommend process changes.
5. Document standard process deviations.

There is a minimum standard risk management process to leverage knowledge between projects and enable project comparisons. The activities performed within each process can vary between projects if standardization occurs at the process output. The following risk management process outputs should be standardized:

- Risk statement.
- Risk list.
- Risk action plan.
- Risk measures.
- Risk database.

I listed the ways in which a project could be considered unique. The following factors can be used to differentiate risk management on projects:

- Size.
- Budget.
- Structure.
- Life cycle model.
- Software development process.
- Level of automation.

16.7   Questions for Discussion

1. List three ways that tailoring options increase the flexibility of a standard process.
2. What are the benefits of a minimum standard risk management process?
3. List five outputs of the risk management process that you should standardize.
4. Give an example of a tailoring option for each process element of the risk management process.
5. Discuss three factors that you can use to describe your project's need for risk management.
6. You are responsible for tailoring the standard risk management process for your project. What is your process for determining your recommendations?
7. In what ways do you consider your current project to be unique?
8. Discuss what might happen if you could not tailor the standard process.
9. List five reasons that you should document the proposed deviations from a standard process.
10. Do you think a defined software process should permit adjustment to unique project needs? Discuss why you do or do not think so.

16.8   References

[DoD95] Department of Defense. *Guidebook for MIL-STD-498 Software Development and Documentation Overview and Tailoring*. Philadelphia: Defense Printing Service, 30 January 1995.

[Humphrey89] Humphrey W. *Managing the Software Process*. Reading, MA: Addison-Wesley, 1989.

17

Assess Risk

cog·ni·tion (kog-nish'en) **1.** *The mental process or faculty by which knowledge is acquired.* **2.** *Something that comes to be known, as through perception, reasoning, or intuition.*
—American Heritage Dictionary

The purpose of assessing risk is to understand the risk component of decisions. When we identify and analyze risk, we assess the probability and consequence of unsatisfactory outcomes. Risk assessment is a method for discovery that informs us about the risk. We are better able to decide based on knowing the risk rather than not knowing it. We invest our experience in the attempt to understand the future. By measuring uncertainty, we are developing an awareness of the future. Future awareness is the result of a cognitive thinking process. When we are cognizant, we are fully informed and aware.

In this chapter, I describe how to identify and analyze the possibilities in the project plan and the remaining work. I discuss how you can discover unknown risk and how to assess risk in a team environment. You will need to draw on the process described in Chapters 4 and 5, the risk management plan described in Chapter 15, and the common sense of this chapter to assess risk.

This chapter answers the following questions:

❏ What are the activities to assess risk?

❏ What software risks are frequently reported in risk assessments?

❏ What is the major challenge that remains in the software community?

17.1   Conduct a Risk Assessment

The project manager is responsible for delegating the task of conducting a risk assessment, which provides a baseline of assessed risks to the project. A risk baseline should be determined for a project as soon as possible so that risk is associated with the work, not with the people. By understanding the worst-case outcome, we bound our uncertainty and contain our fears. Risk assessment helps take some emotion out so we can deal with the issues more logically. The risk assessment should involve all levels of the project because individual knowledge is diverse. Conducting a risk assessment helps to train the risk assessment methods that will be used throughout the project.

There are three main objectives of a risk assessment:

1. *Identify and assess risks.* You can identify and assess risk using different risk assessment methods. Project requirements may call for a less formal or more analytical approach.

2. *Train methods.* You can use the techniques that you learned during risk assessment training throughout the project.

3. *Provide a baseline.* You have a risk aware project team and a risk baseline for continued risk management as the result of a risk assessment.

There are many opportunities to assess risk—for example:

❑ *Phase readiness review.* Have the team identify the top five risks on a risk-appraisal form. As shown in Figure 17.1, the risk appraisal gathers individual perspectives without requiring collaboration or consensus. (The risk statements in this appraisal are concise and readable because they follow the standard notation described in Chapter 4.) *Time*: 15 minutes.

❑ *Team-building session.* Ask the team to identify the top three risks to their success. This exercise is a way to experience collaboration and consensus on risks, and it provides focus for team goals. *Time*: 30 minutes.

❑ *Technical proposal.* A proposal must respond to technical design risk. You can describe technical risk using a risk management form (see Chapter 15 for an example of a completed form), which organizes risk information to help determine the risk action plan. *Time*: 1–2 hours per risk.

❑ *Project start-up.* A rigorous method of formal risk assessment gathers information by interviewing people in peer groups. This method uses a risk taxonomy checklist and a taxonomy-based questionnaire developed at the SEI [Sisti94]. Although there is no limitation as to when to conduct a formal risk assessment, it is most useful at project start-up or for major project changes, such as an engineering change proposal or change in project management. I describe the activities and cost of a typical formal risk assessment below. *Time*: 2–4 days.

Risk Appraisal

1. Check the job category that applies to your role on the project:

Project manager _____ Quality assurance _____ Configuration management _____
System engineer _____ Software engineer _____ Hardware engineer _____ Test engineer __X__
Other (specify) _____.

2. Write the statement of risk and score it according to the following scale:

1   Very low   Risk is an inconvenience without serious impact.
2   Low   Risk has a minor impact to the process or product.
3   Moderate   Risk may disrupt the process or degrade the product.
4   High   Risk seriously disrupts or degrades a major part of the project.
5   Very high   Risk threatens failure of the project.

Score	Risk statement
3	Supplier not colocated • almost certainly • will delay testing.
2	Software fixes • have a very good chance • of affecting other projects.
3	System test • we believe • will uncover problems brought up earlier.
3	Software changes after test • have a better than even chance • of defects.
4	User group • has little chance • of affecting software functionality.

FIGURE 17.1   Individual risk appraisal. The sample risk appraisal requires no prior preparation and is completed without consulting with other personnel. This risk appraisal captures a test engineer's perceptions about five risks in the project.

17.1.1   Activities of a Formal Risk Assessment

The activities of an interview-based risk assessment transform project knowledge into risk assessment results: assessed risks, lessons learned, and a risk database. A formal risk assessment has five major activities:

1. **Train team**
   - ❏ Identify and train assessment team.
   - ❏ Review project profile.
   - ❏ Select interview participants.
   - ❏ Prepare risk assessment schedule.
   - ❏ Coordinate meeting logistics.

2. **Identify risk**
   - ❏ Interview participants.
   - ❏ Record perceived risks.

❏ Clarify risk statements.

❏ Observe process and record results.

3. Analyze risk

❏ Evaluate identified risks.

❏ Categorize the risks.

4. Abstract findings

❏ Sort risks in risk database.

❏ Prepare findings.

5. Report results

❏ Debrief project manager.

❏ Brief project team.

❏ Evaluate risk assessment.

17.1.2   Cost of a Formal Risk Assessment

The cost of a formal risk assessment varies with the number of people involved. I recommend three individuals on the risk assessment team and a minimum of three peer group interview sessions: the first for project managers, the second for technical leaders, and the third for the engineering staff. You should invite from two to five representatives to participate in each interview session. This rule of thumb works for project teams of 50 people or fewer, when 15 representatives constitute 30 percent of the total team. For project teams over 50 people, you will need more interview sessions to maintain a minimum of one-third team involvement. Team representatives should bring input from the other two-thirds to the interview session. Because interviews with a single person do not develop the group dynamics for discovering unknowns, they are not recommended. Individual interviews are analogous to performing a peer review with the author of the source code under review without peers. Yes, there is value in the review—but it is limited.

The formal risk assessment is more expensive than other assessment methods because it provides the most time for communication between project members. The assessment team contributes about half of the cost of the assessment. The value of the risk assessment team is the members' expertise and independence. The assessment team also helps minimize the time the project team spends away from their assigned work. Figure 17.2 shows the schedule of a typical formal risk assessment. Using the above recommendations, the cost for the assessment team is 72 total labor hours. The cost for the project team is 52 total labor hours plus 1 hour for each team member who attends the results briefing.

Time	Day 1	Day 2	Day 3
8:00	Assessment training	Interview 1	Interview 3
8:30			
9:00			
9:30			
10:00		Analysis 1	Analysis 3
10:30			
11:00			
11:30			
12:00	Lunch	Lunch	Lunch
12:30			
1:00	Assessment preparation	Interview 2	Prepare results
1:30			
2:00			
2:30			
3:00		Analysis 2	Manager debrief
3:30			
4:00			Results briefing
4:30			

FIGURE 17.2 Formal risk assessment schedule.

17.2   Develop a Candidate Risk List

You can routinely develop a candidate list of risks by reviewing a risk checklist, work breakdown structure, or a previously developed top ten risk list. These structured lists help you to identify your own set of risks from known risk areas. In addition, you can use techniques to discover unknown risks. When developing a candidate risk list, the focus is on identification of risk and source of risk in both management and technical areas.

17.2.1   List Known Risks

Known risks are those that you are aware of. Communication helps you to understand known risk in the following ways:

❑ *Separate individuals from issues.* Sometimes the right person knows about a risk but is afraid to communicate it to the team, fearing that the team will perceive the individual, not the issue, at risk. In one case, the person responsible for configuration management had no tool training but during the interview session did not raise this as a risk. Fortunately, someone else raised this issue as a risk, so that it could be resolved.

❑ *Report risks.* The most frequently reported software development risks are issues often found on software projects. It is likely that other software projects report risks similar to those found on your project. Section 17.7 lists the top ten risks of government and industry prioritized by the frequency as reported in risk assessments.

❑ *Report problems.* Everyone knows about issues that are pervasive within the organization, such as the lack of a software process. When there are problems without a focus for improvement, these problems are known future risks. If you have problems that are likely to worsen without proper attention, you should add them to the risk list.

17.2.2   Discover Unknown Risks

Unknown risks are those that exist without anyone's awareness of them. Communication helps to discover unknown risk in the following ways:

❑ *Share knowledge.* A team can discover risks by individuals' contributing what they know. The collective information forms a more complete picture of the risk in a situation. Individuals contribute pieces of a puzzle that they could not resolve on their own.

❑ *Recognize importance.* We sometimes identify risks without an awareness of their significance. Discovering the magnitude of the risk helps in prioritizing it correctly. The passing of time helps us to discover risk importance, but only if we are paying attention. When we are not paying attention, risks turn into problems, when it may be too late to repair the damage.

❑ *Cumulate indicators.* A status indicator that is 10 percent off target is generally perceived as low risk. The summation of a small variance in several indicators can add up to a critical risk. Count the number of indicators exceeding threshold and discover the effect of aggregate risk.

17.3   Define Risk Attributes

For each issue listed in the candidate risk list, you should qualify the issue as a risk. If the probability is zero or one, there is no uncertainty, and the issue is not a risk. If there is no consequence of the risk's occurring in the future, the issue is not a risk. Once you believe that you are dealing with a risk, however, you will want to bound the primary risk attributes of probability and consequence.

17.3.1   Bound the Primary Attributes

To bound the primary risk attribute of probability, you can use words or numbers. Table 17.1 provides the mapping from subjective phrases to quantitative numbers. When you are unsure about the probability, you can provide a range for the probability. The range can be broad to provide room for error (e.g., 40 to 60 percent). A five-point risk score can be used in conjunction with a numerical percentage or a perceived likelihood to help group risks.

To bound the primary risk attribute of consequence, you can list the effect on specific objectives. If the risk were realized, what would happen to your objective? For example, if a virus is downloaded from the Internet, system security would be compromised.

TABLE 17.1 RISK PROBABILITY MAP

Five-Point Score	Perceived Likelihood	Numerical Percentage
1	Chances are slight Highly unlikely Almost no chance	Less than 20 percent
2	Little chance Probably not Unlikely	Less than 40 percent
3	Improbable We doubt Better than even	Less than 60 percent
4	We believe Probably Likely	Less than 80 percent
5	Very good chance Highly likely Almost certainly	Less than 100 percent

17.3.2 Categorize the Risk

Risk assessment results are often categorized to communicate the nature of a risk. There are five steps to categorize risk:

1. *Clarify.* Write the risk statement according to the standard notation. Describe the risk in its simplest terms to refine the understanding of the issue.

2. *Consense.* Agree on the meaning of the risk statement. Once everyone understands the issue, you should agree on the scope of the issue as written. Agreement is not about the validity of the issue as a risk but about the meaning and intent of the issue as documented.

3. *Classify.* Select the risk category from a risk classification scheme, such as the SEI software risk taxonomy [Carr93]. If two or more categories describe the risk, the risk may be a compound one. Decompose risks to their lowest level. Note the dependencies that link related risks together.

4. *Combine.* Group risk statements by risk categories. Roll up all the issues in a category and review them to gain a general understanding of this category by the different perspectives documented in the risks.

5. *Condense.* Remove duplicates and summarize related risks. After you summarize the issues in a logical area, you can easily locate and remove duplicates. Then group related risks with other risks by risk category.

17.3.3 Specify the Risk Drivers

Risk drivers are the variables that cause either the probability or consequence to increase significantly—for example, constraints, resources, technology, and tools. The process and environment can also be risk drivers. These forces cause risk to change over time. For example, your SEI Level 3 process can be reduced to an ad hoc SEI Level 1 process over time due to the risk driver of schedule. You would want to specify the schedule constraint as the risk driver that causes the process to be at risk. Because risks are dynamic, it is important to specify the risk drivers to describe the factors that support risk occurrence. Understanding the risk drivers will help you know where to begin to resolve risk. Use the analysis techniques from Chapter 5 to help you determine the risk drivers and the source of risk.

17.4 Document Identified Risk

A risk management form for documenting the risk provides a familiar mechanism that structures how we think about risk. The completed risk management form in Chapter 15 contains all the essential information to understand the risk.

17.5   Communicate Identified Risk

Communicate identified risk to appropriate project personnel to increase awareness of project issues in a timely manner. Examples of good risk statements are
contained in Figure 17.1 and in section 17.7. You can communicate identified risk
by submitting the risk management form. Logging risks in a risk database is one
mechanism to facilitate communication of identified risks. Risks that are logged
into the system can be periodically reviewed. The "Risk Category" and "WBS
Element" fields of the risk management form help to identify the appropriate
project personnel who should review the risk.

17.6   Estimate and Evaluate Risk

Once the risk is clearly communicated, an estimate of risk exposure—the product
of risk probability and consequence—can be made. The estimate of risk exposure
and the time frame for action help to establish a category of risk severity, which
determines the relative risk priority by mapping categories of risk exposure
against the time frame for action. An evaluation of risk severity in relation to other
logged risks determines the actual risk priority. Criteria for risk evaluation should
be established.

17.7   Prioritize Risk

Prioritizing risk provides a focus for what is really important. Your prioritized risk
list will be unique to your role on a specific project. In general, the challenges of
managing software development can be understood by reviewing the current list of
prioritized risks reported by the software community. Government and industry sec-
tors of the software community have different yet interrelated risks. The government
role is primarily that of acquirer (i.e., consumer), while industry is the primary
developer (i.e., producer).[1] By understanding the risks of each sector, we can work
better together as a software community. Through a partnership in helping each
other, we ultimately help ourselves. The remainder of this section reflects on the

---

[1] These roles may be reversed in the future as the general population becomes a significant software consumer and the government helps to develop the information highway.

risks most often reported from risk assessments in the 1990s and how the list has changed since the 1980s.

17.7.1   Government Top Ten

The current issues facing the government sector of the software community depend on whom you ask and when you ask. If you ask a program executive officer (PEO) from a program in the demonstration/validation phase, he or she might say, "Meeting the specified technical performance requirements within cost and schedule."[2] If you ask a PEO from a program in the development/integration phase, the reply might be, "Funding is a major issue due to the lack of sweep-up dollars in the Pentagon."[3] In this case, the difference is a matter of life cycle phase: one software acquisition manager is beginning a five-year program, while the other is maintaining an existing system and developing upgrades simultaneously. Because each life cycle phase has a different focus, issues and risks will vary accordingly.

Formal risk assessments in the government software sector provide insight into risks of a software consumer. The project participants and the independent risk assessment team both rated the issues used to develop the prioritized Government Top Ten Risk List. I added the risk category and summarized the risk statement (according to my standard notation); the project participants provided the risk context.

1. *Funding* (Risk.Management.Project). *Constrained funding • almost certainly • limits the total scope of the project and affects the ability to deliver.* There is no financial reserve. Funding sources face similar constraints. The process used to get additional funding is slow and cumbersome. Inputs to this process are not based on complete or accurate estimates. The project is budgeted at the minimum sustainable level, and budget cuts are a fact of life. Begging for money takes time.

2. *Roles and Responsibilities* (Risk.Management.Project). *Poorly defined roles and responsibilities • almost certainly cause • uncoordinated activities, an uneven workload, and a loss of focus.* Project roles and responsibilities are misunderstood. Lack of communication is caused by not knowing where to go for information. Individuals perform multiple roles, resulting in "context switching." Without a clear understanding of responsibilities, it is difficult to hold people accountable.

3. *Staff Expertise* (Risk.Management.Project). *Shortfalls in staff expertise • are highly likely to continue, causing • lower morale, burnout, and staff turnover.* Shortfalls in expertise are due to a lack of training and difficulties hiring

---

[2] Conversation with direct reporting program manager (DRPM) Colonel James Feigley, USMC.

[3] From a classified conversation.

someone with the right skills through the government hiring system. Replacing personnel is very time-consuming. Turnover from retirement and promotion, combined with turnover expected due to morale and burnout, would cause a further decrease in staff expertise.

4. *Development Process* (Risk.Technical.Process). *Development process definition is inadequate.* • *It is highly likely that procedures followed inconsistently will cause* • *schedule slip and cost overrun.* Existing processes are not well understood or documented. Requirements elicitation process is poor. No method exists for estimating the cost of changing requirements. The change control process is not always followed. Process steps such as testing and configuration management are bypassed due to schedule pressure.

5. *Project Planning* (Risk.Management.Process). *The planning process is not well defined.* • *There is a very good chance that the software estimates are inaccurate, causing* • *difficulty in long-range planning.* There is no integrated project master plan. Work breakdown structure is in bits and pieces, and not communicated. Plans are not based systematically on documented estimates. Contingency planning is informal or nonexistent. Multiple external dependencies drive replanning that is done without understanding the ripple effect of changes to the plan.

6. *Project Interfaces* (Risk.Management.Project). *Multiple project interfaces* • *will likely cause* • *conflicting requirements, technical dependencies, difficulty coordinating schedules, and a loss of project control.* The project interfaces with a number of systems, many of which are under development. Customers have conflicting requirements, both technical and programmatic. Data and communications dependencies exist with other government systems. There are technical dependencies on hardware platform availability and logistic dependencies on hardware delivery and training availability. There are difficult-to-coordinate schedules with a large number of project interfaces and no political clout to control the project.

7. *System Engineering* (Risk.Technical.Process). *Informal and distributed systems engineering* • *will likely cause* • *problems during hardware and software integration.* There is no single point of contact for systems engineering. Systems engineering functions are informally distributed across the project. Interface control documents are lacking with some critical external systems. The impact of system changes is not always assessed. Several areas such as system architecture, human-computer interface design, and security are not assessed efficiently. Extensive reuse and COTS creates a "shopping cart" architecture that causes uncertainty as to whether the software can be upgraded to meet future needs.

8. *Requirements* (Risk.Technical.Product). *Multiple generators of requirements* • *will probably cause* • *requirements creep, conflicting requirements,*

and schedule slip. There are growth of existing requirements, changes to requirements, and new requirements. Requirements grow because they are not fully understood. Derived requirements arise from refining higher-level requirements. Requirements come from a large, diverse customer base, and there is potential for conflict between requirements. Unstable and incomplete requirements are major sources of schedule risk.

9. *Schedule* (Risk.Management.Project). *Constrained schedule • we believe may cause • late system delivery, customer dissatisfaction, erosion of sponsorship, and loss of funding.* The development schedule is driven by operational needs of different user groups whose schedules are not synchronized. Once release dates are set and made public, it sets customer expectations. If the system is not delivered on time for any reason, customer dissatisfaction can lead to erosion of sponsorship and loss of funding.

10. *Testing* (Risk.Technical.Process). *Inadequate testing • has a better than even chance of causing • concern for system safety.* Testing is the primary method for defect detection. The test phase is compressed due to budget and schedule constraints. Test steps are bypassed for low-priority trouble reports. Testing processes are not well defined. Testing is not automated, and existing test and analysis tools are not used effectively. Inadequate regression testing is a safety issue.

17.7.2   Industry Top Ten

What are the current issues facing the industry sector of the software community? It depends on whom you ask and when you ask. Management, if asked, might mention project funding as a particularly high-risk area. Technical staff might say that requirements are changing. In this case, the difference is a matter of conflicting goals. Management is focused on the project profit equation; technical staff has primary responsibility for the product. Each employee has a different assigned task, and the risks will be relative to the task success criteria.

Formal risk assessments in the industry software sector provide insight into the risks of a software producer. The project participants and the independent risk assessment team both rated the issues that were used to develop the prioritized Industry Top Ten Risk List. The risks are described below with their risk category, risk statement, and risk context.

1. *Resources* (Risk.Management.Project). *Aggressive schedules on fixed budgets • almost certainly will cause • a schedule slip and a cost overrun.* Appropriate staffing is incomplete early in project. No time for needed training. Productivity rates needed to meet schedule are not likely to occur. Overtime perceived as a standard procedure to overcome schedule deficiencies. Lack of analysis time may result in incomplete understanding of product functional requirements.

2. *Requirements* (Risk.Technical.Product). *Poorly defined user requirements •*
almost certainly will cause • existing system requirements to be incomplete.
Documentation does not adequately describe the system components. Interface document is not approved. Domain experts are inaccessible and unreliable. Detailed requirements must be derived from existing code. Some
requirements are unclear, such as the software reliability analysis and the
acceptance criteria. Requirements may change due to customer turnover.

3. *Development Process* (Risk.Technical.Process). *Poorly conceived development*
process • is highly likely to cause • implementation problems. There is introduction of new methodology from company software process improvement initiative. Internally imposed development process is new and unfamiliar. The
Software Development Plan is inappropriately tailored for the size of the project.
Development tools are not fully integrated. Customer file formats and maintenance capabilities are incompatible with the existing development environment.

4. *Project Interfaces* (Risk.Management.Project). *Dependence on external soft-*
ware delivery • has a very good chance of causing • a schedule slip. Subcontractor technical performance is below expectations. There is unproven
hardware with poor vendor track record. Subcontractor commercial methodology conflicts with customer MIL spec methodology. Customer action item
response time is slow. Having difficulty keeping up with changing/increasing
demands of customers.

5. *Management Process* (Risk.Management.Process). *Poor planning • is highly*
likely to cause • an increase in development risk. Management does not have
a picture of how to manage object-oriented (i.e., iterative) development.
Project sizing is inaccurate. Roles and responsibilities are not well understood. Assignment of system engineers is arbitrary. There is a lack of time
and staff for adequate internal review of products. No true reporting moves
up through upper management. Information appears to be filtered.

6. *Development System* (Risk.Technical.Process). *Inexperience with the devel-*
opment system • will probably cause • lower productivity in the short term.
Nearly all aspects of the development system are new to the project team.
The level of experience with the selected tool suite will place the entire team
on the learning curve. There is no integrated development environment for
software, quality assurance, configurations management, systems engineering, test, and the program management office. System administration support
in tools, operating system, networking, recovery and backups is lacking.

7. *Design* (Risk.Technical.Product). *Unproven design • will likely cause • sys-*
tem performance problems and inability to meet performance commitments.
The protocol suite has not been analyzed for performance. Delayed inquiry
and global query are potential performance problems. As the design evolves,
database response time may be hard to meet. Object-oriented runtime libraries are assumed to be perfect. Building state and local backbones of sufficient

bandwidth to support image data are questionable. The number of internal interfaces in the proposed design generates complexity that must be managed. Progress toward meeting technical performance for the subsystem has not been demonstrated.

8. *Management Methods* (Risk.Management.Process). *Lack of management controls • will probably cause • an increase in project risk and a decrease in customer satisfaction.* Management controls of requirements are not in place. Content and organization of monthly reports does not provide insight into the status of project issues. Risks are poorly addressed and not mitigated. Quality control is a big factor in project but has not been given high priority by the company [customer perspective]. SQA roles and responsibilities have expanded beyond original scope [company perspective].

9. *Work Environment* (Risk.Technical.Process). *Remote location of project team • we believe will • make organizational support difficult and cause downtime.* Information given to technical and management people does not reach the project team. Information has to be repeated many times. Project status is not available through team meetings or distribution of status reports. Issues forwarded to managers via the weekly status report are not consistently acted on. Lack of communication between software development teams could cause integration problems.

10. *Integration and Test* (Risk.Technical.Product). *Optimistic integration schedule • has a better than even chance of • accepting an unreliable system.* The integration schedule does not allow for the complexity of the system. Efforts to develop tests have been underestimated. The source of data needed to test has not been identified. Some requirements are not testable. Formal testing below the system level is not required. There is limited time to conduct reliability testing.

17.7.3   Top Ten Progress and Challenges

In the 1980s, experienced project managers identified the risks that were likely to compromise a software project's success [Boehm89]. Table 17.2 describes the top ten risk list of the 1980s and shows how the risk priority has changed over time. A review of software risk from the past decade shows both progress and challenges that remain in the industry.

Risk category in the table shows the lack of process focus that typified software development in the 1980s. Progress has been made here. Today we recognize process risk and know how to assess software process. Half of the industry reported risks are related to process.

Current priority in the table shows that risk has increased in priority since the 1980s, which suggests a lack of effective software risk management. Resources, requirements, external interfaces, and design continue as major risk areas. These risk areas should be considered as opportunities for improvement.

TABLE 17.2   TOP TEN RISK LIST OF THE 1980s

Previous Priority	1980s Software Risk	Risk Category	Current Priority
1	Personnel shortfalls	Risk.Management.Project	1
2	Unrealistic schedules and budgets	Risk.Management.Project	1
3	Developing the wrong software functions	Risk.Technical.Product	2
4	Developing the wrong user interface	Risk.Technical.Product	2
5	Gold plating	Risk.Technical.Product	2
6	Continuing stream of require- ments changes	Risk.Technical.Product	2
7	Shortfalls in externally furnished components	Risk.Management.Project	4
8	Shortfalls in externally performed tasks	Risk.Management.Project	4
9	Real-time performance shortfalls	Risk.Technical.Product	7
10	Straining computer science capabilities	Risk.Technical.Product	7

17.8   Summary

In this chapter, I described how to identify and analyze the possibilities in the project plan and remaining work. The following checklist can serve as a reminder of the activities to assess risk:

1. Conduct a risk assessment.
2. Develop a candidate risk list.
3. Define risk attributes.
4. Document identified risk.
5. Communicate identified risk.

6. Estimate and evaluate risk.

7. Prioritize risk.

I presented results from risk assessments performed in the 1990s to use as a list of known risks. The following government and industry top ten risk areas are prioritized by their frequency as reported in the risk assessments.

Government Top Ten Reported Risks

1. Funding.

2. Roles and responsibilities.

3. Staff expertise.

4. Development process.

5. Project planning.

6. Project interfaces.

7. System engineering.

8. Requirements.

9. Schedule.

10. Testing.

Industry Top Ten Reported Risks

1. Resources.

2. Requirements.

3. Development process.

4. Project interfaces.

5. Management process.

6. Development system.

7. Design.

8. Management methods.

9. Work environment.

10. Integration and test.

The 1990s top ten list has changed from the 1980s. These changes indicate where progress has been made and the challenges that remain. For example, progress has been made by identifying process as a new risk. Further comparison reveals that risk priorities have increased in the past decade. The risks of the 1980s have not been resolved. This fact underscores the major challenge that remains in the software community is to follow through with risk control.

17.9 Questions for Discussion

1. Do you think it is important to articulate what we do not know? Discuss the significance of asking questions to become aware of the unknown.
2. Explain why the project manager is responsible for delegating the task of conducting a risk assessment.
3. List three types of risk assessment methods and describe a situation when each would be appropriate.
4. Discuss the extent to which sharing information can discover unknown risks.
5. List the five steps to categorize risk. What is the value of each step?
6. Explain the risk drivers that might cause an SEI Level 3 process to degrade.
7. Do you think it is important to communicate risk in a standard format? Discuss how a standard format might make people more receptive to dealing with uncertainty.
8. Explain how you could measure risk exposure over time and predict risk occurrence.
9. Discuss how you can use time frame for action to determine risk priority.
10. Do you trust your intuition? Give an example of a time when you did and a time when you did not trust your intuition.

17.10 References

[American85] *The American Heritage Dictionary*. 2nd College Ed., Boston: Houghton Mifflin, 1985.

[Boehm89] Boehm, B. *IEEE Tutorial on Software Risk Management*. New York: IEEE Computer Society Press, 1989.

[Carr93] Carr M, Konda S, Monarch I, Ulrich F, Walker C. Taxonomy based risk identification. Technical report CMU/SEI-93-TR-6. Pittsburgh, PA: Software Engineering Institute, Carnegie Mellon University, 1993.

[Sisti94] Sisti F, Joseph S. Software risk evaluation method. Technical report CMU/SEI-94-TR-19. Pittsburgh, PA: Software Engineering Institute, Carnegie Mellon University, 1994.

18

Control Risk

Risk is like fire: If controlled it will help you; if uncontrolled it will rise up and destroy you.
—Theodore Roosevelt

Why do we encounter so many problems while developing software systems? Perhaps because we are not accustomed to thinking ahead or anticipating the worst-case scenario. Hannes Jònsson, a computer science graduate student, wrote a useful example from daily life to illustrate the importance of prevention and early detection in producing high-quality software [Jònsson92]. The example is fire. Every big fire starts as a small one:

Scenario 1: Do nothing. Fires occur occasionally, and there is nothing we can do about it. This will lead to a disaster; there will be losses in both lives and property.

Scenario 2: Rely on fire fighters. Fire fighters will be contacted, but what will happen during the time from when someone called them, until they are on the scene of the fire? As in scenario one, there will be losses in both lives and property.

Scenario 3: Rely on fire extinguishers as a first defense. When a fire is small, it could be put out with a fire extinguisher, and prevented from growing. The property will be saved from further losses. There is one problem with this; it has to be known when the fire starts. If everyone is asleep, no one will report the fire in time; this is now scenario 2.

Scenario 4: Use a fire alarm for early fire detection. If alarmed about the fire in its puberty, it could be put out as in scenario three. There is still one problem; someone has to hear the alarm. The best situation is not to have a fire in the first place.

Scenario 5: Use preventions. By preventing fire there is nothing to worry about. Prevention such as: learning that matches are not a toy, heeding advice from Smokey the Bear, and so on. For example, when the city of Reykjavik changed from heating the houses by burning fuel to heating them with hot spring water, the fire fighters saw a dramatic decrease in house fires. No burning, no fire!

In this chapter, I describe how to plan, track, and resolve the risk in the project plan and remaining work. I discuss how to control risk in a team environment using a creative process. You will need to draw on the process described in Chapters 6 through 8, the risk management plan described in Chapter 15, and the common sense of this chapter to control risk.

This chapter answers the following questions:

❑ What are the activities to control risk?

❑ What makes decisions difficult?

❑ Will the software industry always need risk management?

18.1   Develop Risk Resolution Alternatives

The most creative aspect of risk control is determining the possibilities to resolve risk. In order to develop risk resolution alternatives, you need one or more goals and a list of assessed risks. Goals as well as risks should be prioritized. Knowing priorities helps in planning the allocation of resources. When goals or risks share the same priority, you should divide resources equally.

Consider the activities of controlling risk using a team whose goal is to win the ABC proposal. Objectives include addressing technical design risk in the proposal to support a winning proposal strategy. With the help of a facilitator, the team performed a risk assessment to identify and analyze ABC technical design risks. Table 18.1 shows the top ten technical risks associated with the proposed design. Evaluation criteria and a nominal group technique were used to prioritize the top ten technical design risks. The evaluation criteria were cost, schedule, performance, functionality, reliability, flexibility, and expandability. ABC design risks were analyzed to develop a low-risk technical solution to satisfy ABC system requirements. Risk analysis included evaluation of design objectives, constraints, alternatives, and assumptions prior to developing risk resolution alternatives. The risks were assigned to responsible individuals to develop risk resolution alternatives for the proposal team to review.

The design team worked in small groups—often two and sometimes three people—and individually to determine the events and conditions of a scenario for their assigned risk. The risk scenario would describe how the risk might be realized. The team would capture information on the sequence of events that could lead to risk

TABLE 18.1 ABC TECHNICAL DESIGN RISKS

Top Ten Technical Design Risks	Probability	Consequence	Risk Exposure
1. Correlation processing	5	5	25
2. Software design	5	4	20
3. Radar target extraction	4	4	16
4. Multisensor resolution	5	3	15
5. COTS software modification	4	3	12
6. Hardware acceptability	4	3	12
7. Phase I customer isolation	3	4	12
8. Database performance	3	3	9
9. Real-time performance	4	1	4
10. Lack of hard test requirements	1	3	3

realization and then list the conditions that could perturb the risk situation. They would try to understand the significance of risk occurrence. They would also determine when action would need to be taken to prevent problems. Thinking about how a risk could occur provides clues on what is important to prevent it from occurring.

As an example, the design team considered the risk of real-time performance. Their uncertainty was that the 3-second update rate may not be feasible under the proposed architecture. The consequence if the risk occurs is to buy more expensive hardware. They stated the risk as a fact: *System does not meet real-time performance requirement.* If the team's hierarchical approach adds more overhead than anticipated, a more powerful CPU may be required. Their analysis is based on assumptions for target density and CPU loading and extrapolates based on a few data points. Processing associated with some new data fusion algorithms is also just estimated at this time. The source of risk is the correlation complexity and a lack of validated performance data.

18.2 Select the Risk Resolution Strategy

For the risk scenario that the system did not meet real-time performance requirement, the team discussed potential risk resolution strategies. To prevent the risk from occurring, they could improve their analysis, contain overhead, or buy additional hardware. Not knowing whether this was a complete list of possibilities, the team remembered the seven strategies described in the risk management process. They determined how each strategy might help resolve the risk. For each strategy, the team wrote down a possible approach to resolve the risk. For each strategy and corresponding approach, they discussed the following factors that cause decisions to be difficult [Clemen91]:

- ❏ *Complexity.* Are there interrelated issues that cause this strategy to be complex? Are there multiple alternatives that make this decision difficult? Is there a significant economic consideration of selecting this strategy?

- ❏ *Uncertainty.* Is this strategy high risk? Do the assumptions for choosing this strategy have a high degree of uncertainty? Is the uncertainty based on perceptions of different people?

- ❏ *Multiple objectives.* Are there conflicting goals associated with this strategy? What are the trade-offs in satisfying the objectives? What are the different motivations for or against this strategy?

- ❏ *Different perspectives.* Are there alternatives or variations of this strategy that we should consider? What are the different choices that we could make? What conclusions could we make?

The team scoped the effort for each potential strategy to determine the risk leverage and used the criterion to rank the risk resolution strategies. Table 18.2 shows how the team ranked the strategies from best to worst.

18.3   Develop the Risk Action Plan

The team discussed the top three risk resolution strategies. Selection criteria included minimization of impacts to cost, schedule, performance, and customer satisfaction. They selected the Research alternative based on the need for additional data to support a decision to upgrade the hardware. Improved analysis would assist other aspects of the technical design. The risk action plan they developed included objectives, approach, start date, milestones, due date, responsible person, and resources required. The responsible person documented the risk resolution strategy and the recommended action plan, which would be reviewed by the decision makers. The team believed the managers would agree to the action plan because they calculated significant risk leverage based on the cost of a hardware upgrade. Once approved, there would be a commitment of staff and other resources to support improved analysis. The time frame for action would be dependent on the relative priority of the real-time performance risk.

TABLE 18.2 RANKING OF POTENTIAL RISK RESOLUTION STRATEGIES

Risk Resolution Strategy	Approach to Resolve Risk	Rank (1–7)
Acceptance	Reduce project profit by hardware cost	7
Avoidance	Change the hierarchical development approach	6
Protection	Bid the additional hardware into the proposal	5
Reduction	Contain overhead through requirement allocation	4
Research	Develop a prototype for improved analysis	1
Reserves	Add a percentage of the potential hardware cost	3
Transfer	Give the customer the option to upgrade hardware	2

18.4   Monitor Risk Status

When the risk action plan was presented at the weekly review meeting, the managers were impressed. One wanted to know if the design team thought about using more than one strategy. Another mentioned a project in another division of the company with expertise in writing system simulations. They nodded in agreement that additional analysis would be required. But they took exception to the risk leverage calculation, saying that when the hardware needed to be purchased, it would probably be reduced from the vendor's current quote. Besides, they argued, the customer might want the additional capacity that the more expensive hardware would provide. They debated whether the customer had more funding sources than originally thought by the marketing consultant. The discussion degraded over conjecture regarding the size of the customer's purse. The proposal manager cleared his voice and thanked the design team for their report. He asked for a thumbs-up, -down, or -sideways to indicate management's agreement to monitor the risk. No thumbs went down, a signal that the risk action plan was approved. A trigger was then established that would activate the risk action plan within the established time frame for action.

18.4.1   Send Notification for Triggers

Two months later, notification of the activated trigger came as an e-mail message from the proposal manager to the design team leader. It was brief but the direction was clear: the real-time performance risk was a hot issue at the last management meeting. The design competition in Phase I is clearly cost constrained and under no circumstances could hardware costs increase. Adding cost might jeopardize the entire Phase II contract. The design team was to proceed with the risk action plan as discussed and report risk status at subsequent management meetings.

Before logging off her computer, the design team leader composed a brief message to the systems analyst who was assigned to the real-time performance risk: "Subject: real-time performance risk. We have approval to execute the next step of the risk action plan. Please document the actions taken and results achieved in your weekly status report."

18.4.2   Report Measures and Metrics

Both measures and metrics of risk management effectiveness are needed for reporting on risk status. The proposal team did not report measures and metrics for risk management. They were not trained in this area, though, so we should not be surprised about this fact. Table 18.3 lists measures and metrics of the risk management process that a trained team would use to determine progress in resolving risk. Standard measurement practices must be used to obtain consistent and meaningful risk management results.

Risk measures provide objective and subjective data that can be used to indicate the level of project risk. Objective data consist of actual counts of items (e.g., risks identified). These true counts may cause managers to question their subjective understanding and investigate further. Subjective data are based on an individual's or group's belief of a condition (e.g., significance of risk). They provide critical information for interpreting and validating objective data. Together, objective and subjective data serve as a system of checks and balances to provide project visibility. Measurements of risk and risk resolution should promote the desired action. For example, proper risk management practices will reward most likely estimates of probability and consequence. Worst-case estimates should not be used because they are not as likely to occur.

Metrics are the quantitative result of a measure taken by use of a measurement process. A **measurement process** consists of the activities to define, collect, analyze, report, and interpret metrics. Measurement, the use of a measurement process to determine the value of a measure, has limitations that are worth reviewing:

❑ Metrics are only as good as the data behind them.

❑ Metrics cannot explain or predict anything.

❑ Metrics cannot make sense of a chaotic process.

❑ No single metric can provide wisdom.

❑ Measurement is no substitute for management.

TABLE 18.3   MEASURES AND METRICS OF THE RISK MANAGEMENT PROCESS

Process Element	Measures and Metrics
Identify risk	Number of logged risks Risk category
Analyze risk	Probability Consequence Risk exposure Risk severity Risk priority Risk management index
Plan risk	Risk leverage
Track risk	Current priority Previous priority Number of weeks on Top-N
Resolve risk	Number of active risks Number of resolved risks Return on investment

Metrics provide a means for monitoring the status of an ongoing project while also providing indications of process improvements for future projects. It is important to have a consistent set of metrics that can be used as status comparisons to previous projects and to reduce confusion on the information represented by the metrics. Reporting risk metrics is effective when the measures are timely, validated, economical, and understandable. Three useful risk metrics are the risk forecast, risk index, and the $ROI_{(RM)}$, which are further described below.

Risk Forecast.   The **risk forecast** is a projection of risk exposure for all risks whose time frames for action are short. Weather is a metaphor used to describe the near-term risk exposure of the project. The risk forecast uses available data to predict the chances that the skies are clear, cloudy, or rainy or that a thunderstorm is approaching. Graphics can quickly communicate the project risk forecast like the change of seasons. An explanation of the risk forecast follows with the events and conditions driving the projection. The definition of short term should be calibrated to a specific project.

Risk Index.   The **risk index** is a measure that "rolls up" the risk being monitored by the project. It is calculated by the summation of risk exposure values as a percentage of project cost. It is important not to "game" the metric by discouraging risk identification or not including all identified risk in the calculation. A risk index will help you to recognize when a more rigorous plan is needed to address risk. When the index reads high during the proposal phase, it is important to explain how your approach will address the inherent risk. For example, your plan may include an experienced team with a key personnel clause, or a software organization with a process maturity assessed at SEI Level 3. Knowing that risk exists and having a plan to resolve it is more sophisticated than pretending it does not exist. Savvy customers will recognize the difference.

Plotting the risk index over the life cycle provides a curve that will have a downward trend as risks are resolved. You should expect the risk index to increase dramatically after a risk assessment. When the index remains the same for months, it is an indication of inactivity in risk management. This metric should be calibrated to a business area or product line. The metric can be calibrated only with trusted historical data. The type of project and acceptable profit margin are factors that can be used to adjust the reading of the risk index as high, moderate, or low.

Risk Management ROI.   As shown in Figure 18.1, the $ROI_{(RM)}$ metric grows as project risks are resolved. Early variation of the $ROI_{(RM)}$ indicator will occur based on the diversity of opportunities for risk resolution. The indicator will eventually settle into an average $ROI_{(RM)}$ for the project that will be similar to historical project results. The $ROI_{(RM)}$ metric has a number of uses—for example:

❑ *Planning benchmark for risk leverage.* When planning a risk resolution strategy, $ROI_{(RM)}$ is useful as a benchmark for expected risk leverage. When the expected risk leverage is well below $ROI_{(RM)}$, you may want to spend extra time planning a more effective strategy. When the expected risk leverage is far above $ROI_{(RM)}$, you may want to perform a reality check on your numbers.

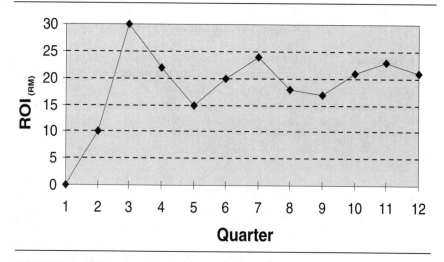

FIGURE 18.1 $ROI_{(RM)}$ trend data. Over time, the cost and savings from risk management yield an $ROI_{(RM)}$ metric that can be used as a standard benchmark.

❏ *Planning benchmark for management reserve.* An understanding of a typical $ROI_{(RM)}$ can be coupled with good estimates of total project risk exposure to set realistic project management reserve levels.

❏ *Project indicator of risk management effectiveness.* For a specific project, $ROI_{(RM)}$ is an indicator of risk management effectiveness. When the project $ROI_{(RM)}$ varies significantly from the organization metric, practices should be investigated for either improvement or lessons learned.

❏ *Organizational measure of risk management utility.* At the organizational level, $ROI_{(RM)}$ is a measure of the value of the risk management practice.

18.5   Execute the Risk Action Plan

Six months later, the systems analyst had dusted off the simulation books from his bookshelf, and even found a new one at the local bookstore. The model had grown from a part-time effort to determine response time, to a full-time effort to impress the customer with a demonstration of system capabilities. It would be a competitive advantage to be able to show the customer the increase in performance by simulating the improved hardware. The systems analyst hoped that he could continue refining the simulation, which was more fun than proposal writing.

18.6   Take Corrective Action as Required

When we encounter unexpected outcomes, we can take corrective action as required. Corrective action is different from risk management, because there is no uncertainty. Corrective action is the specific procedure that is needed to solve a known problem; risk management is a general procedure that is needed to resolve a risk. Risk management is the antithesis of corrective action; where one stops, the other begins. Often the answers to questions lead to further questions. The cycle of risk management and corrective action is as constant as night and day.

When you have the ability to manage risk, does that mean that risk will disappear? No, but it does mean that you will have a measure of control over your outcomes. With the ability to manage risk, you can choose to control existing risk, take on additional risk for potentially higher return, or maximize long-term opportunities. Once you have the ability to manage risk, the choice is yours.

The software industry will always need risk management. The form of risk management will become specialized, as in other industries. Studying risk management in other fields provides insight into how to apply risk techniques in software development. The maturity of agriculture, medicine, transportation, and financial markets provides a wealth of risk management instruments used to control risk. The common thread in these fields is that risk can be averted through quantifiable insurance. Perhaps when software development is insurable at a reasonable cost, the instruments of software risk management will be mature.

18.7   Summary

In this chapter, I described how to plan, track, and resolve the risk in the project plan and remaining work. The following checklist can serve as a reminder of the activities to control risk:

1. Develop risk resolution alternatives.
2. Select the risk resolution strategy.
3. Develop the risk action plan.
4. Monitor risk status.
5. Execute the risk action plan.
6. Take corrective action as required.

I discussed several factors that cause decisions to be difficult:

- Complexity.
- Uncertainty.
- Multiple objectives.
- Different perspectives.

The purpose of developing and executing risk action plans and tracking risk status is to manage software risk. With the ability to manage risk, you can choose to control existing risk, take on additional risk for potentially higher return, or maximize long-term opportunities. Once you have the ability to manage risk, the choice is yours.

The software industry will always need risk management. The form of risk management will become specialized, as it has in other industries. Studying risk management in other fields provides insight into how to apply risk techniques in software development. The maturity of agriculture, medicine, transportation, and financial markets provides a wealth of risk management instruments used to control risk. The common thread in these fields is that risk can be averted through quantifiable insurance. Perhaps when software development is insurable at a reasonable cost, the instruments of software risk management will be mature.

18.8   Questions for Discussion

1. Write a progressive five-level scenario that illustrates the importance of prevention in daily life. Use any subject that is a routine experience, such as brushing your teeth, driving a car, or saving for retirement.

2. Explain how a risk scenario removes uncertainty. What do you think happens when you state a risk as though it were a known fact?

3. Explain the factors that cause decisions to be difficult.

4. Do you think it is important to think through all seven risk resolution strategies for a given risk? Discuss why you do or do not think so.

5. When would you use a combination of risk resolution strategies? Explain your answer.

6. What triggers might you use to provide notification to execute a risk action plan?

7. Discuss the importance of training in risk management measures and metrics.

8. Explain the significance of corrective action when you encounter unexpected outcomes.

9. With the ability to manage risk, you can choose to control existing risk, take on additional risk for potentially higher return, or maximize long-term opportunities. Once you have the ability to manage risk, what will you do?

10. Do you think risk is like fire? Discuss why you do or do not think so.

18.9   References

[Clemen91] Clemen R. *Making Hard Decisions: An Introduction to Decision Analysis.* Belmont, CA: Wadsworth Publishing, 1991.

[Hall95] Hall E. *Software Risk Management and Metrics*, Arlington, VA: Software Program Managers Network, October, 1995.

[Jònsson92] Jònsson H. *Quality Assessment Using Factor Analysis of Survey Data.* Masters thesis, Computer Science Department, Florida Institute of Technology, Melbourne, FL August 1992.

PART V

People in Crisis and Control

The objective is not to be excellent, because "to be" implies a stasis and there is no place to stand anymore; the only excellent firms are those that are rapidly evolving.
—Tom Peters

Part V provides five software project case studies about risk management experiences. The projects range from small to large, and from commercial to government system development. Each chapter provides consecutive levels of personal development in managing risk, from novice to expert. In each chapter I describe an overview of the project and the risk management practices, and then I summarize the results.

Chapter 19, "Stage 1: Problem," describes what happens when risk identification is not seen as positive and people are too busy solving existing problems to think about risks that may occur in the future. Read Chapter 19 to understand why some people see only problems at work. I wrote this chapter from a process consultant's perspective.

Chapter 20, "Stage 2: Mitigation," details results when risk concepts are introduced. Read Chapter 20 to understand the shift from crisis management to risk management. I wrote this chapter from a project manager's perspective.

Chapter 21, "Stage 3: Prevention," discusses what occurs when managers understand that risk management is a dynamic process that cannot be performed in isolation. Read Chapter 21 to understand the shift from risk management viewed as a manager's activity to a project team activity. I wrote this chapter from a system engineer's perspective.

Chapter 22, "Stage 4: Anticipation," describes when the project team and customer use risk management to quantify risks with reasonable accuracy to focus on the right priorities. Read Chapter 22 to understand the shift from subjective to quantitative risk management through the use of measures to anticipate predictable risks. I wrote this chapter from a measurement analyst's perspective.

Chapter 23, "Stage 5: Opportunity," details results when people expect to do better than planned. Read Chapter 23 to understand the power of risk management when it is everyone's responsibility to manage risk. I wrote this chapter from a software engineer's perspective.

With the knowledge of how to develop a risk management philosophy provided in Part V, you will be ready to manage opportunities, risks, and problems in your life.

19

Stage 1: Problem

Life is just too complicated to be smart all the time.
—Scott Adams

In this chapter, I describe the practices that characterize the problem stage of risk management evolution. People are too busy solving problems to think about the future. They do not address risks and, in fact, act as if what they do not know will not hurt them. Management will not support communication regarding risks. Reality is viewed as pessimism, where it is unacceptable to estimate past the dictated time to market. The team works very hard, yet product quality is low. Quality assurance is performed by the product buyers, which tarnishes the company's reputation. Management has unrealistic expectations of what is achievable, which causes the team to feel stress. When significant problems of cost and schedule can no longer be ignored, there is a reorganization. This is what we observe in the problem stage project. (The project name is withheld, but the people and their experiences are genuine.)

This chapter answers the following questions:

❑ What are the practices that characterize the problem stage?

❑ What is the primary project activity at the problem stage?

❑ What can we observe at the problem stage?

19.1   Problem Project Overview

The project is developing a state-of-the-art call-processing system for wireless communications. The project infrastructure is a commercial corporation. The project has a 20-month iterative development schedule. The team consists of over 40 engineers, approximately half of them subcontractors. The estimated software size is 300K lines of code plus adapted COTS (commercial off-the-shelf software). Software languages used are C, C++, Assembly, and a fourth-generation language.

19.2   The Process Improvement Initiative

The corporation is laying the foundation for the implementation of a quality management system (QMS), based on the requirements of the ANSI/ASQC Q9001 quality standard [ASQC94], the Six Sigma method of metrics and quality improvement [Motorola93],[1] and the SEI CMM for Software [Paulk93]. To help with the initiative, a process consultant was brought on board. She prepared a statement of work (SOW) that describes the effort required to achieve SEI CMM Level 2.[2] The goal of SEI Level 2, the repeatable level, is to institutionalize effective management processes. Effective processes are defined, documented, trained, practiced, enforced, measured, and able to improve. The scope of the SEI Level 2 key process areas (KPAs) has been expanded to include systems engineering and hardware.

19.2.1   Vision and Mission

Through discussions with the employees, the process consultant understood the quality vision and mission as follows:

> The quality vision is to lead the wireless communications industry by becoming a world-class organization and achieving a reputation for innovative, high-quality products. The quality mission is to commit to customer satisfaction and continuous improvement through total quality management and adherence to international (i.e., ISO 9001) and industry (i.e., SEI CMM) benchmarks for quality.

---

[1] As a corporation, Motorola's goal is to achieve Six Sigma Quality for all operations: 99.99966 percent of output must be defect free. In other words, for every million opportunities to create a defect, only 3.4 mistakes occur.

[2] This chapter describes the risks of process *improvement*, not the risks of product *development*.

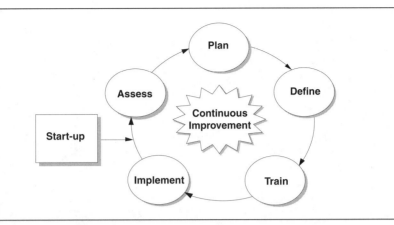

FIGURE 19.1   Proposed improvement strategy. Continuous improvement is an evolutionary approach based on incremental improvement. The proposed improvement strategy has six phases: start-up, assess, plan, define, train, and implement.

Continuous improvement is iterative in nature. The continuous improvement model shown in Figure 19.1 can be used to understand the major activities of the QMS. The corporation is currently in the start-up phase.

19.2.2   Roles and Responsibilities

The corporation began the initiative by establishing a steering committee to guide the objectives associated with continuous improvement. As shown in Figure 19.2, the planned improvement organization has several components that work together to achieve the business objectives.

To define roles and responsibilities clearly, the process consultant mapped the phases of continuous improvement to the improvement organization shown in Table 19.1. Detailed descriptions of the roles and responsibilities follow to describe completely how the work is accomplished.

Senior management—the chief executive officer (CEO) and the vice-presidents—has primary responsibility for establishing the quality vision for the organization by understanding the existing practice and allocating resources for continuous improvement. Senior management reviews findings from audits and assessments, approves the QMS plan, provides motivation to the organization through execution of the reward and recognition program and communicates commitment to quality by their written and spoken words and their actions.

The *steering committee* members are the directors from each business area. This committee has primary responsibility for designing the foundation of the

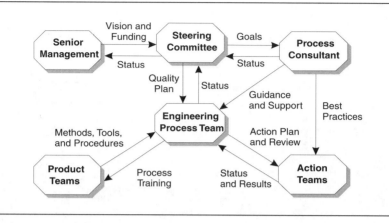

FIGURE 19.2   Proposed improvement organization.

QMS, commissioning audits and assessments, and developing the QMS plan to achieve ISO 9001, SEI maturity levels, and Six Sigma goals. The steering committee provides incentives for sustained improvement by establishing an employee reward and recognition program and ensures communications within the organization by reviewing status and reporting results to senior management, creating posters, and promoting a quality culture.

The *process consultant* is an experienced process champion from an ISO-certified and SEI Level 3 organization. This person is responsible for under-standing the corporation's goals and priorities and facilitating process develop-ment. This is accomplished by performing a **process assessment**, establishing the

TABLE 19.1   ORGANIZATION ROLES AND RESPONSIBILITIES, BY PHASE

	Start-up	Assess	Plan	Define	Train	Implement
Senior management	X	X				
Steering committee	X	X	X			
Process consultant	X	X	X	X	X	X
Engineering process team			X	X		X
Action teams				X	X	
Product teams		X			X	X

baseline, and assisting in process improvement plan development. Other activities include defining the top-level process from SEI CMM requirements, creating action team notebooks, training action teams, facilitating action team meetings, reviewing action team products, reporting status, and helping to train the process to the product teams.

Engineers from various levels in systems, software, and hardware are on the *engineering process team*. This team has responsibility for characterizing the existing process, establishing a metrics program, developing the process improvement plan, and maintaining the process asset library. Other activities performed include establishing the priority of action teams, reviewing action team process status and products, approving the defined process, and handling change requests.

The practitioners from the organization are the *action team* members. These teams are responsible for executing the action plan to analyze and define the CMM key process areas. Cross-functional volunteers meet periodically and coordinate with existing process definitions to complete their objectives. They maintain a team notebook, distribute meeting minutes, and report status and recommended solutions to the process team. Then they document and update products based on review comments, as well as define training modules and instruct training sessions.

The *product team* members are the practitioners with product responsibilities. These teams are responsible for implementing the defined process. They help to describe existing methods, tools, and procedures; measure the process; collect the metrics; and evaluate the process for improvement. Product teams also feedback comments and improvement recommendations to the process team.

19.2.3 Statement of Work

The process consultant's SOW assumes that the corporation has taken a holistic view of process improvement and wants to expand the scope of the SEI model to include systems and hardware. Software is not developed in isolation, and the engineering process is assumed to be inclusive. Two process models for systems engineering were reviewed by the managers for their utility: the System Engineering Capability Maturity Model (SE-CMM) version 1.0 [Bate94] and the Systems Engineering Capability Assessment Model (SECAM) version 1.41 [CAWG96].

Resource constraints of time, budget, and staff were factored into the SOW. The assessment process was streamlined and focused on providing the inputs required for the process improvement plan. Staffing issues were addressed by scheduling a minimum number of action teams in parallel and allowing for incremental training.

Risks to institutionalizing effective engineering management processes were identified by the process consultant. These risks, described in Table 19.2 are typical of improvement initiatives. These risks have been evaluated and prioritized by their risk severity. Risk severity accounts for the probability of an unsatisfactory outcome, the consequence if the unsatisfactory outcome occurs, and the time frame for action.

A risk resolution strategy has been incorporated into the SOW for each of the risks identified in Table 19.2. As shown in Table 19.3 these strategies are necessary but not sufficient for the success of the initiative. When executed, these strategies will go a long way to ensuring the success of the initiative goals of a repeatable process.

TABLE 19.2 KNOWN PROCESS IMPROVEMENT INITIATIVE RISKS

Priority	Risk	Probability	Consequence	Time Frame
1	Low employee motivation	> 80%	Critical	Short
2	Lack of management commitment	60–80%	Critical	Short
3	Weak organizational communication	60–80%	Critical	Medium
4	Inefficient process definition	40–60%	High	Medium
5	Poor process implementation	40–60%	High	Long

TABLE 19.3 RISK RESOLUTION STRATEGIES

Risk	Resolution Strategy
Low employee motivation	Establish a reward and recognition program for effort and progress toward initiative objectives. Associate employee performance appraisal with initiative participation and results. Certificates, luncheons, awards, trophies, and pins given in a timely fashion help to sustain employee motivation.
Lack of management commitment	Reward management for their participation and leadership of the initiative. They are responsible for support and encouragement of employees activities for the initiative.
Weak organizational communication	Establish communication channels and clearly define and adhere to organizational roles and responsibilities. Establish on-line process documentation that is faster, easier, and cheaper to maintain than hard copy documentation.
Inefficient process definition	The process consultant is to provide the standard process notation, process improvement process, and top-level process definitions to action teams as an efficient starting point.
Poor process implementation	Establish the engineering process team as an ongoing group of practitioners with a rotational assignment to serve as keepers of the process assets. Maintain the process and mature the organization's capability to engineer quality systems to achieve the business objectives.

19.3   Process Assessment

A process assessment would be necessary to understand the current engineering practices and identify areas for improvement. Prior to the process assessment, the process consultant sent a letter to the CEO with the following counsel: "The road to Level 2 should not be underestimated. Industry data from September 1995 reported the percentage of assessed companies at SEI Level 1 was 70%. False starts due to lack of long-term commitment only make subsequent efforts more difficult to initiate."

The CEO approved a process assessment of the project. Assessment objectives included the initiation of process improvement with the completion of the following activities:

- ❏ Provide a framework for action plans.
- ❏ Help obtain sponsorship and support for action.
- ❏ Baseline the process to evaluate future progress.

19.3.1   Assessment Process

The assessment process was streamlined to reduce the cost, effort, and time to achieve the stated objectives. As shown in Figure 19.3, the process is a tailored version of the mini-assessment process used by a subset of Kodak product development organizations [Hill95].[3] The streamlined assessment included a one-hour assessment overview presentation to the entire project team that described the assessment goals and process. The process improvement organization and the roles and responsibilities of both the assessment team and the project practitioners were also discussed. A one-hour CMM tutorial followed to explain the vision of process improvement with an emphasis on the key process areas of SEI Level 2. Six hours were spent in assessment team training identifying assessment risks and learning the details of the assessment process. The SEI maturity questionnaire was given to each assessment team member, and a week later the results were reviewed at the response analysis meeting. During this meeting, discussion scripts were prepared to validate the maturity questionnaire responses. By dividing assessment team members into three teams that worked in parallel, the project discussion was accomplished in one

---

[3] Kodak developed the mini-assessment in 1993 to reduce the cost, effort, and time frame associated with traditional SEI Software Process Assessments (SPAs). After performing 12 mini-assessments, Kodak reported the assessment cost at 10 percent to 13 percent of the cost of a traditional SPA.

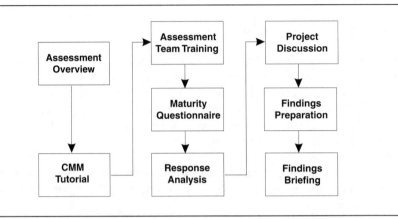

FIGURE 19.3   Streamlined assessment process.

day. Findings preparation lasted eight hours to condense the assessment results down to 20 viewgraphs for the one-hour findings briefing.

19.3.2   Reasons for Improvement

As part of the assessment overview briefing, the process consultant devised an exercise to document the organization's rationale for process improvement. The people attending the briefing were given ten minutes to complete the following directions:

1. Think about the benefit of process improvement.
2. Think about how the organization would benefit from improving its processes.
3. Write one reason that you think the organization should improve.

As part of its training, the assessment team was asked to sort the reasons, which had been written on index cards. Using an affinity diagram process to group similar reasons for improvement [Brassard94], the following six categories emerged:

❑ *Gain the competitive advantage.* To produce a better product and be able to identify what changes are incorporated into a release. Time to market is very critical to the bottom line.

❑ *Produce a quality product.* So we can effectively delight our customers and improve stakeholder value. Process needs improvement to improve future products' quality. Improved process can benefit in producing a better-quality product in less time. We are in the market with world-class companies. For us to survive, we must improve the quality of our products *NOW*. There is no tomorrow for small companies. Improve the coding cycle of multiple reviews of documentation and prelim-code. Get away from coding on the fly. Lower risk of meeting deadlines.

- *Develop efficiency.* More efficient use of resources (people's time, lab equipment, development workstations, licenses for various development software). Gain process efficiency and shorten cycle time. Efficiency in how we operate—we get a lot done in a short time only because of the extra hours and commitment by employees. We do not work efficiently or do the same thing consistently. Process improvement is required so that we can reduce the time wasted in correcting problems caused by lack of a good process (e.g., in design, in test, in code). Allow the company to spend money on new development versus maintenance! To improve our concept of time and not publish unrealistic schedules. Need to reduce "fire drills." No person or organization or product can ever be better than the process it followed.

- *Repeat quality.* Capability to recreate exactly pieces for maintenance support (e.g., find library items despite changes in personnel). The company needs this to provide a means to develop quality products consistently! To be competitive and succeed in the marketplace, we *must* consistently produce high-quality product and services in a predictable and timely manner. We should improve how we maintain software to incorporate enhancements or corrections into our product more easily.

- *Reduce learning curve.* Clearly documented and trained process reduces the learning curve for new team members and maintains process focus as team players change. This facilitates team flexibility.

- *Clarify expectations.* The organization's processes are not well defined, written down, and available to the engineering staff. Employees will have a clear definition of process for their individual task, and understand what is required to work effectively, instead of individuals working within vacuums. Expectations of individual processes are not clear. Intermediate work products do not always meet expectations or easily fit together. Process improvement is necessary to ensure the company's long-term viability, because it first defines and documents the process, and second works the process toward more profitability.

19.3.3   Process Assessment Risks

The assessment team was asked to identify their top three risks to a successful assessment. The assessment team had 30 minutes to complete the following directions:

1. Divide into three teams.
2. Brainstorm risks to a successful assessment.

3. Come to a consensus on the top three risks.

4. Spokesperson presents and leads discussion including mitigation strategies.

The exercise helped the assessment team focus on what they needed to do. The assessment team listed the following risks to a successful assessment:

1. Clear definition of the assessment outcome.

2. Time management.

3. Interpersonal conflicts.

4. Is there any value? Will this be taken seriously? Will anything change? *Mitigation*: Management support through actions.

5. Proper time allocation to task with everything else on our plate! *Mitigation*: Plan consistent with workload demands.

6. Truthful feedback. Concern of negative ramification to person or group. *Mitigation*: Anonymous results.

7. Consistent management support for action plans.

8. Inaccurate and inappropriate measurements. *Mitigation*: Take time up front to identify measurements to be made, and clearly define the measurement procedures.

9. Failure to communicate findings correctly. *Mitigation*: Tailor findings to the audience. Communicate plan for correcting shortcomings.

10. Lack of cooperation from staff. *Mitigation*: Provide free lunches. Get buy-in from all concerned.

The process consultant anticipated several additional assessment risks and reviewed them with the assessment team:

❑ *Assessment overview*: Employees have seen similar, unsuccessful initiatives. The assessment team should be sensitive to this.

❑ *Response analysis*: Because the team is too large [it had ten members], consensus will likely be laborious. Conclusions will be strong before discussion begins.

❑ *Project discussion*: Assessment team familiar with project can lose objectivity. Direct reporting relationships can cause subordinates to hold back their inputs. Single project focus may miss different aspects of software projects. Software-intensive project may lack hardware and systems input.

❑ *Findings briefing*: Employees fear that nothing will be done with the inputs. Team feeling that they are finished when they have only just begun. Reactionary response by management could have negative impact on employee willingness to be involved.

19.3.4   Assessment Team Discussion

After the team completed the maturity questionnaire response analysis, they were prepared for the interview sessions. The assessment team was asked to summarize their thoughts on what was needed. The process consultant added her concern to the list.

- ❑ Everyone brings old quality baggage. It does not have to fail.
- ❑ We have a chance to change this. It is not a bitch session.
- ❑ Focus on key issues. Start small to achieve success.
- ❑ Look for success. Everything we do is a step forward.
- ❑ Maintain momentum. Do not let them wonder what happened to the initiative.
- ❑ Plan for beyond SEI Level 2. Need individuals to push.
- ❑ Listen to gather good information.
- ❑ Communicate to the lowest level.
- ❑ Support from management and time to accomplish goals.
- ❑ Need reward and recognition for action teams.

19.4   Process Assessment Results

An important part of the assessment was that the people discover the results for themselves. The answers to the following two questions sum up the distance between "as is" and "should be":

1. Where are we? There is no organization-wide definition or documentation of current processes.
2. Where should we be? The organization should describe all processes in a standard notation. The organization should train processes to the management and staff, and follow them as standard procedure. The organization should measure and monitor processes for status and improvement.

19.4.1   Engineering Process Baseline

The final findings summarized the engineering process baseline as follows:

Strengths

   The organization is rich in the diversity of the staff.

   Productivity is very high.

Everyone wants to do a good job.

Open to ideas and suggestions for improvement.

Weaknesses

Lack of communication with management.

Schedule estimates tend not to be realistic.

Lack of well-defined engineering processes and procedures.

Lack of clear roles and responsibilities.

19.4.2 Participants' Wish List

At the close of each interview session, the facilitator asked the following question: "If you could change one thing, other than your boss or your paycheck, what would it be?" Project leaders said:

"Reality is viewed as pessimism."

"Vendors and customers serve as quality assurance."

"The development process is iterative code, design, test."[4]

"Do not sacrifice quality."

"Focus on company priorities, process."

"Senior management is not looking for quality; it is schedule driven."

Software functional area representatives said:

"Change requests should be tracked for system test."

"Appoint a software watchdog to oversee project to facilitate consistency and reuse."

"Software CM tool to be changed."

"Senior management has unrealistic expectations of people who are working on several projects with priorities changing daily."

"This assessment will not be of benefit, as senior management will ignore it."

"Integration and system test should be started much earlier."

"Mixing C and C++ is a mistake, as we do not have staff skilled in both."

"Senior management is committed to deadlines, not quality; hence this assessment is meaningless."

Test and configuration management functional area representatives said:

"More planning for demos. Put hooks in the schedule."

---

[4] This order implies that the development process was broken.

"More hours in the lab. During the day, there is no schedule. It is first come, first served. Typically, a management person owns the system. Get bumped regularly by demos. Easily lose half the morning by the demo."

"More flexibility in adjusting schedules. Worked overtime every week, 24 hours around the clock for three demos."

"More feedback from upper management. More of a large-company mentality. Feel like more of a small company. The CEO told us what he told the shareholders. We do not get that feedback anymore. Closed-door attitude."

Hardware functional area representatives said:

"I would like to see a more unified top-level structure and more focus at the company level."

"More information from the top on company direction and progress. Need status on projects."

"More procedures established. More consistency in purpose and operation. Each department needs charters so that senior management will know who is responsible for what job. Basically it should define what the job is and what results are required."

"I am looking for more direction. I need distinct goals. What are my personal goals? What are the company's strategic goals? All I am doing right now is fire fighting."

19.4.3 Findings and Recommendations

The findings and recommendations were briefed by the assessment team leader, who was project manager. The findings were summarized according to the SEI CMM Level 2 KPAs:

Requirements management. Requirements do not drive the development (e.g., system requirements were approved one year after the project started). There is no policy for managing requirements, and no method for tracing requirements through the life cycle. *Recommendations*: Ensure that requirements are entry criteria for design and provide for buy-in from developers.

Project planning. Developers are not adequately involved in the planning process (e.g., the schedule was inherited, and estimates are allowed only if they fit). There is no methodology used for estimating. There is no schedule relief for change in scope and resources. Schedule is king—the project is driven by time to market. *Recommendations*: Adopt scheduling methodology to involve all affected parties.

Project tracking. Project status is not clearly communicated in either direction (i.e., up or down). There is "no room for reality" with a "sanitized view of status reported." Milestones are replanned only after the date slips. Schedules are not adjusted by the missed dependencies, so the history is not visible. *Recommendations*: Improve data and increase circulation of project review meeting minutes. Also, communicate reality and take responsible action.

Subcontract management. Validation of milestone deliverables is ineffective because milestones are completed without proper verification. Transfer of technology is not consistently occurring since it is not on the schedule and inadequate staff are assigned. *Recommendations*: Establish product acceptance criteria and a plan for transfer of technology.

Quality assurance. There are no defined quality assurance engineering activities. There is no consistent inspection of intermediate products. Product quality is ensured by final inspection and, in some cases, by our vendors and customers. The project depends on final testing to prove product quality. There is no quality assurance training for engineering. *Recommendations*: Define quality assurance checkpoints as part of the engineering process.

Configuration management. No companywide configuration management (CM) plan. For example, systems, hardware, and software do not use the same CM tool. There is a lack of advanced CM tool training. The CM tool does not satisfy the project's needs because the developers go around the tool to do their job. *Recommendations*: Fix or replace the tool, and provide more in-depth tool training.

19.5   Initiative Hindsight

There is much to learn from the experience of others.

19.5.1   Assessment Team Perspective

The assessment team was asked to think about the engineering process assessment from their own perspective. They were given 15 minutes to answer the following questions:

1. What worked?
2. What did not work?
3. What could be improved?

For each question, the team members shared their views with the other assessment team members. At the executive briefing, their lessons learned were presented to senior management.[5]

---

[5] The executive briefing was not on the assessment process diagram but was necessary because several senior managers were unable to attend the findings briefing.

What Worked

In retrospect, preparation, organization, and timing were key to several successes identified by the assessment team members. Training helped each assessment team member develop the skills they needed to be prepared for the project discussion. The organization of the assessment team into three subteams helped make the discussion groups feel more comfortable and know that this was not an inquisition. The timing of the findings briefing the morning after the findings preparation enabled the assessment team to easily recall specific examples to support the findings. These successes are further described below.

Assessment team training. Organization of training material, group interaction, and involvement through exercises and rotation of groups of people was good. The team practiced sharing results, and the people wanted to be there. The team built momentum, enthusiasm, spirit, and camaraderie by using the consensus process. The consensus process worked well to get more buy-in and much less dissatisfaction after a decision was made.

Project discussion. Candid discussions with honest thoughts and feelings were possible due to the emphasis of confidentiality in the introduction script. The assessment team preparation of potential interview pitfalls helped. The listening skills of the assessment team were good; there was genuine caring by the assessment team. Grouping assessment team members so their skill mix more closely matched the peer group led to cohesive discussions. Dividing the assessment team into three subteams enabled five interview discussions to finish in one day.

Findings briefing. The timing of the briefing was immediately after the assessment, when thoughts were fresh. Questions were answered quickly, because the examples were easily recalled by the team. Asking for participation on the action teams was good because everyone was there, and they signed up for specific teams to be involved in.

What Did Not Work

Informing the staff about the SEI CMM in the one-hour tutorial did not work because not everyone was aware of the SEI maturity model. Only those who participated in key functional areas were aware of what the assessment team was doing. In general, there was no relief from the assessment teams' assigned work. Phone calls in the conference room were an interruption to other team members. There was no encouragement from management to focus on the assessment. There was too much pressure on the assessment team to get assessment training and conduct the assessment in one week without dropping any project tasks.

Project discussion. The focus on the assessment was disrupted by people wanting to get organizational issues off their chest.

Response analysis. The meeting was too long because ten people is too many for an assessment team. By the end of the analysis meeting, many people had lost focus and were suffering from burn-out. There was a feeling of "hurry up and finish."

Findings briefing. Management was surprised by the results and took the results personally. This defensive posture on the findings added a negative aspect to the assessment results. The assessment was to help people to own the results, but management made a speech that essentially said they were responsible, and they would fix the problems.

Informal hall talk. Interviewees thought the presentation was watered down. Interviewees know that nothing will change.

Executive briefing. The executive briefing was held over a month after the assessment results briefing, which was not timely.

What Could Be Improved

The assessment team also noted areas that could be improved as follows:

Assessment process. The assessment team and participants can be more effective by planning meetings with enough time so the process is not rushed. Using PCs for notes would make efficient use of time.

Findings briefing. The presentation should not be a surprise to senior management. Perhaps involving them in a dry run would allow them to prepare a response better. Emphasize that no names are associated with the results, and explain that the assessment team notes are shredded. If key managers cannot attend the results briefing, then reschedule the briefing.

Follow-through. There needs to be immediate follow-up and ongoing demonstration of the progress being made to define the engineering process standards. Upper management must do more to support process improvement than just talk about it.

19.5.2   Process Improvement Risks

The process consultant attempted to move the initiative forward into the planning phase of continuous improvement. There was a baseline process and a framework for action plans. Twenty-five people signed up as action team volunteers. At the executive briefing, the steering committee asked the CEO, "Where do we go from here?" The CEO replied, "SEI Level 5." But when the subject of resources, specifically time and people, came up, the CEO said, "Quality is free." The number two risk—lack of management commitment—had just become the number one problem. This risk was predicted in the SOW with a high probability and critical consequence.

Six months after the assessment, a reorganization removed a layer of senior management. Within a year after the assessment, the CEO was ousted by the board of directors. The rationale for the reorganization was not a failed process improvement initiative but rather a lack of product results. Perhaps the lack of product results was caused by the lack of process results. If this were true, management commitment to process improvement might have prevented the reorganization. Hindsight is, as they say, 20/20.

19.6   Summary and Conclusions

In this chapter, I described the practices that characterize the problem stage of risk management evolution. These practices include managing problems, not risks. Management is driven by time to market, and as a result, products are shipped with problems. Risks identified through the efforts of a process consultant are not taken seriously by the organization. Attempts to improve ad hoc procedures fail as management expects the team to improve in their spare time.

The primary project activity in the problem stage is hard work. Long and frustrating hours spent in the work environment make even the most intelligent people work inefficiently. Blame for this situation is assigned to management, who must suffer the consequences.

At the problem stage, we observed the following:

❏ *Smart people*. The project had many intelligent individuals working on state-of-the-art technology.

❏ *Burnout*. Many people worked 50 hours or more each week. The stress of the work environment was evident in the frustration level of the people.

❏ *Reorganization*. Management took the blame when the company did not meet its goals. Six months after the assessment, a reorganization removed a layer of senior management. Within a year after the assessment, the CEO was ousted by the board of directors.

19.7   Questions for Discussion

1. How does improving a process improve the quality of future products? Do you think process improvement is a risk reduction strategy? Explain your answer.

2. Do you agree that false starts due to lack of long-term commitment make subsequent improvement efforts more difficult to initiate? Discuss why you do or do not agree.

3. Write your top three reasons for improving an ad hoc process. Describe your reasons in terms of their effect on quality, productivity, cost, and risk of software development.

4. Given an SEI Level 1 organization, discuss the likelihood for high productivity and low quality.

5. Explain the consequence of the statement, "Reality is viewed as pessimism."

6. You are a hardware engineer with an invitation to be a member of a process assessment team. Your supervisor gives you permission to participate in the assessment as long as it does not affect your regular work. Describe your feelings toward your supervisor.

7. You are a senior manager responsible for purchasing a configuration management tool costing $100,000. At the process assessment results briefing, the recommendation was made to fix or replace the tool. Discuss how you will or will not support this recommendation.

8. You are the chief executive officer of a commercial company. At an executive briefing, a project manager informs you that your organization is SEI Level 1. Discuss how you will respond.

9. Do you think it is easier to replace people or to change the way they work? Explain your answer.

10. Why do people become stressed? How could you help people reduce their stress at work? Do you think people work better under stress? Discuss why you do or do not think so.

19.8   References

[Adams96] Adams S. *The Dilbert Principle*. New York: HarperCollins, 1996.

[ASQC94] American National Standard. *Quality Systems—Model for Quality Assurance in Design, Development, Production, Installation, and Servicing*. Milwaukee, WI: ASQC. August 1994.

[Bate94] Bate R, et al. *System Engineering Capability Maturity Model (SE-CMM) Version 1.0*. Handbook CMU/SEI-94-HB-04. Pittsburgh, PA: Software Engineering Institute, Carnegie Mellon University, December 1994.

[Brassard94] Brassard M, Ritter D. *The Memory Jogger II*. Methuen, MA: GOAL/QPC, 1994.

[CAWG96] Capability Assessment Working Group. *Systems Engineering Capability Assessment Model (SECAM) Version 1.41*. Document CAWG-1996-01-1.41. Seattle, WA: International Council on Systems Engineering, January 1996.

[Hill95] Hill L, Willer N. A method of assessing projects. *Proc*. 7th Software Engineering Process Group Conference, Boston, May 1995.

[Motorola93] Motorola University. *Utilizing the Six Steps to Six Sigma*. SSG 102, Issue No. 4. June 1993.

[Paulk93] Paulk M, et al. Capability Maturity Model for Software. Version 1.1. Technical report CMU/SEI-93-TR-24. Pittsburgh, PA: Software Engineering Institute, Carnegie Mellon University, 1993.

20

Stage 2: Mitigation

Ignorance remains bliss only so long as it is ignorance; as soon as one learns one is ignorant, one begins to want not to be so. The desire to know, when you realize you do not know, is universal and probably irresistible.
—Charles Van Doren

In this chapter, I describe the practices that characterize the mitigation stage of risk management evolution. An introduction to risk concepts occurs at the mitigation stage. Contact is made with individuals from other organizations, who share their experiences in risk management. Through this initial contact comes an awareness of risks and the realization that what we do not know may hurt us. People's knowledge of risk management is limited. They seek independent expertise to help them get started managing risk. This is what we observe in the mitigation stage project. The project name is not given due to the first rule of risk assessment: Do not attribute any information to an individual or project group. In accordance with this rule, I use job categories (instead of individual names) to discuss the people in the project. The people and practices of the project are authentic.

This chapter answers the following questions:

❑ What are the practices that characterize the mitigation stage?

❑ What is the primary project activity to achieve the mitigation stage?

❑ What can we observe at the mitigation stage?

20.1   Mitigation Project Overview

The project is a $10 million defense system upgrade that has a 21-month development schedule. Software (30 KLOC) is being developed in Ada on SUN Sparc10s using Verdix software tools. Custom hardware is being developed with embedded code. The project organization and the system concept of operation are described below.

20.1.1   Review the Project Organization

The project is staffed through a functional matrix organization, with a functional manager responsible for staffing, performance appraisal, training, and planning promotions. After assignment to the project, the staff take direction through delegation from the project manager. The project manager believes that having two bosses is a problem. From his perspective, there is no apparent incentive for functional management to make projects successful.[1]

The organization chart in Figure 20.1 depicts the relationship among the project personnel. The relationship between systems and software engineering is a cooperative one. Systems engineering is responsible for the overall technical integrity, system concept, system analysis, requirements management, functional allocation, interface definition, and test and evaluation of the system. Software engineering participates in definition and allocation of system-level requirements, project planning, and code estimation. It is led by a chief software engineer, who is responsible for overseeing software production, managing software requirements and resources, specialized training, and development tools. Quality assurance works with the project personnel but has an independent reporting chain. Test engineers control the formal baseline with support from software engineers until system sell-off.

Contractually, the project's organization is the prime contractor, who is responsible for requirements analysis through development and sell-off. A subcontractor will train customer personnel and perform operations and maintenance. A preferred list of vendors is used for other procurements to promote a cooperative supplier relationship.

20.1.2   Review the System Concept of Operation

The latest technology is being used to replace the 1970s-vintage command processor. The project will replace existing equipment, increase system performance, and

---

[1] The project manager speculates that the real incentive for functional management is to keep people off overhead.

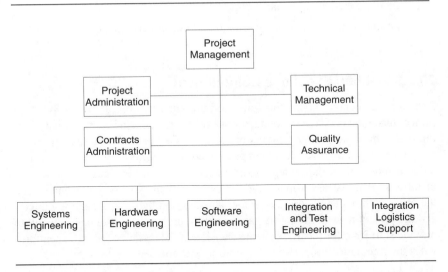

FIGURE 20.1   Project organization chart. The project personnel worked within a matrix management division of a Fortune 500 company.

condense existing hardware by a factor of seven. Important system-level requirements have been derived from over 30 existing specifications, both hardware and software. The concept of operation is that embedded software will control all system functionality. The majority of system requirements map to software functionality. There are key performance requirements for command and authentication processing. The high-technology system does not have much of a human-machine interface. The system's primary function is to process digital data for the next 10 to 15 years. It must also have the capability for future expansion to the next-generation system.

20.2   Risk Assessment Preparation

An organization standard procedure requires the identification of risk and problem analysis and corrective actions as a component of monthly project reviews. The operating instruction does not require the use of a particular method to identify and analyze risk. Through the organization's process improvement activities, a new policy was written that requires a risk assessment at the beginning of a project. The project team began preparation for their risk assessment two months after contract award. The key activities to prepare for a risk assessment are the following:

❑ Obtain commitment from top management.

❑ Coordinate risk assessment logistics.

❑ Communicate assessment benefits to the project participants.

20.2.1   Obtain Executive Commitment

Risk management is about the future of present decisions [Charette89]. The project made the decision to conduct a risk assessment during an executive briefing that communicated the benefits of such an assessment. Individuals from the SEI, whose work involves developing, evaluating, and transitioning risk management methods, made the presentation. SEI representatives explained the concepts of software risk, risk assessment, and risk management to the project manager and the organization's engineering director. The decision by the engineering director and the project manager to participate as a pilot project reflects a commitment to provide staff time for the assessment. The signed risk assessment agreement provides the foundation for future collaboration with the SEI.

20.2.2   Coordinate the Risk Assessment Logistics

After the managers signed up for the risk assessment, the task of coordinating logistics was delegated. Assessment team members were selected and team roles and responsibilities allocated. A site coordinator was chosen to select and invite the participants[2] and to schedule the required facilities. The site coordinator used e-mail to communicate with the participants regarding the risk assessment schedule.

20.2.3   Brief the Project Participants

Before the risk assessment, a participants' briefing was held to provide information and answer questions on the risk assessment activities. The risk assessment objectives—to identify software risks and train mechanisms for risk identification—and benefits—to prevent surprises, make informed decisions, and focus on building the right product—were explained. The risk assessment principles were emphasized:

❑ *Commitment.* Demonstrate commitment by signing the risk assessment agreement.

❑ *Confidentiality.* Emphasize confidentiality by making a promise of no attribution to individuals.

---

[2] Approximately 25 percent of the project personnel were invited to participate in the interview sessions.

❑ *Communication*. Encourage communication of risks during the risk assessment.

❑ *Consensus*. Show teamwork through the consensus process that the risk assessment team operates by.

20.3   Risk Assessment Training

To conduct the risk assessment as professionals, assessment team members spent two days in training at the SEI.[3] (The risk assessment training material was that used by the SEI in 1993, which was revised as Software Risk Evaluation [Sisti94].) The following major activities were used to train assessment team members:

❑ Review the project profile.

❑ Learn risk management concepts.

❑ Practice risk assessment methods.

20.3.1   Prepare the Assessment Team Members

Expectations for the risk assessment training included understanding the techniques used, learning how risk assessment fits into the risk management paradigm [VanScoy92], and determining the value of risk assessment to the business bottom line. A team-building exercise was used to interview and then to introduce the assessment team members.

The project profile was presented to ensure that assessment team members understood the project context. The project overview covered the operational view of the product, how the project was structured, contractual relationships, organization roles, software staff, software characteristics, and project history. The project profile was used to set the context and vocabulary for communicating with the project team during the risk assessment.

20.3.2   Learn the SEI Taxonomy Method

A taxonomy is a scheme that partitions a body of knowledge and defines the relationships among the pieces. It is used for classifying and understanding the body of knowledge. A software development **risk taxonomy** was developed at the SEI to

---

[3] Just-in-time training is best. Team training occurred two weeks before the risk assessment.

facilitate the systematic and repeatable identification of risks [Carr93]. The SEI taxonomy maps the characteristics of software development into three levels, thereby describing areas of software development risk. The risk identification method uses a taxonomy-based questionnaire to elicit risks in each taxonomic group. Risk areas are systematically addressed using the SEI taxonomy as a risk checklist. An interview protocol is used to interview project participants in peer groups. Peer groups create a nonjudgmental and nonattributive environment, so that tentative or controversial views can be heard.

20.3.3   Practice the Interview Session

With an understanding of the SEI taxonomy method, the risk assessment team practiced for an interview session by acting out each of the required roles:

- ❑ *Interviewer.* The interviewer conducts the group discussion using an interview protocol in a question-and-answer format.
- ❑ *Interviewee.* The interviewees (project participants) identify risks in response to questions posed by the interviewer.
- ❑ *Recorder.* The recorder documents the risk statements and results of the preliminary risk analysis.
- ❑ *Observer.* The observer notes details of the discussion, the group dynamics, and overall process effectiveness. The observer monitors the time to ensure the meeting ends on schedule.

20.4   Project Risk Assessment

From the risk assessment team's perspective, there was a tremendous amount of information to collect, correlate, and synthesize in a limited amount of time. From the project participants' perspective, this would be a chance to say what they thought, to hear what other people thought, and to discuss upcoming project issues. The major activities to perform the risk assessment are the following:

- ❑ Conduct the interview sessions.
- ❑ Filter the identified risks.
- ❑ Report the assessment findings.
- ❑ Obtain assessment team feedback.
- ❑ Obtain project management feedback.

20.4.1   Conduct the Interview Sessions

Three interview sessions were conducted that lasted three hours each, with between two and five project participants per interview session. Project participants were interviewed in peer groups with no reporting relationships. They considered risks that applied to the project as a whole, not just their own individual tasks. The first interview group consisted of project managers, the second of task leaders, and the third of engineering personnel.

The project managers identified twice as many project risks as either process or product risks. The task leaders identified more product risks than project risks by a factor of 10. And the engineering personnel identified the same number of product risks as process risks. These results are not by coincidence, but in part by design of the SEI taxonomy method [Carr93].

Each interview session began with a set of questions structured according to a different taxonomy class:

- ❑ *Product engineering*, the intellectual and physical aspects of producing a product. In the interview session, task leaders began by responding to questions from this class of the taxonomy.

- ❑ *Development environment*, the process and tools used to engineer a software product and the work environment. In the interview session, engineering personnel began by responding to questions from this class of the taxonomy.

- ❑ *Program constraints*, the programmatic risk factors that restrict, limit, or regulate the activities of producing a product. In the interview session, project managers began by responding to questions from this class of the taxonomy.

20.4.2   Filter the Identified Risks

On average, over six issues were identified by each participant. For each identified risk on the candidate risk list, interviewees were asked to evaluate the risk according to four criteria: risk consequence, likelihood, time frame, and locus of control. These criteria determine whether the issue is documented as a risk. The risk evaluation is determined by a series of yes-no questions:

- ❑ *Consequence*. Does this risk have a significant consequence? Will the outcome affect performance, function, or quality?

- ❑ *Likelihood*. Is this risk likely to happen? Have you seen this occur in other circumstances? Are there conditions and circumstances that make this risk more likely?

- ❑ *Time frame*. Is the time frame for this risk near term? Does this require a long lead-time solution? Must we act soon?

❑ *Locus of control.* Is this risk within the project control? Does it require a technical solution? Does it require project management action?

Responses were consolidated from all interview sessions and results tabulated by sorting the risk evaluation criteria, which helps to prioritize the issues. A significant difference was observed in response to the question regarding the project locus of control. Figure 20.2 shows this disparate perception of control among the interview sessions. The following risks were evaluated as outside the project's locus of control:

❑ *Project managers.* This group believed that 47 percent of their identified risks were in the project's control. They evaluate staff expertise, technology, and customer issues (e.g., government-furnished equipment) as outside the project locus of control.

❑ *Task leaders.* This group believed that 55 percent of their identified risks were in the project's control. They evaluated a new development environment and process, customer closure on requirement definitions, and the inefficient interface with functional management as outside the project locus of control.

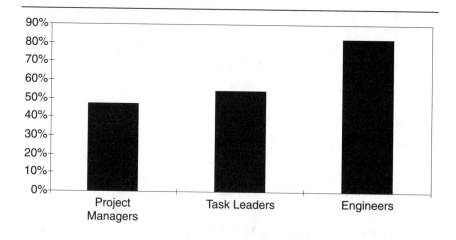

FIGURE 20.2   Perception of project control. Of the risks they identified, project managers evaluated 47.1 percent in the project's control, task leaders 54.5 percent, and engineers 82.3 percent. Engineers were more likely to perceive that risks were in the project's control, because there were two levels of management above them that could resolve the issues. The issues facing project managers (the project externals) were less likely to be perceived as in their control. If project managers included two levels of management above them (i.e., functional management and the customer), they would have a higher percentage of control over their project.

❑ *Engineering personnel.* This group believed that 82 percent of their identified risks were within the project control. They evaluated vendor-supplied hardware, limitations of time, deliverable formats, acceptance criteria, and potential morale problems due to layoffs as outside the project locus of control.

The risks were classified according to the SEI taxonomy. Sorting the risk by the taxonomy classification provided a grouping of issues raised in a specific area. Grouping similar risks identified by all the interview groups helped to summarize the findings and prepare the results briefing.

20.4.3 Report the Assessment Findings

A summary of the risk assessment activities and results was presented to the project team. Findings were summarized in ten briefing slides, each containing the topic area at risk, several risk issues with specific supporting examples, and consequences to the project. There was surprise from the engineering director, who did not expect to hear about so many risks so soon after contract award. The tone of the meeting was mostly somber. No positive comments or solutions were presented. The project manager was assured there would be a point of contact for the project to continue risk management of the baselined risks.

20.4.4 Obtain Assessment Team Feedback

A meeting was held with the risk assessment team to provide feedback on the assessment experience. Observations of what worked were discussed and documented:

❑ *Cooperative project management.* There was value-added by interviewing the project manager and the functional manager together. For example, the project manager learned that he could obtain a waiver for organizational standard processes that did not suit the project. The functional manager became sensitive to the staff skill mix required by the project.

❑ *Peer group synergy.* The reason to interview peer groups is that they share common concerns and communicate at the same level in the project hierarchy. People can empathize better with others if they know what the others' concerns are.

❑ *Earlier is better.* A direct relationship exists between the time assigned to a task and the attribution associated with an individual responsible for the task. Project teams should perform a risk assessment as soon as possible to avoid retribution to the individual team members.[4]

---

[4] Avoiding retribution is not necessary in advanced stages of risk management evolution.

Observations of what did not work were also discussed and documented:

❏ *Required solutions*. Most engineers and managers felt competent when they were solving problems. The presentation of risks without a corresponding solution made the project team feel uncomfortable.

❏ *Negative results*. Presenting risks without a plan in place to address the critical risks left the project team with a negative feeling. Positive comments can make the project team feel good about taking the first step to resolving risks. An announcement should be made at the risk assessment results briefing about a meeting to move the results forward into risk management.

❏ *Abandoning risks*. Everyone should resist the temptation to address an easy risk first and abandon a difficult risk because it was not in the perceived locus of control. The team could expand its locus of control by including the functional management and the customer as part of the project team.

20.4.5   Obtain Project Management Feedback

Three months after the risk assessment, the SEI representative returned to facilitate a discussion on the value of the risk assessment to the project and to the organization. The most important points the project manager made are summarized below:

❏ *The customer's reaction was positive*. The customer reaction to reviewing assessed risks at the system requirements review was positive. The customer wanted to keep the issues out in front, to avoid surprises, and to work toward the same set of goals.

❏ *There is no reward for reducing risk*. Customers were sensitive to the consequences for the risks presented, but the customers themselves did not receive a grade on decreasing risk.

❏ *Risks are programmatic in nature*. The top 16 risks had little to do with software. The risk assessment identified risk projectwide.

❏ *Take the time to do risk management*. Within the organization, there needs to be pressure to take the time to do risk management. Otherwise, the problems at hand, meetings, and tomorrow take precedence.

The most important points made by the organization assessment team members are summarized below:

❏ *Collaboration saved time and money*. Collaborative risk assessment was of great benefit to learning and leveraging existing methods to improve the risk management process [Ulrich93].

- *Proposals need risk assessment.* Proposal teams should use the risk assessment method during the proposal phase. Early identification means there is more time to work the issues.

- *Risk assessment is the first step.* Lack of follow-through on risk items gives a bad name to volunteering risk items. Risk assessment is not sufficient to resolve risk.

20.5   Project Risk Management

The independent risk assessment paved the way for the project to continue risk management. As a result of the risk assessment activities, the project possessed the following assets:

- Senior management commitment.

- A baseline of identified risks.

- The nucleus of a risk aware project team.

From the organizational perspective, there were several opportunities that existed after the risk assessment:

- Support the project in managing identified risks.

- Develop and refine methods of systematic risk management.

- Share lessons learned throughout the organization.

20.5.1   Pilot the Risk Management Process

The task leaders began to present the top risks at project reviews. They decided to address risks every other week at their top-level staff meeting on Monday morning for half an hour. Every month at their all-hands meeting, risks were reviewed with the entire project team. For these meetings, an independent facilitator from the software engineering process group (SEPG) led the group discussion on risks. The project manager later gave testimonial to the value of the facilitator role: "A facilitator was invaluable. The facilitator gives a common, consistent approach. It served as a forcing function. The project would not have otherwise done it."

Prioritization of the risks occurred using the nominal group technique [Brassard94], a consensus approach that involved the project manager and task leaders. Each person ranked all the critical risks from 1 to N. As shown in Table 20.1, the results of the individual risk scores showed unilateral disagreement. Risk action plans were informal—discussed but not documented.

TABLE 20.1   RANKING OF IDENTIFIED RISKS

Log number	Program manager	Test engineer	System engineer	Hardware engineer	Logistics support	Quality assurance	Configuration manager	Software engineer	Contract administrator	Score	Rank
38	9	1	3	2	5	3	3	7	10	43	1
13	2	4	4	3	12	8	9	2	5	49	2
18	1	7	1	6	10	11	7	4	7	54	3
31	4	5	7	8	13	1	12	10	2	62	4
28	15	15	8	4	4	7	1	8	3	65	5
12	5	2	6	1	7	12	15	14	6	68	6
11	7	3	5	7	6	9	14	5	12	68	7
22	14	13	2	13	3	6	6	3	11	71	8
27	10	8	11	5	11	10	11	6	4	76	9
43	8	6	15	9	14	2	13	11	1	79	10
9	6	11	14	10	16	4	8	1	14	84	11
29	11	9	13	11	1	14	2	16	9	86	12
45	13	12	12	12	2	13	5	12	15	96	13
14	3	14	10	16	15	15	10	9	8	100	14
10	12	10	9	14	9	5	16	13	13	101	15
21	16	16	16	15	8	16	4	15	16	122	16

20.5.2   Sign the Technical Collaboration Agreement

Six months after the follow-up visit with the SEI representative, a technical collaboration agreement (TCA) was signed with the SEI. The focus of the collaboration was to participate in the development and deployment of the self-administered risk assessment process. The organization had learned many useful techniques and had leveraged the SEI material through reuse on over ten projects and proposals. High marks were received on the risk section of one winning proposal, to the tune of over $100 million in new business. Software risk management was a niche capability that appeared to have competitive advantage.

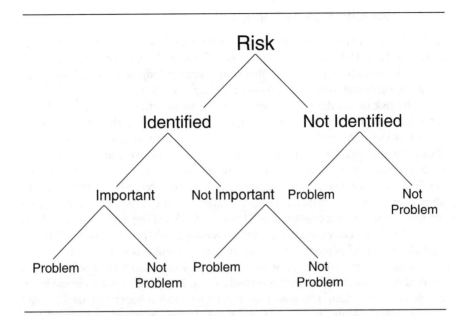

FIGURE 20.3   A risk may turn into a problem. Risk exists regardless of whether anyone identifies it. A risk consequence does not depend on an assessment of its importance. Only the action taken to resolve risk may prevent a risk from becoming a problem.

20.6   Project Risk Retrospective

One year after the risk assessment, the project manager presented the project lessons learned. The project was in the hardware-software integration and testing phase—behind schedule, but making good progress. There were no known major technical issues but several minor issues. The project manager said they had stopped performing risk management when they reached the test phase because the remaining risks had already turned into problems. How did some of the project risks turn into problems? As shown in Figure 20.3, there are three distinct paths a risk can take to end up as a problem:

❑ Identify a high risk and do nothing about it.

❑ Identify a low risk and later it changes into a high risk.

❑ Do not identify a risk and later it becomes a problem.

20.6.1   Identify Risk as Important

Risks that are identified and assessed as important have the greatest chance of being resolved. Unless risk assessment (see Table 20.2) is followed up with risk control, it would be naive to think that simply acknowledging a risk's importance would be sufficient to prevent it from becoming a problem.

The risk of building the wrong product was identified as important due to incomplete requirements. Several statements were captured during the risk assessment that supported this as a legitimate issue. Some requirements were missed during the proposal phase. Existing system requirements were incomplete due to inadequate documentation, interface documents that were not approved, and inaccessible domain experts. To compound the issue, requirements for software reliability analysis, data formats, system flexibility, and acceptance criteria were unclear. Each risk was evaluated as having a significant impact that was likely to occur. The combined evaluation for these issues was 100 percent impact, 100 percent likelihood, 83 percent time frame, and 100 percent locus of control.

Requirements risk was prioritized by the project as incomplete requirements (ranked 4) and unclear requirements (ranked 10). These risks were addressed, and the priority was later reassessed as incomplete requirements (ranked 7) and unclear requirements (ranked 16). Both risk issues decreased in their relative importance because the project perceived that progress had been made in resolving the risk. The consequence that had been described in the risk assessment findings briefing never materialized. The project manager reported that some requirements baseline design concepts were not solidified by the preliminary design review and that some requirements documentation was developed out of preferred order but that problem was largely due to staffing issues.

20.6.2   Identify Risk as Not Important

Risks that are identified and assessed as not important may change in significance over time. The dynamic nature of risk does not depend on an assessment of its importance. Our assumption that we have correctly assessed a risk merely adds to the risk that a significant risk will be overlooked. Risks with significant consequences may not appear important when the likelihood is low or the time frame is later.

Such was the case with the seven issues identified in test and integration during the project risk assessment. The combined evaluation for these issues was 86 percent impact, 14 percent likelihood, 14 percent time frame, and 57 percent locus of control. Six of the seven issues were presented at the results briefing. Two months later, the project manager and the task leaders reviewed the baseline risks at a staff meeting. One risk was accepted when the consensus was reached that they could live with the risk consequence, and the other six were reevaluated. The increase in importance given to these issues was 100 percent impact, 17 percent likelihood, 50 percent time frame, and 100 percent locus of control. Two weeks later, the project manager and eight task leaders ranked each risk using a nominal group technique. Priority was determined by risk score, a summation of all ratings from 1 to N. There was no correlation in these ratings. The project manager mentioned that results of the risk scores showed unilateral disagreement of the different concerns in the project.

The next month, the quality assurance specialist issued a phase readiness review memo to the project personnel to report on the readiness to proceed into the detailed design phase. The project manager, chief system engineer, chief software engineer, and chief hardware engineer were interviewed. There were some concerns expressed about not having a full-time test engineer on the project. This was not viewed as an immediate risk, but the recommendation was that it be studied. The six test and integration issues were monitored over six months. As Table 20.3 shows, most of the issues had increased in their relative priority since the initial risk ranking. Over time, these issues were assigned to various individuals, combined as similar issues, and changed from test issues to issues of schedule and staff.

TABLE 20.2   LIST OF ASSESSED RISKS

Rank	Log #	Risk Item
1	38	Tight schedule leading to SRR, PDR, CDR
2	13	Test fixture not simulated realistically
3	18	Development tool unfamiliar
4	31	Existing system requirements incomplete
5	28	GFE baseline in flux during development life cycle
6	12	Not enough time for software integration
7	11	Optimistic schedule for HW/SW integration
8	22	Personnel changes could result in loss of critical capability
9	27	Unproved I/O board; poor vendor track record
10	43	Some missed requirements
11	9	Key test personnel not identified
12	29	May have to train the trainer
13	45	Process demands not adequately planned in estimates
14	14	Sell-off is required in operational requirement
15	10	Integration success depends on key personnel
16	21	Request for proposal may impact staffing

TABLE 20.3   PRIORITY CHANGES OF TEST AND INTEGRATION ISSUES

Log Number	Risk Item	Previous Priority	Current Priority
13	Test fixture not simulated realistically	2	6
12	Not enough time for software integration	6	1
11	Optimistic schedule for HW/SW integration	7	1
9	Key test personnel not identified	11	6
14	Sell-off is required in operational environment	14	6
10	Integration success depends on key personnel	15	2

The project manager noted that they had underestimated the need for a software test engineer. Problems occurred as a result (e.g., conflicts over limited test bed resources, and a compressed site installation schedule). A $500,000 per month spend rate would overrun the project if they were unable to close on the schedule and destaff the project. The bottom line is that risks, even when they are identified early, may become problems when they are not viewed as important enough to resolve.

20.6.3   Do Not Identify Risk

Risks that are not identified have the greatest chance of becoming problems. The project experienced problems in an area the participants had not been concerned about: hardware. The team had difficulty finalizing mechanical product design and drafting well beyond critical design review and completing the custom circuit card design and debugging it. Staffing was a probable cause for the problems experienced in hardware. The hardware task leader arrived late to the team, was pulled away part-time to a previous job, and did not have experience in coordinating manufacturing, material, product design, and drafting. The result was that the project lost focus in hardware design, and when other functions tried to help, their areas got into trouble. A vicious cycle of replanning and workarounds ensued. Perhaps the problems the project experienced in hardware could have been minimized if they had been identified early as risks and perceived to be important.

20.7   Summary and Conclusions

In this chapter, I described the practices that characterize the mitigation stage of risk management evolution. These practices include risk identification with subjective and superficial risk evaluation. A risk list is prioritized and updated infrequently. Risks are assigned to either the project manager or the task leaders. There is no evidence of documented risk action plans. The major activity is risk assessment, with little follow-through for risk control.

The primary project activity to achieve in the mitigation stage is a risk assessment that is conducted early in the project's life cycle. The risk assessment is the key to introducing risk management concepts at a time in the life cycle where there is no blame assigned to individuals. The involvement of the entire project personnel is minimal, but they become more aware of the risks inherent in their plans and work.

At the mitigation stage, we observed the following:

- *A lack of volunteers.* Identifying risk is a relatively new concept for most of the staff, and they are not very comfortable raising issues without a corresponding solution. One of the task leaders said during the risk assessment, "Participating in the risk process is risky. It is less risky to share risks with the customer than management."

- *Improvement costs.* You pay a price to learn a new process. There is a cost to develop the process, and another cost to tailor it to meet the needs of the project. There may be time spent resisting the process and trying to build a case against its use. You must invest the time to learn the process before you will see productivity increase.

- *Testimonials.* After the risk assessment, the project manager said, "Risk assessment helps flush out potential problems early, so that action may be taken to avoid problems. It brings the staff together to work on project issues as a whole, rather than as individual concerns, which results in team building." After the project development, the project manager said, "We have not learned our lessons, and continue to repeat history. We see the problems but do not have good solutions that work."

20.8   Questions for Discussion

1. List four resources a manager should provide for a risk assessment. Discuss why a manager would provide these resources.

2. Do you think there are any disadvantages of using a software risk taxonomy to identify risks? Explain your answer.

3. Discuss three classes of software risk. How do these classes describe the different roles and responsibilities of people on software projects?

4. List ten general categories of software risk that you would expect to find early in the project. Would you expect that most projects that perform a risk assessment early in their life cycle have the same logical grouping of risk? Explain your answer.

5. Discuss three emotions you would feel if you were the project manager and the risk assessment findings had nothing positive to report.

6. Do you agree that interviewing people in peer groups is synergistic? Discuss why you do or do not agree.

7. Are all risks programmatic in nature? Discuss the differences between risk assessment results in the requirements phase versus the coding phase.

8. What are three opportunities that exist after a risk assessment? Describe your plan to create these opportunities.

9. List five barriers to risk control. Discuss a contingency plan for each barrier.

10. What is the difference between ignorance and awareness? Explain your answer.

20.9   References

[Brassard94] Brassard M, Ritter D. *The Memory Jogger II*. Methuen, MA: GOAL/QPC, 1994.

[Carr93] Carr M, Konda S, Monarch I, Ulrich F, Walker C. Taxonomy based risk identification. Technical report CMU/SEl-93-TR-6. Pittsburgh, PA: Software Engineering Institute, Carnegie Mellon University, 1993.

[Charette89] Charette, Robert N. *Software Engineering Risk Analysis and Management*. New York: McGraw-Hill, 1989.

[Sisti94] Sisti F, Joseph S. Software risk evaluation. Technical report CMU/SEl-94-TR-19. Pittsburgh, PA: Software Engineering Institute, Carnegie Mellon University, 1994.

[Ulrich93] Ulrich F, et. al. Risk identification: Transition to action, Panel discussion, *Proc.* Software Engineering Symposium, Pittsburgh, PA: Software Engineering Institute, Carnegie Mellon University, August 1993.

[Van Doren91] Van Doren C. *A History of Knowledge*. New York: Ballantine, 1991.

[VanScoy92] VanScoy R. Software development risk: Problem or opportunity. Technical report CMU/SEI-92-TR-30. Pittsburgh, PA: Software Engineering Institute, Carnegie Mellon University, 1992.

21

Stage 3: Prevention

If you do not actively attack the risks, they will actively attack you.
—Tom Gilb

In this chapter, I describe the practices that characterize the prevention stage of risk management evolution. Prevention is a transitional stage, when the risk management approach changes from reactive avoidance of risk symptoms to proactive elimination of the root cause of risk. Individuals on the project team are aware of basic risk concepts, and most of them have experience in risk assessment. They have already learned a valuable lesson: assessed risks will be realized unless action is taken to prevent them. Through this insight comes the realization that what we do not know will hurt us. Most people are comfortable identifying risks but are unsure how to quantify them. They define a process to help them follow through for risk control. Managers acknowledge the paradox that control is best achieved by first accepting the lack of it. They recognize that only the technical staff can control technical risk, which is often the source of cost and schedule risk. To achieve risk control, managers know they must delegate the responsibility of assessing risk to the team. There is a shift from risk management viewed as a manager's activity to a team activity. This is what we observe in the prevention stage project that I discuss in this chapter. The people and practices of the project are authentic, but the project name remains anonymous.

This chapter answers the following questions:

❑ What are the practices that characterize the prevention stage?

❏ What is the primary project activity to achieve the prevention stage?

❏ What can we observe at the prevention stage?

21.1   Prevention Project Overview

The project is a $100 million command-and-control center upgrade. The prime contractor, subcontractor, and the customer are colocated at the development site. The system concept of operation is a complex turnkey system incorporating communications, telemetry processing, timing, command and control, and data processing. There are special constraints for safety-critical equipment with requirements for no single point of failure. Software is being developed in Ada 95 using an object-oriented tool set. There are approximately 2,000 classes in the object model. Reuse on the 220K total lines of code is estimated at 15 to 20 percent.

The prime and subcontractor formed an integrated team to leverage organizational resources, which include a quality philosophy and software process assets. The team also inherited relevant experience in risk management from previous projects. The foundation of the project's risk management practice has the following elements:

❏ A risk-driven development model.

❏ Quality management techniques.

❏ Organizational process assets.

❏ Previous project experience in risk management.

21.1.1   Use a Risk-Driven Life Cycle Model

The project required the use of a spiral development model [Boehm88]. In response to this requirement, the project software standards manual described a rigorous risk management process that is a key element in the successful use of the spiral life cycle model. Before the start of each product development cycle, spiral model management activities were used to permit a more opportunistic approach to be developed based on the current project situation and knowledge gained from previous product development cycles and risk mitigation activities. The management activities included identifying the objectives, constraints, and alternatives using the worksheet shown in Table 21.1. (This worksheet is a modified version of that presented in [Boehm88].) Objectives provide focus on specific requirements, constraints provide a basis for scoping the work to be performed, and alternatives for achieving the objectives and

TABLE 21.1 OBJECTIVES, CONSTRAINTS, AND ALTERNATIVES WORKSHEET

Section	Information to Be Presented
Header	Product development cycle identification Date Review dates Author(s)
Objectives	Key objectives of the pending product development cycle Products to be generated Formal reviews
Constraints	External and internal requirements on the product development: product dependencies; standards; interfaces; key cost, schedule, staff constraints.
Alternatives	Description of each identified approach to achieving objectives. For each alternative: description of the approach, estimated cost and schedule, advantages of the approach, risks inherent to the approach.
Decision	Select alternative
Rationale	Document the rationale for the decision based on the results of the risk management activities. Complete the rationale prior to initiation of a product development cycle.

the tasks necessary for each strategy are outlined. The approaches are evaluated, and the best alternative is selected.

21.1.2 Reuse Quality Management Techniques

The team believed that a major factor contributing to the success of prior projects was corporate commitment to the total quality management (TQM) initiative. Total quality management is the vision, guiding principles, and philosophy that form the foundation of organizational improvement with respect to people, processes, and products. Both the prime and subcontractor organizations were industry leaders in TQM and were registered ISO 9001. Each organization had received several quality awards for leadership, performance, and excellence on projects. The team was built on a TQM philosophy, with 100 percent of the team trained a minimum of eight hours in quality management. The team reused the following quality techniques in risk management:

❑ Brainstorming.

❑ Causal analysis.

❑ Consensus process.

❑ Delphi process.

❑ Nominal group technique.

❑ Problem-solving process.

21.1.3   Leverage the Software Process Assets

Management procedures for software development were derived from the prime contractor standard software management process. Both prime and subcontractor organizations held an SEI Level 3 rating.[1] As the project team found out, some of the assets of an SEI Level 3 organization enable development of risk management practices:

❑ *Engineering process group*. A separate process group that provides a focus for process definition and process improvement.

❑ *Process asset library*. A repository that maintains hard copy and soft copy resources such as a template for a risk management plan, risk assessment handbook, and historical project risk databases.

❑ *Training material*. A course that teaches managers and developers a common vocabulary and a standard process.

Several key process areas in the SEI CMM require risk management practices [Paulk93]. The prime contractor organization had enhanced division risk management practices through a software risk management action team in order to comply with SEI Level 3. The standard risk management process was subsequently trained in a software project management course.

21.1.4   Build on Previous Risk Management Experience

The prime and the subcontractor organizations had previous experience using risk management techniques. Projects that were relevant to this one showed prior success through the use of various risk management strategies. The past performance of these projects provided documented evidence of an assortment of experiences using risk management.[2] Table 21.2 shows the organizations' previous risk management experience. The results from use of risk management on these ten projects were favorable. Some of the risk management practices were contingencies and workarounds using common sense. Others show the implementation of more progressive strategies, which achieve team goals through collaboration of people.

---

[1] There is not a correlation between SEI software process maturity levels and risk management evolutionary stages.

[2] Of the prior projects, 80 percent were performed by the prime contractor.

TABLE 21.2   PREVIOUS RISK MANAGEMENT EXPERIENCE

Project	Risk	Risk Management	Accomplishments
1	Subcontractor delivery schedules	Fixed price subcontracts with delivery incentives	All deliveries ahead of schedule
	Accuracy of tracking data	Analysis and testing program in plant and on site	Tracking accuracy exceeded contract expectations
	Critical project schedules	Integration laboratory formed to facilitate early completion or workarounds	Completion three months ahead of schedule
2	Software and directed changes	Determination of the delays that would adversely affect the project and identification of the potential changes early	Substantial cost ($2 million) and schedule (four months) savings
	Transition to operational status	Close working relationship with customer and end user personnel	No impact to ongoing operations
3	Developmental system	Early identification and resolution of project problems and issues	All project milestones to date successfully met
	Expected technical changes	What-if analysis to identify potential areas of risk	Received award fee of 95 percent
	Many users	Partnership between the customer and contractor	Active participation of user community in the decision process
4	Lack of scheduling definition with potential mission impact and a loss of fiscal year funds	Scheduled meetings with sponsor to jointly review the status of plans	All critical deadlines met

(CONTINUED)

TABLE 21.2 PREVIOUS RISK MANAGEMENT EXPERIENCE *(CONTINUED)*

Project	Risk	Risk Management	Accomplishments
5	Lack of risk control after early emphasis on identification and characterization of risk items at project start-up review	Project engineer as risk manager and author of project risk management plan	Abatement events occurred in analysis, test, simulation, prototyping, second sourcing, and trade studies to implement the project in an integrated management structure and integrated team environment
6	Ada development with complex integration schedule	Probable areas of risk identified and risk probabilities defined as part of project management responsibilities	Large (over 300 racks of hardware) system that met or exceeded all design requirements
7	High probability of design deficiencies	Engineering teams to analyze each element of the design and all associated system and equipment requirements	Rapid assessment and redesign when potential design problems with the build-to-print documentation became reality
8	That facilities would not be completed in time for the operational test bed	Establishment of a center to perform functionality on an interim basis until the required infrastructure was established andtested	Customer fielded new technology 18 months prior to delivery of the electronic support infrastructure
9	Systems and network loading	Scientific and Engineering Software (SES) workbench used to model the network dynamically before implementation	Risk templates were employed as a tool to identify, highlight, and track all areas of concern; data shared with the customer, included as an active team member
10	Software integration risk from the reuse of over 80,000 lines of FORTRAN and Assembler code	Incremental software builds with multiple design reviews, detailed estimates to complete, and what-if scenarios	Demonstration of the total compliance with all system and software requirements at the customer's facility

21.2   Risk Assessment Results

A risk assessment was performed early in the project by an assessment team consisting of three members of the organization SEPG. At the participants' briefing, risk was explained as an uncertainty with defined probability and impact. The benefits to cost and schedule through risk management would be potential problem avoidance and opportunity awareness. Project participants were informed of their SEPG point of contact and that there would be a risk champion on every project. The policies, procedures, methods, and training available for risk management were explained. The diagrams for both the risk assessment and risk management processes were reviewed. The SEI risk taxonomy [Carr93], risk evaluation criteria, and risk assessment schedule were given as part of the briefing handouts to the participants. Risk assessment ground rules were discussed as follows:

- ❑ *Be on time.* You cannot participate in the group if you arrive late. Disruptions affect the systematic approach to risk discovery and are unfair to those who are on time. Ask the assessment coordinator to replace you if you cannot be on time.

- ❑ *Stay in assigned group.* Do not switch groups or send alternates. If you cannot attend, you should notify the assessment coordinator as soon as possible.

- ❑ *Do not attribute risk to people.* Do not discuss or attribute risk items surfaced in the meetings with others.

- ❑ *Submit risk appraisal.* Understand that the risk groups are a representative sample of the project personnel. The remaining individuals are not being ignored. Everyone should submit risk appraisals now and throughout the life of the project.

21.2.1   Involve the Project Team

Forty-five participants were interviewed in ten peer groups, each with three to five people. Approximately 50 percent of the entire team participated, including customer and subcontractor representatives. The original risk assessment schedule is shown in Table 21.3.

21.2.2   Analyze the Distribution of Risk

Each individual identified six or more risks. The number of risks identified in each peer group ranged from 16 to 41, with an average of 28 risks per interview session. The project participants scored the risks using the risk evaluation criteria shown

TABLE 21.3   RISK ASSESSMENT SCHEDULE

Event	Date	Time	Place	Personnel
Preparation	April 4	7:30	Bldg. 1, Rm. 56	Risk assessment team
Project profile	April 4	8:00–8:30	Bldg. 1, Rm. 56	Project manager, assessment team
Participant briefing	April 4	8:30–9:00	Auditorium	All peer groups
Interview group 1	April 4	9:00–12:00	Bldg. 3, Rm. 24	Customer project managers
Interview group 2	April 4	2:00–5:00	Bldg. 3, Rm. 24	Prime contractor project managers
Interview group 3	April 5	8:00–11:00	Bldg. 3, Rm. 24	Subcontractor project managers
Interview group 4	April 6	8:00–11:00	Bldg. 3, Rm. 24	Customer technical leaders
Interview group 5	April 7	1:00–4:00	Bldg. 3, Rm. 24	Prime contractor technical leaders
Interview group 6	April 11	8:00–11:00	Bldg. 3, Rm. 24	Subcontractor technical leaders
Interview group 7	April 11	1:00–400	Bldg. 3, Rm. 24	Customer technical staff
Interview group 8	April 12	8:00–11:00	Bldg. 3, Rm. 24	Prime contractor technical staff
Interview group 9	April 12	1:00–4:00	Bldg. 3, Rm. 24	Subcontractor technical staff
Analysis	April 13	8:00–5:00	Bldg. 1, Rm. 56	Risk assessment team
Project debriefing	April 15	8:00–11:00	Auditorium	Project team

in Table 21.4, and the risk assessment team classified the risks according to the SEI software risk taxonomy. The risk frequency distribution by taxonomy element is shown in Figure 21.1.

21.2.3   Report the Sources of Risk

In response to questions raised by the project participants during the interview sessions, the term *risk* was further defined in the assessment debriefing:

TABLE 21.4 EVALUATION CRITERIA FOR RISK SCORING

Evaluation Criteria	1: Minimal	2: Low	3: Moderate	4: High	5: Critical
Potential loss to project	Inconvenience: No adverse affects	Minor obstacle: May not adversely affect customer satisfaction, budget, schedule, or system performance	Obstacle: Potential customer dissatisfaction, cost overrun, schedule slip, system degradation	Major obstacle: Significant customer dissatisfaction, cost overrun, schedule slip, system degradation	Serious threat: Severe customer dissatisfaction, cost overrun, schedule slip, system degradation
Probability of occurrence	Not likely: Range is 1–20%	Possible: Range is 20–40%	Probable: Range is 40–60%	Likely: Range is 60–80%	Very likely: Range is 80–100%
Time frame for action	Never	Later	Near term	Urgent	Immediate
Overall risk impact	No problems expected	Few problems expected	Minimal problems expected	Problems likely	Problems assured

- ❑ A risk is a potential problem.
- ❑ A risk is an uncertainty with a probability and impact.
- ❑ A risk may be an existing problem that is allowed to continue.
- ❑ A risk may be failure to take advantage of an opportunity or improvement.

Eleven viewgraphs captured the major risk categories with specific risks and associated database log numbers. Significant sources of risk were reported in the following areas:

- ❑ *Schedule*. Waterfall management and spiral development.
- ❑ *Process*. Inconsistent awareness and understanding, follow-through, and commitment.
- ❑ *Tools*. New, unfamiliar, and unproved.
- ❑ *Meetings*. Too many, conflicting and overlapping, agendas, interruptions, action items not tracked.

An experienced risk assessment team knows to present both strengths and weaknesses. By observation and recording participant comments, the assessment

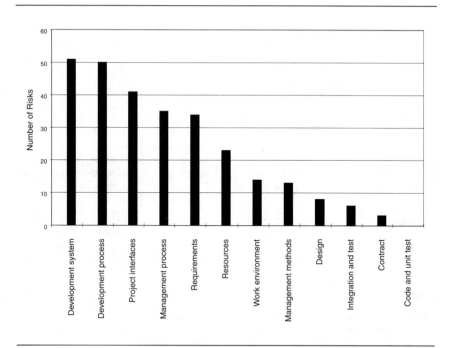

FIGURE 21.1 Frequency distribution by taxonomy element. The total number of risks identified in each of 12 elements of the SEI software risk taxonomy highlights the need for risk management in these areas.

team was able to report more strengths than sources of risk. Sources of strength were noted as follows:

- ❑ Team effort in risk assessment interviews. Good communication and support for each other.
- ❑ Commitment to ensure quality products.
- ❑ Enthusiasm to apply new process and methods.
- ❑ Innovative process and technologies expanding customer and contractor capabilities.
- ❑ Commitment to provide the team with tools and training.
- ❑ Abundant system and software engineering experience.
- ❑ Existing risk management, as evidenced by a documented process, commitment, and implementation (management review board and project tracking).

21.3 Risk Manager

A risk manager has responsibility for coordinating risk management activities. The part-time position of risk manager (about 25 percent of a full-time position) was assigned to a senior technical person on the project. Over a three-year period, the same risk manager championed the risk management process. According to the risk manager, "I have seen it go from a project manager who did not understand what this whole process was about, to a project manager who uses it as a central element of how he manages each of his task leaders." The key ingredient to the project's success over the three years was the central focus provided by assigning the role of risk manager.

The view of the risk manager is that risk management is a systems engineering process required by the customer for project control. In the risk manager's opinion, the role of a risk manager is needed to achieve objectives in the following areas:

- ❑ *Methods for risk management.* Provide methods for systematic identification, mitigation, and tracking of long-term issues. The idea behind risk management is to look into a project and see where the sensitive areas are—likely places for problems—and to do something about them.

- ❑ *Focus for management.* Provide the project management team with a tool to focus on immediate project problem areas. The engineering staff generates risk information largely by their work in designing the system. Risk management flushes this information up to the management team, where the process is addressed.

- ❑ *Insight for the customer.* Provide customer insight into problem resolution. Management and the customer are always after insight as to how the project is doing. Risk management offers insight into technical performance.

- ❑ *Trend information.* Look at where your estimate at completion (EAC) trend is going. Very seldom do we have enough knowledge to say we know what the end item cost of the project is going to be. The cost climbs because of problems that need to be solved, and that costs money. This process helps provide trend information.

In general, the risk manager must be able to command respect from senior-level management and technical individuals for them to listen to the judgment of the risk manager. The risk manager should be a senior-level technical person with a broad enough background to understand all the variation of risks that come up and have the ability to discuss these with the people involved. The risk manager does not need to be an expert, because he or she is not responsible for mitigating the risk.

The risk manager on the project worked for the chief systems engineer, who did not have the time for the role of risk manager. The risk manager was a conduit back to management on the 20 to 30 risk issues that management had neither the attention nor the time to chase individually. The risk manager worked with the subcontractor and customer as much as anyone else on the project. The risk manager was given the responsibility and authority for administering the risk management process. This responsibility included ensuring:

- *Complete documentation.* Document the definition of risk coherently on a risk management form.

- *Consistent evaluation.* Evaluate each risk consistently to enable comparison with other risks.

- *Correct mitigation plan.* Develop a **mitigation plan** to reduce the probability and consequence of a risk that is accurate and makes sense technically. Back up the numbers presented by supporting data or rationale.

- *Coordinate responsibility.* Tag the risk to someone to ensure that none of it becomes lost. Hold those who are responsible accountable for risk management.

From the risk manager's perspective, the implementation of risk management on the project posed a significant number of problems, most having to do with how the engineering teams themselves viewed risk management and went about accomplishing it. In this section, the risk manager describes antidotes that provide an understanding of the practices and problems that were encountered.

21.3.1   Focus the Integrated Product Team

The project was organized as an integrated product team, with risk identification a responsibility of the system engineers, project leaders, and project management as a group. The risk management responsibility for each job category was as follows:

- *Management review board.* The management review board reviewed all the risks on a monthly basis.

- *Customer.* The customer was part of the review process, not separate from anyone else in terms of looking at the data. The customer saw all of the assessments and understood all of the risks. Some risks were under the customer's domain (e.g., providing the support services needed for test).

- *Project manager.* The project manager provided direction back to the team as to what to do about the risk issues. The project manager used the process to focus resource allocation.

- *Technical leaders.* Technical leaders provided the basic information to the management review board, including where the team was going with the risks and how they were doing with risk management.

- *Project engineers.* The responsibility of resolving risk rested with the project engineers assigned to a technical task and the project manager who controlled the entire project.

21.3.2   Describe Risk Management Practices

The project risk management process can be described as a set of activities to identify and resolve risks. The risk manager described the risk management process in five steps:

1. *Risk identification.* We think of risk identification as ongoing. You identify risks whenever you can. As you learn more and more about the project over time, you certainly identify the risks. Any person, at any time, can submit a risk item to the system engineer by completing the risk management form. Project leaders also maintain a list of watch items. **Watch items** are issues that tend to be long term and may be resolved by the normal engineering process. The other thing you should do is a survey. Most projects ask you to do a survey at the start. We found that periodic surveys are required. We conduct a survey every six months or upon major engineering change proposal or redirection.

2. *Risk analysis.* We ask project leaders to assess the impact of risk and put it down on paper using the risk management form. We evaluate watch items monthly to determine if they have diminished, or if they should be escalated to a project risk level. The management team reviews project risk on a monthly basis.

3. *Development of a mitigation plan.* The project management and system engineer develop an action plan. The action plan identifies alternatives and selection criteria if appropriate. The action plan identifies the person responsible for implementing the action plan. The action plan itemizes additional resources necessary to perform the plan. The management team reviews action plans that are documented and summarized on a risk management form.

4. *Mitigation plan execution and tracking.* Once you have a risk that you understand, you have to look at it on a monthly basis. This is a conversation between the project manager and the task manager that owns the risk—not a conversation between the engineer and engineer, because they should be doing what they are told. The project manager needs to know exactly how the mitigation plan is turning out, what is happening to that risk. Is it getting bigger or getting smaller? Then you have the plan adjustments, because the risk goes up and down as you look at it over time. We track about 15 to 25 risks on the watch list, but the focus is on the top ten. The rest migrate up or down over time.

5. *Risk closure.* You close a risk when it is mitigated or when circumstances are modified so the risk is redefined or eliminated. When the risk is mitigated as far as possible but some residual impact exists, project management determines the impact to project EAC. Unmitigated risk impacts EAC. Of course, there are always instances in which EAC does increase as a result of closing out a risk. Then it is there—that is why you have overspent. We try to resolve small risk in two months, medium risk in four months, and huge risk in about six months. Any longer than that, there is something major wrong, and you are probably in a situation where your whole project plan is in jeopardy.

21.3.3 Describe Risk Management Pitfalls

Early on, the project management did not understand how to use the data and how to make the risk be a central part of the way they managed. As time went by, they found problems associated with the risks they had identified and started seeing that their management efforts were focused around resolving these risks. The risk manager observed, "Within the last year and a half, project management has been very committed to holding cost and schedule, and the only way they are going to do that is risk management." Some of the problems and how the project addressed them are described below.

Scaling the Spiral Model.   Software development began with an object-oriented analysis that took about six months. The engineers wrote a preliminary set of requirements based on the results of that analysis. The requirements for the software and hardware components took almost two years to negotiate. The whole spiral was not implemented because they never completed the requirements phase. The project threw out their adaptation of the spiral model[3] but maintained the orientation of risk as a driving factor in system development.

Believing in the Process.   If a group in the project believes risk management is just a bunch of paper, they are only going to pay lip-service to the process. Fundamentally, three things happen: the discipline goes away, the organization is uncovered for major problems, and insight into that portion of the project is lost. The project manager must use this whole process to focus on how to apply project resources. If the project manager does not believe in risk management, everyone is wasting time. You get out of it what you put into it.

Overreacting to Risk.   Risk management offers insight into technical performance and provides a sense that you are telling about problems that you have. The reaction to risk can often exacerbate the problem rather than help to solve the problem. Without sensitivity in discussing risk, you can get a project in trouble, get your customer in trouble, and get yourself in trouble. The way to discuss risk with the customer has to be in terms of a forum where everybody understands the definition of all of the terms.

Lacking Control of Risk.   Risks do not include items that go beyond the contract. If something outside your control is affecting the project, one response is to tell the customer that the project does not have the resources to go beyond the contract. Let the customer decide whether to attack these risks.

---

[3] The spiral model was originally developed for an internal research and development project [Boehm96]. Difficulties with the original spiral model led to the WinWin Spiral Model, which provides for identification of stakeholders and negotiation of win conditions [Boehm97].

Tracking Long-Term Issues. One of the major problems with the risk management process is how long-term issues are tracked. Early assessment of risk means not knowing whether that risk is going to take place. The project used a watch list. People were wasting so much time looking at things that were a low probability of occurring that the management team's confidence began to drop. The watch list effectively tracked issues over the long term.

21.4 Risk Practice Survey

Every new process should be piloted and evaluated for improvement, and risk management is no exception. A risk management survey was given to those who participated in the baseline project risk assessment. The purpose was to improve risk management practices through feedback from individuals using the risk management process. The project manager was interviewed to describe the use of risk management and to approve the survey for distribution and collection. To maintain anonymity, distribution and collection of the surveys was performed by the project manager's secretary.

21.4.1 Categorize Survey Participants

The risk management survey was designed to assess the state of the practice in risk assessment and risk management by asking survey participants to identify their perceptions of the performance and importance of risk practices on the project. Only 2 percent of the surveys were returned initially. After the project's engineering director sent an e-mail message requesting project support, the return climbed to 42.8 percent (18 survey respondents). On the average, the respondents had over 11 years of experience on software projects. Figure 21.2 illustrates the survey participants' roles as a percentage of the total surveyed.

21.4.2 Summarize Risk Practice Performance

Figure 21.3 charts the team's perception of the importance and performance of risk management practices. Importance was rated significantly higher than project performance, indicating the perceived need for risk management in all process elements.

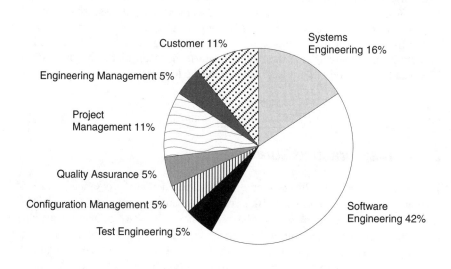

FIGURE 21.2   Risk management survey participants.

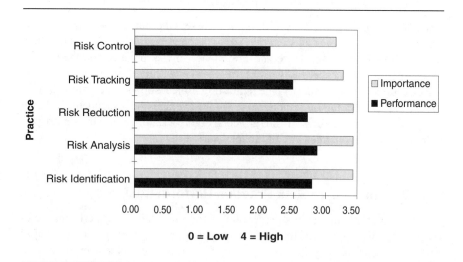

FIGURE 21.2   Risk management practice. On a five-point scale, the importance of risk management practices is rated higher than the corresponding practice performance.

21.5   Risk Practice Observations

Risk management survey results included responses to five open-ended statements. Following are some of the comments:

1. *Some effective risk management practices are*:

   "Identify risks consistently and constantly. Just having a risk program in place is a major step in the correct direction."

   "Identification and documentation of well-known risks."

   "Management review board."

   "Regular activities planned to evaluate risks and identify new ones. Includes risk management in project plans, test plans, and transition plans."

   "Tracking the top 10–20 project risks."

2. *Some ineffective risk management practices are*:

   "Identification and documentation of new risk—some have not been brought to the project level."

   "Risks tend to be identified bottom up. Systems-level architectural risks are not visible."

   "Leaving it up to only a few assigned 'experts' on the project."

   "Since the IPTs do not see a direct benefit (and they are pressed with other duties) the risk management is seen as a hoop to jump through. This has resulted in risks not being presented because the process levies what is seen as extra work."

   "Focus on development almost exclusively for nominal flight conditions. Worst-case scenarios are important to the development of robust software and are effective at revealing faulty and/or inadequate designs."

3. *One thing needed in my work group is*:

   "Some better ways of quantifying the real risks identified."

   "For the integrated product teams to address and restructure risks."

   "More visibility into project risks. More input into risk identification and quantification, especially software."

4. *The risk management lessons learned on the project are*:

   "Must be more proactive in seeking out risks."

   "Just having a risk management process is not enough. It has to be used and dynamic."

   "Be careful about tightly coupling project contractual dollars to risk assessments. Identification of 'potential' overruns makes everyone uneasy."

5. *Other comments regarding software risk management are*:

"It [risk management] needs to be generated and used below the systems level."

"Overall good job identifying risks, not so good doing something about them."

"Risk management statements apply to the project and system level now. Software-specific definitions will not start for several months."

"Risk management is much more effective than management by objective, and a definite step in the right direction. It focuses all on the important problems at hand much earlier in the life cycle than other techniques. More efficient means are needed to collect and evaluate metrics."

21.6   Summary and Conclusions

In this chapter, I described the practices that characterize the prevention stage of risk management evolution. These practices include a documented project risk management plan, written to satisfy customer requirements for risk management. Risk identification occurs at any time using a risk management form. Risk assessment is performed monthly at project management reviews, at six-month intervals using a survey method, and occasionally at an all-hands meeting off-site. Risk is defined in terms of low, medium, and high risk. Risk mitigation plans are documented and assigned to a responsible person. A watch list is maintained that tracks long-term risk. Risks are assigned to the technical leaders, and a risk manager coordinates action items among the various functional groups within the integrated product team. Quality management techniques are reused in risk management to determine the root cause of risk. The organization provides risk management process training as part of a software project management course. A risk practices survey is used to capture feedback for process improvement.

The primary project activity to achieve the prevention stage is the systematic application of a risk management process. Involvement of the people and root cause analysis are two quality principles that are used to prevent risk. Understanding the source of risk is the key to risk prevention. The involvement of the entire team is necessary to identify risk in all project areas.

At the prevention stage, we observed the following:

❑ *A risk management champion.* A senior technical person fills the part-time position of risk manager to coordinate the risk management plan implementation and act as a catalyst for risk management activities. The risk manager has the authority and responsibility to ensure the integrity of the risk management process.

❑ *Process discipline.* The risk management process is a tool for insight into implementation problems that may affect the estimated project cost at completion. To achieve insight, all project elements must participate. Management supervision is important to force process consistency.

❑ *Problem prevention.* The project manager knows that risk management can be used to avoid problems. Reflecting on this fact, the risk manager said, "The project manager believes in it. There is no guarantee, except that you know where most of your problems are."

21.7 Questions for Discussion

1. List five techniques of a quality philosophy that can be reused in risk management. Describe the advantages of each technique.

2. In what ways does experience in risk management increase the likelihood of success in managing risk? How likely do you think it is to expect success in managing risk the first time you try?

3. In your own words, define the term *risk*.

4. Summarize three methods for risk identification that would be cheaper than a formal risk assessment interview session. Include the percentage of team involvement using each method.

5. Improvement means better, faster, cheaper—among other qualities. How would you improve the formal risk assessment method in each of these three areas? List the other ways you could improve the method.

6. Discuss the advantages and disadvantages of a project risk manager position.

7. As an individual contributor and team member, you have a risk that is outside your control. Describe the risk, and discuss how you will handle the situation.

8. Give five reasons that it is important to obtain feedback from people. How could you increase the percentage response using a survey method to obtain feedback?

9. Why is risk prevention cheaper than problem detection? Discuss the consequence of risk prevention. Discuss the consequence of problem detection.

10. Do you agree that you should actively attack risk? Discuss why you do or do not agree.

21.8 References

[Boehm88] Boehm B. A spiral model of software development and enhancement. *IEEE Computer*, 21(5): 61–72, 1988.

[Boehm96] Boehm B. *Software Management & Economics.* Computer Science 510 Video lecture. Los Angeles, CA: University of Southern California, 1996.

[Boehm97] Boehm B, Egyed A, Kwan J, and Madachy R. Developing Multimedia Applications with the WinWin Spiral Model. *Proc.* Sixth European Software Engineering Conference and Fifth ACM SIGSOFT Symposium on the Foundations of Software Engineering, Zürich, Switzerland, September 1997.

[Carr93] Carr M, Konda S, Monarch I, Ulrich F, Walker C. Taxonomy based risk identification. Technical report CMU/SEl-93-TR-6. Pittsburgh, PA: Software Engineering Institute, Carnegie Mellon University, 1993.

[Gilb88] Gilb T. *Principles of Software Engineering Management.* Reading, MA: Addison-Wesley, 1988.

[Paulk93] Paulk M, et al. Capability Maturity Model for Software. Version 1.1. Technical report CMU/SEI-93-TR-24. Pittsburgh, PA: Software Engineering Institute, Carnegie Mellon University, 1993.

22

Stage 4: Anticipation

Wherever mankind has been able to measure things, which means to transform or reduce them to numbers, it has indeed made great progress both in understanding and in controlling them.
—Charles Van Doren

In this chapter, I describe the practices that characterize the anticipation stage of risk management evolution. Individuals from the project team receive training in a measurement process and risk metrics. Measures are used to quantify risk and anticipate predictable risks. Through the application of a measurement process to risk comes an appreciation of the value of risk metrics and the insight that you cannot manage what you cannot measure.[1] People know that risk can be quantified. Metrics are reported to provide insight into the risk management process. The value of risk metrics lies in the ability of aggregated data to confirm or deny estimates. Estimates are refined over time using the Living Lifecycle Model [Gorsuch97]. Risks are shared and acted on cooperatively by both project management and the customer. Status indicators are used to trigger corrective action. This is what we observe in the anticipation stage project. The project name was omitted. The account of the people, measures, risks, and analysis of the project was not.

This chapter answers the following questions:

❑ What practices characterize the anticipation stage?

---

[1] In his book, *Controlling Software Projects*, Tom DeMarco said, "You can't control what you don't measure." [DeMarco82]

❑ What is the primary project activity to achieve the anticipation stage?

❑ What can we observe at the anticipation stage?

22.1   Anticipation Project Overview

The project is a central database for tracking assets distributed across the country. The technical challenges for the system include a very large database with fast response time, a national network with multiple protocols, improvement of accuracy and speed for complex asset identification algorithms, and custom development (hardware and software) for asset scanning. The customer's primary concerns were technical functionality and initial operating capability in 30 months after receipt of order.

The software development organization recently had been assessed at SEI Level 3 [Paulk93]. The project was won by the organization as a technically compliant, schedule-compliant, lowest-cost bidder. The organization's proposal included a constructive cost model (COCOMO) development model, which completely characterized the expected software development task [Boehm81]. The development was divided into four components: central processor, user terminal, identification algorithms, and input firmware. The total size of the effort was estimated at over 360K nominal source lines of code (SLOC). The model was optimistic on the talent and teamwork available for the project. The capability and experience parameters of several components in the model were rated highly, as was the team cohesion, which included customer involvement. The architecture was considered well on its way to being complete given that a feasibility prototype demonstration was performed as a part of the bidding process. The central processor (CP) development effort would take advantage of a fourth-generation language (4GL) COBOL development tool. All of these factors were included in the as-bid development model. The software portion of the development was expected to require 33.7 months, $27 million, and 45 developers to complete.

22.2   Proactive Risk Management

Even with good intentions and well-formulated plans, any software development effort includes an element of risk. Management knew that a proactive approach to risk would be required to win and execute the contract, and they understood that how well they managed their risks would make the difference between project success and failure. In this section I discuss how risk was reduced in the proposal phase to win the contract and how the project team was organized to manage risk.

22.2.1   Propose Requirements for Risk Management

Prior to contract award, a proved, low-risk design demonstrated system performance by a functional prototype built with commercially available technology. The project team proposed a team-building conference upon contract award and customer participation in the project risk management organization. They also offered electronic on-line access to the project team and all project activities. Early in the proposal phase, schedule, technical, and cost risks were analyzed, and a risk reduction plan was baselined. The risk reduction plan described the plan to reduce risk to an acceptable level. To reduce schedule risk, the project development was extended over 30 months. To reduce technical risk, key technologies not available in commercial products were demonstrated. To reduce cost risk, realistic bases of estimate were used from a cost history database, which increased confidence in the accuracy of the cost forecast.

22.2.2   Develop the Risk Management Approach

After contract award, risk management became an integral part of the system management approach. The risk management methodology was developed and documented in a risk management plan. The chief systems engineer prepared the plan by tailoring the soft copy plan maintained in the software engineering process group (SEPG) repository. The roles and responsibility for risk management were tailored by defining a hierarchical structure shown in Figure 22.1. Overall responsibility for ensuring that the risk management plan was peer reviewed, managed, and controlled was assigned to the project manager. The roles and responsibility defined for each organizational element are described below:

- ❏ *Risk review board.* Composed of key project leaders, the board directed the risk management process. The members also assigned responsibility and resources to high-priority risks and reported status to senior management regularly.

- ❏ *Risk management committee.* A **risk management committee** is a group of people with responsibility for directing risk management activities. The committee, composed of representatives from the project team and customer, analyzed identified risks, made recommendations, and prepared action plans.

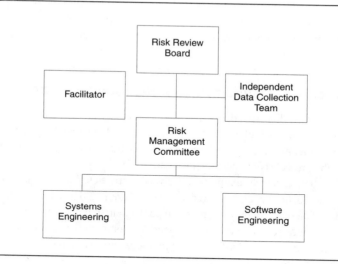

FIGURE 22.1   Risk management organization. The risk management structure comprises five organizational elements and a facilitator.

They also assigned responsibility and resources to implement the risk action plan and reported status to the risk review board monthly.

❑ *Independent data collection team.* Composed of members of the organization SEPG, representatives from the project team, and the customer, the team collected data on risks in an open and nonthreatening environment. They also prepared the baseline risk database and reported their findings to the project team at major milestones.

❑ *Chief systems engineer.* The chief systems engineer was responsible for ensuring that systems aspects of the risk management plan were addressed.

❑ *Chief software engineer.* The chief software engineer was responsible for ensuring that the software aspects of the risk management plan were addressed managing the software risks. This person was the link between the risk management committee and the technical staff.

The risk management approach included identification of programmatic and technical risk by everyone on the project. Early in the project, customer and subcontractor organizations were included in a project risk assessment. The independent risk assessment provided the team with a baseline of identified risks for the project to manage.

22.3   Organization Measurement Practices

The organization's measurement procedures were defined in three guidebooks. The software development handbook related the organization's policies and standards with an overview of required practices and introduced the need for the detailed software management and software engineering guidebooks. The software management guide covered project planning and management, configuration management, development environment, and quality assurance guidebooks. It dealt with software project management and was the primary source of measurement guidance. The software engineering volume included requirements analysis, design methods, coding standards, integration and test, peer review, and software reuse guidebooks. Other functional areas (e.g., project management and systems engineering) also developed and adopted procedure guidebooks, which were integrated with the software procedures.

22.3.1   Collect Core Measures

The organization's measures and metrics were defined in the software management guide. The organization core measures for software management were size, hours, and defects. The project collected all three measures on a regular basis.

Size of the software was estimated according to the SEI line of code counting definitions [Park92]. The organization had procedures for estimating size of new development, reuse code, and nondevelopment item or commercial off-the-shelf (COTS) software. An automated code counter program, defined and maintained by the SEPG, was required for all projects. Initial size estimates were developed by a group of experts using a delphi consensus process and reviewed at all major milestones. Indicators of expected effort versus actual effort with respect to a development phase and software component were used to trigger intermediate-size estimate updates. The SEPG accumulated organization-wide size metrics, including development language, estimate and actual variation, reasons for variation, and changes in expected COTS and reuse usage.

Hours expended on a project were collected through time cards and the corporate cost history database. Separate work detail numbers were allocated for each development phase, software product component, and functional activity. Hours expended per task were compared monthly to hours estimated for the task. The SEPG collected hours expended on a project phase basis.[2] Rework measures were also collected using a work order number established as part of the cost history database.

---

[2] The SEI has developed a framework for counting staff hours [Goethert92].

Defects are found primarily in requirements, design, and code. Defect data were collected through a configuration management tool.[3] A useful indicator of product quality and expected rework is the number of defects relative to the norm for each project phase. Higher-than-norm defects are often an effect of inaccurate estimation and a catalyst for project oversight. Defect measures were categorized by project phase, defect type, defect severity, and correction priority.

22.3.2   Indicate Return on Investment

The three core measures of size, hours, and defects were used by the project team to improve performance and refine estimates. The measures were accumulated by the SEPG at the end of each development phase to develop cross-project trend data for evaluating improved processes and return on investment. Trend data are necessary for estimating future development efforts. The core measures were the only ones aggregated for the organization, although additional measures may be collected by project teams to facilitate project control.

Some averages from early metrics analysis for the organization showed a need for an established, repeatable process. One such metric was the size estimation accuracy per phase. Proposal submission size estimates averaged 56 percent of the final product size. Through awareness and a defined process, this metric improved as the organization matured. Another revealing metric was the productivity by language type, which varied by a factor of four among the organization's common languages of Ada, FORTRAN, C, C++, Pascal, and PL/1. An indicator of process improvement return on investment was the average software productivity, which improved by 29 percent over the five years of the organization's software process improvement initiative.

22.4   Risk Management Committee

The risk management committee received all potential risks submitted on a properly completed identification section of a risk management form. All identified risks were logged in the project risk database and maintained in the risk database for measurement and evaluation. The risk management committee assessed the risk as high, moderate, or low. Risk action plans were developed for moderate- and high-risk areas, and low-risk areas were monitored and managed through weekly project control meeting action items. The risk management

---

[3] The SEI has developed a framework for counting defects [Florac92].

committee was scheduled to meet weekly through system design, twice monthly during preliminary design, and monthly during development, integration, and test. Fewer than ten people served on the committee. Unfortunately, these people were not colocated.

22.4.1   Use Innovative Methods

One of the problems with addressing risk is how to communicate the issue with all the assumptions and associated uncertainty. You might believe that face-to-face verbal communication is not possible when two parties are not located in the same room. The risk management committee thought that it *was* possible and met using a videoconferencing system. The risk agenda, risk minutes, and risk ranking list were all sent by fax prior to the meeting. Using technology, the risk management committee could discuss new risk, coordinate risk issues, and report on progress in an efficient manner.

22.4.2   Quantify the Risk Index

New processes should be piloted before being mandated on projects. The same is true of process metrics. The project was selected by the system engineering process team to pilot process metrics. The purpose of the metrics pilot program was to evaluate the validity and usefulness of metrics in measuring the effectiveness of the system engineering process. Benefits of the pilot program included training in the measurement process and the ability to influence the organization's set of mandatory process metrics. The project was required to collect data on seven metrics over a three-month period:

1. Requirements stability.
2. Requirements clarity.
3. Action item response.
4. Risk count.
5. Risk management index.
6. Phase end report.
7. Cost history.

The project was required to provide feedback on the effort and usefulness of the metrics. A metrics evaluation form was written for each metric. The evaluation categories and questions from the metrics evaluation form are shown in Table 22.1. Feedback from the chief systems engineer was that the risk management index was the most significant of the piloted metrics in terms of customer satisfaction.

TABLE 22.1   METRICS EVALUATION

Category	Evaluation Questions
Purpose	Is there a clear understanding of why these data are being collected? Have the likely causes of an increase or decrease in the metric been identified? Have the customers of the metric been identified? Is there a clear method to analyze the results? Does the metric lend itself to a clear and unambiguous presentation?
Relevance	Is there a clear association between the metric and cost and schedule objectives? Is the metric representative of the project's activities? Have the customers agreed that the metric is meaningful? Has a goal for the optimum value of the metric been agreed on?
Reliability	Would different people measure identical values? Will the metric exist if the process is modified?
Process	Does a graph of the metric indicate the good direction? Is the metric available in a timely manner? Are you measuring something that is within your capability to change? Are the factors that may influence the metric clearly recorded? Can the metric be used as a benchmark for performance comparison? Can the metric measure change in the process?
Efficiency	Is there a clear method to collect the metric? Is the cost of gathering the data reasonable and acceptable? Can the data be gathered with available resources?

The risk management index quantifies the risk exposure for all active risks as a percentage of the total program cost. The chief systems engineer had presented quantifiable risk data to the customer at project reviews.

22.5   Living Lifecycle Model

The project had proceeded nominally per plan with typical perturbations up to the middle of the code and unit test phase. At that point, an analysis of current status indicators predicted problems meeting the original project estimates. The analysis consisted of updating the original development model parameters based on the current project status. A **Living Lifecycle Model** is one where the cost model is updated using actual measures to predict project completion. An analysis of the variance between estimates and actuals served as a trigger for corrective action.

This section describes how low-risk items, when summed together, can cause critical project risk that requires management attention.[4]

22.5.1   Analyze Status Indicators

Major project risk was discovered by comparing the as-bid development model to the current project status. As shown in Table 22.2 most indicators were less than 20 percent off expectations. However, the number of indicators exceeding threshold flagged a serious problem.

TABLE 22.2   TRACKING STATUS OF INDICATORS (Source: [Gorsuch97])

Indicator	Status	Formulation
Milestones	10% behind	(Planned – claimed)/planned milestones
Unit coding	10% behind	Planned units versus completed ((1,400–1,250)/1,400)
Hours by phase	20% growth	Requirements and design each overran hours by 20%
Costs	Same labor rate	Supply of programmers exceeds demand
Software size	10% growth	Extrapolated from LOCs/units completed to date
Requirement changes	75% changes	Total of 3,200 changes to date for 4,300 requirements
Reuse/4GL use	20% less reuse	Extrapolated from units completed to date
Data size	Same data size	Some negotiating on message content, TBD
Number of defects	2x expected	Total of 300/140K LOC versus 170 140K LOC to date
CPU utilization	Much higher, 90%	System simulation and performance tests (CP only)
Memory utilization	Higher, now 75%	Per 4GL data efficiency experiments (CP only)
SEI CMM Level	Level 2 practices	Per mini-assessment of the project

---

[4] Special permission to reproduce an example of the Living Lifecycle Model is granted by Level 6 Software.

TABLE 22.3 LIVING LIFECYCLE MODEL PREDICTION

COCOMO 2.0	STATUS	Schedule Milestones (10% behind)	Unit Coding Status (10% behind)	Hours by Phase (20% CUT growth)	Actual vs. Plan Costs (same labor rate)	Software Size (10% growth)	Requirement Changes (75% changes)	Size Decomposition (20% less reuse)	Size of Data (same data size)	Number of Defects (2x expected)	CPU Utilization TPM (much higher, 90%)	Memory Usage TPM (higher, 75%)	Process Maturity (operating at level 2)	As Bid	At Status	Corrected
Size (ESLOC)				+		++		++						362,879	503,801	503,801
Breakage							++			+				0%	10%	10%
Labor Rate					++									$18,000	$18,000	$18,000
DRIVERS	PREC	+												N		
	FLEX												+	N		
	RESL													H	L	N
	TEAM						+							H	N	
	PMAT												++	N	L	N
FACTORS	RELY									+				- - - -		
Product	DATA								++	+				VH - - -		H - - -
	CPLX	+								+	+			- - H H		
	RUSE					+		++						- - - -		
	DOCU		+							+				- - - -		
Platform	TIME										++			- - - -	VH - - H	- - - H
	STOR											++		- - - -	- - - H	
	PVOL													- - - -		
Personnel	ACAP			+			+							H - - -	L - - -	- - - -
	PCAP	+		+			+							H - - -	- - - -	
	AEXP						+							- - H -	- - - -	
	PEXP		++				+			+				- H - -	L - - L	- - - L
	LTEX	+					+			+				H - - -	- - - -	
	PCON													all H	L H H H	
Project	TOOL	+					+			+	+			H - - -	- - - -	
	SITE			+										H - - -		
	SCED	++		+										all L	L - - -	- - - -
SCHEDULE	(months)													33.7	75.7	58.2
COST	(millions)													$27	$130	$68
SW STAFF	(FSWP)													45	94	65

Source: [Gorsuch97].

Table 22.3 key:

Scaling Drivers:
PREC   precedentedness
FLEX   development flexibility
RESL   architecture/risk resolution
TEAM   team cohesion
PMAT   process maturity

Product Factors:
RELY   required software reliability
DATA   data base size
CPLX   product complexity
RUSE   required reusability
DOCU   documentation match to life cycle needs

Platform Factors:
TIME   execution time constraint
STOR   main storage constraint
PVOL   platform volatility

Personnel Factors:
ACAP   analyst capability
PCAP   programmer capability
AEXP   applications experience
PEXP   platform experience
LTEX   language and tool experience
PCON   personnel continuity

Project Factors:
TOOL   use of software tools
SITE   multisite development
SCED   schedule

Note: Other acronyms from Table 22.3 are listed below but should appear in the text.

COCOMO   constructive cost model
ESLOC   equivalent source lines of code
CUT   code and unit test
CPU   central processing unit
TPM   technical performance measurement
SW   software
FSWP   full-time software personnel
L   low
N   nominal
H   high
VH   very high

Using the Living Lifecycle Model, it became obvious that the original completion plan could not be met. As shown in Table 22.3, the Living Lifecycle Model maps the project status to COCOMO parameters according to a cross-reference to predict project completion. Three different development models show the parameter inputs for COCOMO:

❏ *As bid*—the proposed project cost and schedule.

❏ *At status*—the current phase (i.e., code and unit test) status check.

❏ *Corrected*—the predicted set of parameters after corrective action.

The scaling drivers are the same across all four components of the system. The product factors for the four components are grouped together in a single cell. For example, "- - H H" represents "nominal, nominal, high, high" settings for central processor, user terminal, identification algorithms, and input firmware, respectively. Dashes are used for "nominal" to enhance readability. Moving to each model at the right, only changes are listed. For example, the at-status model changed team cohesion from high to nominal. The schedule, cost, and staff numbers at the bottom are recorded from the COCOMO model [USC96] using the listed parameters. The line of code summary is included in Table 22.4.

The at-status COCOMO parameters were modified from the as-bid parameters per the cross-reference table. For example, input parameters were changed as follows:

❏ Team cohesion (TEAM) dropped to nominal based on high tension due to excessive requirements change.

❏ Architecture/Risk resolution (RESL) dropped to low based on excessive requirements volatility.

❏ Process maturity (PMAT) dropped to SEI Level 2 based on a mini-assessment of the project.

❏ Execution time constraint (TIME) was increased to very high for the central processor based on CPU utilization technical performance measure.

❏ Analyst capability (ACAP) dropped to low for the central processor based on excessive requirements changes and extended effort to complete the requirements phase.

❏ Personnel continuity (PCON) dropped to low for the central processor due to high turnover at the subcontractor.

The majority of the changes took place in the central processor and input firmware. The central processor changes were due to requirements growth, observed lack of analyst and programmer experience, and the lowered performance margins due to the inefficient code generated by the 4GL. Using a development model update to study the effects of accumulated indicator variances is quite startling. As can be seen from the model summary data at the bottom of the

TABLE 22.4   LINE OF CODE ESTIMATES AS BID AND DURING CODE AND UNIT TEST

Component	As Bid			At Status and Corrected		
	Estimated SLOC	% Reuse	Nominal SLOC	Estimated SLOC	% Reuse	Nominal SLOC
Central processor	390,430	43	258,152	429,473	34	361,684
User terminal	90,094	50	52,254	99,103	40	75,873
Identification algorithms	39,219	27	33,210	43,141	22	42,937
Input firmware	19,263	0	19,263	21,189	0	23,307
Total	**539,006**		**362,879**	**592,907**		**503,801**

Source: [Gorsuch97].

table, the effects are significant. The modeled schedule increased from 33.7 months to 75.7 months (over 6 years). The cost grew from $27 million to $130 million. The staff required grew from 45 to a potential need for 94 developers.

22.5.2   Take Corrective Action

The severity of the potential problems was anticipated through analysis of a complete set of project indicators. Each indicator reviewed in isolation would not have identified how far off course the project was. Only the system perspective—the big picture—showed the extent of the change necessary to get the project back on track. This is the point where corrective action was taken to save the project from certain failure. Table 22.5 lists the changed COCOMO model parameter and corresponding corrective action required to change the parameter and save the project. The result of the replan was a 56-month schedule, $64 million software cost, and need for 63 developers.

22.5.3   Predict Project Performance

Through the use of the Living Lifecycle Model, the project management team was able to identify the necessary replan. The return on investment for this schedule risk was calculated as cost avoidance relative to the cost of the required risk management activity. The cost avoidance was calculated as two months down the wrong path for each of the project engineers. The risk management cost included the routine risk management activities and the research to investigate the effects of multiple small variances in project indicators using the Living Lifecycle Model.

TABLE 22.5   MID COURSE CORRECTIONS

Model Parameter	Corrective Action
RESL to nominal	Contractor and customer acceptance of problem and agreement to work together
PMAT to nominal	SEPG support of project to bootstrap practices back to SEI Level 3
CP-DATA to high CP-TIME to nominal	Replacement of original mainframe with higher-performance, greater-memory-capacity model
CP-ACAP to nominal	Replacement of system analysts with mainframe expert analysts
CP-PCAP to nominal	Additional training and mentoring of the system programmers with mainframe expert programmers
CP-SCED to nominal	Relaxing the schedule to nominal conditions

Source: [Gorsuch97].

(The replan costs were not included; they were assumed to be inevitable at a later date.) The calculations show that the project $ROI_{(schedule\ risk)}$ was 23 to 1:

> *Savings*: 25,600 labor hours cost avoidance (2 months x 80 engineers x 160 hours/month).

> *Cost*: 1,120 labor hours:

> > 480 hours meetings (10 engineers x 1 hour/week x 48 weeks).

> > 320 hours assessment (40 hours x 8 engineers on average).

> > 320 hours model research (1 engineer x 320 hours).

> $ROI_{(schedule\ risk)}$ = 25,600 labor hours/1,120 labor hours.

> > > = 23 to 1.

The project was completed at an overall cost of $110 million with about $65 million for software development. The initial operating capability was achieved in 4.5 years from the start date. Without the measurements, indicators, and project risk analysis, the project would surely have continued to the point of no return and then been written off as a failure. Updating the development model with accumulated effects of the project indicators amplifies the danger and provides an early warning system.

22.6   Summary and Conclusions

In this chapter, I described the practices that characterize the anticipation stage of risk management evolution. These practices include training a measurement process and quantifying risk exposure. Risk metrics are reported to the customer. Core measures are collected and periodically analyzed together with refined development model parameter inputs to predict the completed project in terms of cost, schedule, and staff. The projection using actual measures yields a more accurate picture of the future. By this early warning system, anticipated problems are avoided through corrective action.

The primary project activity to achieve the anticipation stage is training of the measurement process and definition of measures used to evaluate risk quantitatively. Piloting the metrics for process improvement is the key to reporting risk management metrics that provide management insight. The involvement of the customer in collaborating on risk issues provides a shared understanding of project issues. The Living Lifecycle Model accumulated indicators during the development life cycle. The results show how the model can predict the project's future. The model improves the utility of measurement practice.

At the anticipation stage, we observed the following:

- ❏ *Several risk management champions.* Approximately 20 people participated in the organization to identify and manage project risks. The organization had three major elements—a risk review board, a risk management committee, and an independent data collection team—and a facilitator.

- ❏ *Measurement process discipline.* A set of core measures provided data to assess status and risk quantitatively. Return on investment of 23 to 1 for a significant schedule risk provided assurance that a costly replan was worthwhile. Automated tools such as a project scheduling tool, configuration management tool, and cost history database ensured process consistency (i.e., standard definition and regular collection).

- ❏ *Problem prediction.* Analysis of the project cost model showed how the summation of a small variance (e.g., 10 percent) in several status indicators yields a large risk. This prediction triggered corrective action because of the faith in the accuracy of the refined cost model.

22.7 Questions for Discussion

1. What software process assets does an organization assessed at SEI maturity Level 3 possess? In your opinion, how valuable are these assets?

2. Do you agree that a proactive approach to risk makes the difference between success and failure? Discuss why you do or do not agree.

3. Discuss the similarities and differences between a risk management committee and a single risk manager. Which would you choose for your project? Explain your answer.

4. Give five reasons that a measurement process is important. How could you ensure that the measurement process is cost-effective?

5. List the minimum set of measures required to know whether to change a plan. Discuss the relationship among these measures.

6. Discuss the value of a risk metric. What would you expect the graph of the risk metric to show over the project life cycle?

7. Why should the project cost model parameters be updated based on the current status? Do you agree that using current parameters can predict project completion? Discuss why you do or do not agree.

8. Explain how the summation of a small variance (e.g., 10 percent) in several status indicators yields a large risk.

9. You are a measurement analyst who is responsible for project variance reporting. Your analysis concludes that although no thresholds have been exceeded, corrective action is needed. Recommend the corrective action based on your measurement data. Use a cost model to support your findings.

10. Discuss how measurement makes known that which was previously unknown. In your opinion, what are the consequences of measurement?

22.8   References

[Boehm81] Boehm, B. *Software Engineering Economics*. Englewood Cliffs, NJ: Prentice-Hall, 1981.

[DeMarco82] DeMarco T. *Controlling Software Projects*. New York: Prentice-Hall, 1982.

[Florac92] Florac W, et al. Software quality measurement: A framework for counting problems and defects. Technical report CMU/SEI-92-TR-22. Pittsburgh, PA: Software Engineering Institute, Carnegie Mellon University, September 1992.

[Goethert92] Goethert W, et al. Software effort and schedule measurement: A framework for counting staff-hours and reporting schedule information. Technical report CMU/SEI-92-TR-21. Pittsburgh, PA: Software Engineering Institute, Carnegie Mellon University, September 1992.

[Gorsuch97] Gorsuch T. Dynamic project measures in a living-lifecycle model. *Proc.* Eighth International Conference on Applications of Software Measurement, Atlanta, October 1997.

[Park92] Park R. Software size measurement: A framework for counting source statements. Technical report CMU/SEI-92-TR-20. Pittsburgh, PA: Software Engineering Institute, Carnegie Mellon University, September 1992.

[Paulk93] Paulk M, et al. Capability Maturity Model for Software. Version 1.1. Technical report CMU/SEI-93-TR-24. Pittsburgh, PA: Software Engineering Institute, Carnegie Mellon University, 1993.

[USC96] USC Center for Software Engineering. *USC COCOMO 2.0 Reference Manual*. Los Angeles: University of Southern California, 1996.

[Van Doren91] Van Doren C. *A History of Knowledge*. New York: Ballantine, 1991.

23

Stage 5: Opportunity

The world would be a better place if we could insure against every future possibility. Then people would be more willing to engage in risk taking, without which economic progress is impossible.
—Kenneth Arrow

In this chapter, I describe the practices that characterize the opportunity stage of risk management evolution. Risk (the chance of a bad outcome) is associated with every opportunity (the chance of a good outcome). When people know how to manage risk, they are prepared to take on more difficult assignments with greater opportunities. But perfect knowledge of risk management cannot guarantee success. Managers give people permission to fail because they know there is no progress without risk. People have a positive belief under conditions of uncertainty when they are not afraid to try. In general, not trying is perceived as the only sure way to fail. Individuals learn from past mistakes—not just their own, but those of other companies, countries, and even other centuries. For example, René Descartes (1596–1650) created a scientific method to achieve certainty by doubting everything except the doubter (*Dubito ergo sum.* "I doubt; therefore I am."). By abolishing preconceptions and reducing all problems to mathematical form, Descartes revolutionized science and the material world in which we live.[1] Those who understand Descartes' scientific method realize that you do not know what you do not know. Previously accepted beliefs are questioned in the name of science and progress. The responsibility for managing risk is distributed to everyone,

---

[1] Before Descartes, the focus of the world was spiritual, not material.

which creates opportunity at all levels of the organization. Management empowers the people to share what they do not know, and risk is resolved because someone else knows. That is what we observe in the opportunity stage project. The project name is covert, but the people, their perceptions, practices, and results are overt.

This chapter answers the following questions:

❑ What are the practices that characterize the opportunity stage?

❑ What is the primary project activity to achieve the opportunity stage?

❑ What can we observe at the opportunity stage?

23.1   Opportunity Project Overview

The objectives of the project were to build the highest-quality product given the resources and contractual requirements. The ultimate goal was to produce the product within budgeted cost and schedule in a manner that would please the customer and provide the company with profit.

23.1.1   Review the Organization Structure

The organization behind the project is shown in Figure 23.1. Each of the two divisions within the company provided resources to project teams using matrix management. Project management requested human resources from various centers of expertise centralized in sections, and the section managers reviewed available human resources and matched them to requests generated by project management. The project used resources from two divisions and eight sections and hired four independent subcontractors.

23.1.2   Review the Project Structure

The project had 45 people divided into six functional groups. The project structure is shown in Figure 23.2. Twenty people were assigned to the five major tasks of the software engineering group, with task groups ranging in size from two to four people. Ten people formed the mechanical integration group. The other functional groups consisted of one to three people.

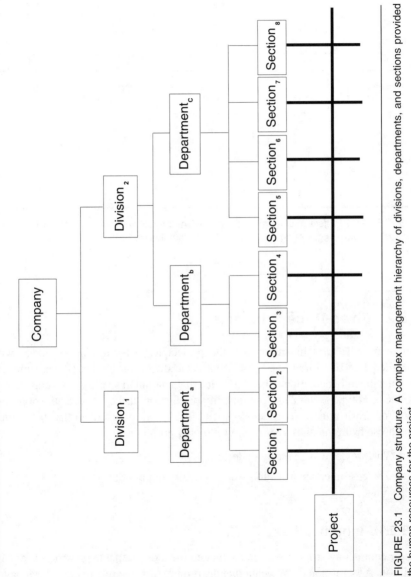

FIGURE 23.1   Company structure. A complex management hierarchy of divisions, departments, and sections provided the human resources for the project.

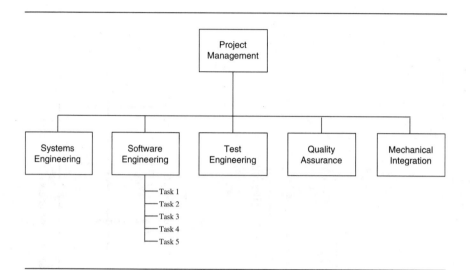

FIGURE 23.2   Project management structure. The project was divided into six functional groups. Software engineering was further divided into five major task groups.

23.2   Fixed-Price Problems

There were several incentives for the project to perform. The company was awarded the $10 million fixed-price contract as the lowest bidder. (It was rumored that the incumbent company had bid twice that amount in an effort to recoup a loss on the prototype system.) A low-quantity production further reduced the opportunity for profit after system development. This section describes the difficulties that arose from the discovery of the following problems:

- ❏ The project was severely underbid.
- ❏ The customer specification was physically impossible.

23.2.1   Inherit a Risky Business

After contract award, the project calculated the most probable project cost at $14 million. A $4 million delta meant that the project was severely underbid. Management performed a root cause analysis (the engineers called it a "witch hunt") to determine how the situation had occurred. They held several meetings with the proposal team and the project team, trying to reconcile the following questions:

- What caused the discrepancy between the two estimates?
- Did the project team change things that were unnecessary?
- Did the proposal team forget things?
- Did the proposal team underestimate the cost of some components?

Eventually people realized that the proposal team just missed the mark on some of the items. Since it was a fixed-price contract, the company (as the contractor) had to deal with the difference. For a business area of that size, $4 million was the expected profit for a whole year. Early on, the customer was made aware of this discrepancy. Since it was a fixed-price contract, the customer was afraid that the team was going to cut corners. From the beginning, the customer relationship was poor. It became apparent that the project had inherited a risky business.

The climate within the company was that management, all the way to the corporate vice presidents, accepted the most probable cost of $14 million and accepted that the company was going to lose $4 million. That atmosphere was probably the most important single item in making the project as successful as it was. If management had refused to accept the most probable cost, the project would have had high turnover. Everyone would have thought that it was impossible; they would give up. But when management said, "It is what it is; do your best," they inspired everyone to achieve the most probable cost.

It could have gone the other way. Management did not say, "It is $14 million, but we are only going to give you $12 million." In response, the engineers would devise a schedule based on $12 million and would likely overrun both budget and schedule. It is a different philosophy of management that says, "All right; it is $14 million. Now underrun." That philosophy enables the team to feel as if they are exceeding their own goal, not meeting an unrealistic goal set by management. Management enabled the team by saying, "The most probable cost is the most probable cost." It left to the engineering team to figure out if they could do better or not rather than setting out an unrealistic goal.

23.2.2   Discover an Impossible Specification

By the design review, the team showed that some of the requirements were beyond the state of the art—beyond physical possibility. The customer had a difficult time accepting that. It seemed to think that even if the specification was physically impossible, the team was bound by contract to develop the system. The customer did not want to renegotiate any of the specifications because renegotiation on any specification opens the door for cost consideration. As long as the specification remains the same, there is no cost growth to the customer. The relationship between the customer and contractor became hostile. The design review ended prematurely, with the contracting officer threatening to sue the contractor.

23.3   Routine Risk Management

The project used a simple process to discover ways to do better than their plan. Initially, the management team used programwide risk management. One of their biggest areas of cost concern was software. The software team had a large risk of overrun and also potential for cost savings, because the software cost was 50 percent of the total project. A separate team was spawned to work on software possibilities for cost savings. This team implemented software risk management. Other functional groups held risk management meetings and reported results to programwide risk management. These groups used a similar process and met on an as-needed basis. Risk meetings had three major parts:

1. *Review status.* Review minutes and status from the previous meeting. The minutes included a list of issues, who the volunteers were, and proposed solutions (or resolutions).

2. *List risk and opportunity.* List roadblocks to the project progress and list opportunities to do better.

3. *Brainstorm solutions.* Brainstorming solutions usually got the most qualified person to volunteer to take on that solution. For example, if the solution was that the team needed to meet with the antenna designer to help improve the specifications, then the project manager might approve the trip. The project manager was not the right person to go see the antenna designer.

The risk meeting had no leader, only a scribe and a facilitator. The purpose of the weekly risk meeting was to list risks and brainstorm opportunities and solutions. (This is different from the staff meeting, whose purpose was to review progress, status, plans, and problems.) The team had to quantify either negative or positive cost and schedule impacts, as well as the solution cost. Each month, management reviewed the team's cost savings in terms of cost avoidance and cost reduction.

23.3.1   Quantify Negative Consequences

Cost avoidance is a quantification of the negative outcome of risk. It includes costs that could happen to the project. The major risk previously discussed was that the customer was ready to sue the contractor after hearing that one of the items in the specification was physically impossible. The team could get close to the specification at a significant cost (millions of dollars). If the project was terminated for cause, the contractor would have to refund to the customer any money invested in the project, including procurement costs. If the contractor had invested $3 million into the project, it would lose the entire sum. Actual legalities of such a situation are complex, and the team considered some of that in a calculation of cost avoidance. This was a big risk: the customer was irate and threatening to sue.

In response, the team got the customer involved in order to mitigate the risk. The team always saw the solution as their responsibility, even though it was a customer problem. Because the specification was impossible, they could have said, "There is nothing the team can do. It is an impossible specification." Instead, they always assumed that they had to do something—in this case, educate the customer on why the specification was impossible.

Most of the core customer team members were not experts in the area of the impossible specification and did not understand that it was impossible. They believed it was possible because they had a previous breadboard system, and it performed to the specification. Nevertheless, the project team knew it was physically impossible and offered to test the breadboard system to see if there was something they could learn from it. During those tests, they were able to observe that the breadboard system operated differently from the specifications. Whoever had written the specification for the production system misinterpreted what the breadboard system was doing. The customer then was willing to change the specification, although it could not permit cost growth because it did not have more money to give the contractor. Eventually the system capability was renegotiated. The customer reduced functionality for all the money the contractor had spent pursuing the impossible specification. Where the risk consequence could have been a big money loser, it ended up a break-even situation.

23.3.2   Quantify Positive Consequences

Cost reduction, a quantification of the positive outcome of opportunity, includes opportunities to exceed metrics. For example, the team believed they could create cost reduction through the use of new technology to increase productivity. The opportunity to improve productivity was presented to management. The engineers said the personal computers (PCs) they were using were inefficient as a development station, because the PC allowed only one window up at a time. The software tools supported multiple windows, but only with an X–Windows terminal. The team brought the issue to management and said, "Productivity could increase if the team had SparcStations or X–terminals to do our coding." The engineers presented their case quantitatively based on the profit equation, in terms that management understood. If management could spend $300,000 on SparcStations and it reduced their fixed price cost by $500,000 because productivity went up, then they would save $200,000. Since it came out of the same pool of money, it was still profit. Spend $300,000 on SparcStations or $500,000 on project loss: the decision was obvious. Management came up with the money, and the engineers bought SparcStations and had them installed. The improved technology significantly helped software productivity. The engineers eventually quantified the increase in productivity after the SparcStations versus before the SparcStations and used that calculation on the spreadsheet that showed cumulative cost reduction.

23.4   High-Performance Engineering

The engineers had an adage that they said in the hallways: "No complaining." Obviously the engineers *could* complain about the project because it was a difficult assignment. Even at $14 million, the project was an aggressive bid. Nevertheless, the engineers said, "No complaining outside the software risk management meeting. If you have a complaint, then bring it to the meeting." They posted a sign designating the development lab a "Positive Thinking Area." Despite the difficulty of the project, or perhaps because of it, the engineers took responsibility for managing risk and set a goal to beat the most probable cost estimate by $1 million. In this section, the engineers describe why they volunteered their time to manage risk, how they worked to improve productivity, and how they quantified risk management effectiveness.

23.4.1   Develop a Volunteer Team

Although the programwide risk management meeting had mandatory attendance, the software risk management meeting attendance was voluntary. Because software risk was within their locus of control, the engineers cared about risk management, so attendance at the software risk management meeting needed no enforcement.

A nonautocratic management style that enabled people to voice concerns was a by-product of quality management training, and everyone on the team had quality management training. As a result, engineers who came to the software risk management meeting said whatever they wanted to say. They held the meeting for an hour over lunchtime. In any given week, there were between seven and ten people at the meeting. The meeting held an attraction for the engineers to attend. Like visiting a psychiatrist, the engineers sought help in what was troubling them at work and saw the meeting as an opportunity to improve their work environment. They shared their concerns and knew they were not alone; there was help at the meeting. Group therapy worked. By not having somebody be held responsible, everyone became responsible for managing risk.

23.4.2   Improve Software Productivity

Each week the team would work on improving productivity. They would come up with subopportunities and sublevel solutions. At any given time, software risk management tracked approximately 30 issues on the status list. Most of the meetings were focused on the following questions:

- ❑ What could go wrong?
- ❑ How could we do better than the plan?

During the coding phase, the team had an objective of increasing productivity by 10 to 20 percent. The team knew that the productivity bid was based on division metrics and wanted to do better than that, so they talked about how to improve productivity every week for an hour. One way the team improved productivity was a midcourse correction of coding standards. They quantified the inefficiency of a coding standard in the following manner: If it is aggravation for 20 people and it slows them down by 10 minutes per day, that is 200 minutes per day, or 867 hours per year.[2] At a labor rate of $100 per hour, that adds up to about $87,000. The cost of changing a few lines in the coding standards was zero. Somebody volunteered to do it, and because the coding standards were on-line, it was easily done. The team saved roughly $87,000 by changing a few coding standards.

23.4.3   Quantify Risk Management Effectiveness

The team cumulated their cost savings as well as their cost of performing risk management activities. The process required the estimates for risk probability and consequence to be most likely (not worst-case) estimates. These estimates were updated whenever significant changes occurred in the estimates or when a change in resolution strategy occurred. The project leader reported the return on investment as an indicator of the team's risk management effectiveness. The calculations show the project $ROI_{(RM)}$ was 22 to 1:

Savings: $8 million ($6 million cost avoidance and $2 million cost reduction)

Cost: $370,000 ($150,000 programwide risk management, $100,000 software risk management, and $120,000 risk resolution cost)

$ROI_{(RM)}$ = $8 million/$370,000.

= 22 to 1.

---

[2] This calculation is based on a nominal 40-hour work week. The coding phase on the project lasted one year.

23.5   The Power Pyramid

Empowerment is maximizing power and opportunity for success by enabling people. Diane Tracy, author of *The Power Pyramid: How to Get Power by Giving It Away*, outlines ten principles necessary to achieve empowerment [Tracy90]. The primary premise of *The Power Pyramid* is that managers can greatly increase their power by enabling all members of the organization to achieve their maximum potential.

A survey was performed to study the teams' level of empowerment. The survey consists of 63 statements derived from Tracy's book. The survey statements are subtopics of the ten power principles introduced in the book. The survey maps each of the ten power principles to several statements to determine the level of perceived empowerment. The survey participants were instructed to read the statements and reflect on the experience of their current assignment and project. Allowing 20 minutes, survey participants were to list their response to each statement based on a five-point scale. All information received was confidential, and the participants' name or other identifying information was not required. Completed surveys were returned by interoffice mail.

The survey results were used to understand the teams' perspective of how they were empowered. Figure 23.3 shows the average score for each of the ten empowerment categories. The lessons learned from the survey results were used by the software manager to help improve job satisfaction and team performance. To provide additional insight into the project practices, the software manager and a software engineer summarized their feelings on how they were empowered.

The software manager, responsible for 22 engineers, observed the following actions that management took to empower the team:

- ❏ *Admit weaknesses.* "Individuals feel proud when they are given responsibilities above the level they feel they deserve. In order to be successful, we had to rely on each others' strengths and admit our weaknesses."

- ❏ *Eliminate waste.* "I encourage my subordinates to produce at levels that exceed current company benchmarks. I ask them to nominate for elimination any process or procedure that does not directly add to improved output. (Improved output includes equal product at reduced cost.)"

- ❏ *Discuss failures.* "Failure can become a personal experience that impacts productivity when the individual involved believes that others will be judgmental. For example, we have equipment and cabling problems that we must solve during subsystem integration. These problems exist due to an inadequate amount of time spent in testing these items at subsystem levels.

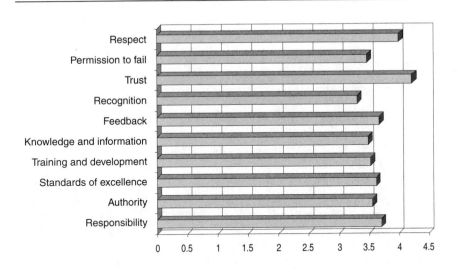

FIGURE 23.3   Empowerment survey results. An average score above 3.0 is considered better than expected based on previous experiences. Averages below 3.0 indicate less than expected empowerment. The average team score shows a high level of trust and respect.

The temptation is to lay blame on responsible parties, which is a nonproductive exercise. I promote an attitude of, 'We will do what it takes to fix whatever needs fixing.' "

The software engineer brought team-oriented beliefs from experience gained at a small company. The software engineer observed that management empowered the team members in the following ways:

❑ *Expand knowledge.* "The company promotes training through a center for training and development. The educational assistance program is another opportunity for employees to expand their knowledge and skills."

❑ *Show appreciation.* "After working hard for over six months on a technical design, our customer refused to speak with us due to overriding contractual issues. The software engineering team felt unrecognized and unappreciated. Upper management arranged to provide the team with an off-site party. Management gave the team jackets with their names and project logo embroidered on them."

❏ *Take chances.* "Management allows the team to try things that are less than certain. When we did not succeed, it was treated as a positive experience, and we were encouraged to explore why we did not succeed."

23.6   Summary and Conclusions

In this chapter, I described the practices that characterize the opportunity stage of risk management evolution. These practices include positive expectations for success, even under difficult circumstances. Management creates an environment for success, which includes realistic cost estimation, calculated risk taking, and team empowerment. Posters designate the development lab a "Positive Thinking Area." Because the top ten project manager risk list is different from the top ten software engineer risk list, the team does both programwide risk management and software risk management. The same risk management techniques are used at different project levels. Software risk management provides focus for small risks with big multipliers (e.g., daily 10-minute time wasters for 20 people) to eliminate risks of process inefficiencies that add up. Risks are assessed at a weekly meeting where everyone is responsible because there is no leader, only a facilitator. Risk action plans are developed at the meeting and implemented by volunteers. A survey is used to capture feedback on team empowerment, and the results are used to improve productivity and job satisfaction.

The primary project activity to achieve the opportunity stage is the positive expectation of using risk management to exceed established goals. Placing simple principles for managing opportunity and risk in the hands of the project team empowers them. In the hands of the many, a simple risk management philosophy becomes a powerful weapon. The final software risk management spreadsheet showed $6 million in cost avoidance and $2 million in cost reduction. Quantitative, cumulative, and positive results propagate cost savings to make the team's goal a reality.

At the opportunity stage, we observed the following:

❏ *Management expectations.* Management accepted the most probable cost estimate and then challenged the team to underrun. Management expected to hear about opportunities, risks, and problems and to see cost savings quantified on a monthly basis. The practice of quantifying results as abstract as empowerment enabled the team to give back to the organization positive process improvement findings.

❏ *Team empowerment.* Sharing concerns at a weekly lunchtime meeting enabled volunteers to choose the risks that they wanted to resolve. The team believed they were empowered through responsibility, authority, standards of excellence, training and development, feedback, and, above all, respect and trust.

❑ *Positive results*. The ultimate test of any philosophy (what you know) or attitude (how you feel about what you know) is objective results. The team's productivity exceeded the organization metric by 10 percent. The team underran their budget by $2 million. Without their efforts, the project cost at completion could have been $6 million over budget. The project $ROI_{(RM)}$ was 22 to 1. The system worked in the field, and the customer was happy.

23.7   Questions for Discussion

1. Do you think the ability to manage risk prepares you to take on more difficult assignments? Discuss why you do or do not agree.

2. List three reasons for distributing the responsibility to manage risk. Describe your reasons in terms of their effect on productivity, cost, and risk of system development.

3. Discuss the risk and the opportunity of a fixed-price contract.

4. How does a realistic estimate of the software development effort enable the team to succeed? In your opinion, what are the consequences of an unrealistic estimate?

5. Compare and contrast programwide risk management and software risk management.

6. Explain the difference between cost reduction and cost avoidance. Give examples of cost reduction and cost avoidance from your own experience.

7. Discuss the paradox of getting power by giving it away.

8. What could you do to ensure that feedback was analyzed and used for improvement?

9. Why should results be quantitative, cumulative, and positive? Explain the disadvantages of having each without the other two.

10. Why is economic progress impossible without risk taking? Explain your answer.

23.8   References

[Arrow71] Arrow K. *Essays in the Theory of Risk-Bearing*. Chicago: Markham, 1971.

[Tracy90] Tracy D. *The Power Pyramid: How to Get Power by Giving It Away*. New York: Morrow, 1990.

EPILOGUE

Managing Risk: Methods for Software Systems Development introduces three new methods to promote understanding of software risk management: the 6-D Model, the P^2I^2 Success Formula, and the Risk Management Map. The 6-D Model extends the Deming PDCA cycle by adding the ability to reveal risk and opportunity. Conceptually more powerful than a Turing machine, the 6-D Model is a requisite set of properly coordinated disciplines because it describes the four quadrants of human awareness. The ability to perceive risk exists in our right brain, where there is no faculty for processing speech. Perhaps that is why we often make decisions based on a few facts loaded with emotion. The P^2I^2 Success Formula is a cause-effect diagram that relates the factors influencing risk management capability. We can distribute the task of managing risk according to four major factors: people, process, infrastructure, and implementation. Using this divide-and-conquer approach, parallel efforts can speed the adoption of risk management within an organization. The Risk Management Map synchronizes these efforts by providing direction through five evolutionary stages: problem, mitigation, prevention, anticipation, and opportunity. To achieve the next stage of our development on the road from novice to expert, we need the vision, goals, and strategy provided by the map. Risk management capability increases through the accomplishment of each goal, which enhances the ability to manage risk.

Risk management is not the grail of the software community. However, the search to understand how risk fits into the big picture of managing software development led to its discovery. The grail was found within each one of us, it is the essence of what makes us human. Should we be surprised to find a tree when looking at the forest? No. We should expect that an effective approach to thinking, created by millions of years of evolution, would scale from individuals to teams, projects, organizations, the software community, and beyond. Feeding the grail (i.e., reading this book) will not resolve your risks. Results come only from application of knowledge and development of skills through practice. To obtain the results we desire as a software community, we must use the grail to resolve our prioritized risks, for that is where the opportunity lies.

This book is about results from application of risk management methods in software systems development. The opportunity-stage project is an example of a project with excellent risk management results. To achieve these results, the project team worked hard. Risk management does not make difficult work go away. The project is not intended to serve as an example of the best risk management process, because the best process is the one that is tailored for a custom fit. Ultimately, results matter more than process. The project quantified $ROI_{(RM)}$ at 22 to 1. That is risk management nirvana.

Let us briefly recap the important conclusions offered in *Managing Risk*:

1. *Risk identification is a right-brain activity.* Effective methods and tools to identify risk will allow for the specialized way the right brain processes information.

2. *The grail is our brain.* The meaning of life and perception of risk, housed within the grail, is different for each person. The productivity of any organization is based on individual performance. Performance is relative to perceived importance.

3. *Results matter more than process.* The product is a measure of process value. Users, not process, measure product value. The process is never more important than the product. The product is never more important than the user. This is the engineering food chain.

4. *The benchmark for $ROI_{(RM)}$ is over 20 to 1.* A best-in-class standard for risk management return on investment is over 20 to 1. Working to achieve this benchmark will maximize opportunities within an organization.

5. *Negative thinking is positive.* Positive results prove that negative thinking is positive. This paradox destroys the illusion that the best results come only through positive thinking. Managing risk is negative thinking that has positive results.

GLOSSARY

acceptable risk   When you can live with the risk consequence.

anticipation stage   The fourth stage of the Risk Management Map, which describes the shift from subjective to quantitative risk management through the use of measures to anticipate predictable risks.

Bayes theorem   Determines the probability of event B given new evidence A by the following equation, which reads, "The probability of B given A equals the probability of A given B times the probability of B divided by the probability of A."

$$P(B|A) = \frac{P(A|B)\,P(B)}{P(A)}$$

benchmark   A reference point or standard by which products, practices, or performance may be judged.

best practice   A routine activity that enables excellent performance.

causal analysis   Determination of the relation between an effect and its possible causes to get to the root cause of risk.

chaos theory   The theory that chaos and uncertainty are a source of market opportunities with competitive advantage.

collaboration   Dialogue in working with others to develop a shared understanding.

concern   Anxiety, uneasiness, or worry related to a possible bad outcome.

condition   The component of a risk scenario that describes the circumstance that enables a future event.

consensus   The decision-making process of a mature team that ensures everyone can live with the decision.

consequence   The loss of risk occurrence; the effect of an unsatisfactory outcome.

continuous improvement   Betterment of an existing product or service.

corrective action   Activities required to solve a problem.

cost   The cost of risk management is the total investment in resources for risk assessment and risk control. Resources include time spent in risk management meetings, the cost of reporting risk information, and the staff to develop a risk action plan.

cost-benefit analysis   Evaluation of the costs and benefits to determine whether the return was worth the investment.

cost avoidance   A technique for cost savings that decreases the anticipated cost growth. Cost avoidance is the difference between possible cost without risk resolution and the actual cost with risk resolution.

cost reduction   A technique for cost savings that decreases the estimated planned cost. Cost reduction is the difference between planned and actual costs.

cost savings   Money or other resources not spent. Cost avoidance and cost reduction are techniques for cost savings.

creative process   The transformations required to generate new ideas.

creativity   Inventiveness in originating ideas.

creativity theory   A theory for generating opportunities that uses knowledge and imagination to develop ideas that are either original (previously unknown) or novel (extensions of known).

crisis management   Ad hoc and reactive management that wastes resources, increases cost, and decreases customer satisfaction.

decision   The passing of judgment on an issue under consideration.

decision analysis   Use of influence diagrams, decision trees, and other techniques to characterize options by their possible outcomes in terms of risk exposure.

decision theory   A theory for decision making under conditions of uncertainty that uses probabilities to determine outcomes.

decision tree   A risk analysis technique useful in structuring a decision model and showing the details.

discipline   A body of theory and technique that must be studied and put into practice to be mastered.

disciplined risk management An approach to assessing and controlling risk by developing the skills to master six disciplines: Envision, Plan, Work, Measure, Improve, and Discover.

Discover A discipline for seeking to know the unknown, identifying uncertainty in the plan and the work, assessing risk and opportunity, understanding the possibilities, and becoming aware of the future.

diversification A policy for risk resolution that reduces risk by distribution of resources.

empowerment Maximizing power and opportunity for success by enabling people.

enigma Information that does not make sense. The information may be mysterious, ambiguous, puzzling, paradoxical, or obscure.

Envision A discipline for transforming ideas into goals and objectives.

estimation An appraisal of the risk probability and consequence.

evaluation An assessment of the options using defined evaluation criteria.

event The component of a risk scenario that describes what must happen for the risk to occur.

evolution A process of gradual growth and change.

external view The part of a process definition that describes the process controls, inputs, outputs, and mechanisms.

force field analysis A technique to understand the positive and negative aspects of change.

formal risk management A practice of assessing and controlling risk throughout the life cycle. Practices include developing a risk management plan, establishing a risk database, defining triggers for metrics-based tracking, allocating resources for risk resolution, and reporting risk status at management reviews.

future awareness To reason about possibilities, both positive (e.g., opportunities) and negative (e.g., risk).

game theory A theory for decision making that uses heuristics to determine which alternatives to explore in large search spaces.

gap analysis Analysis that shows the difference between two variables. Results can be sorted by magnitude of the difference.

gauge A graphic display of a status indicator, a quantitative target, and a threshold warning level.

goal The success criteria, purpose, or aim to be achieved; the criteria for completion, achievement, and success.

IDEF0 A standard process definition notation.

implementation The project methodology and plan used to perform risk management.

Improve A discipline for learning from past experience.

indicator Implies a value without specifying the quantity directly (e.g., the number of complaints is a quality measure that indicates customer satisfaction; the number of function points is a size measure that indicates software complexity). A composite of measurement data that provides information (e.g., planned versus actual cost). Groups of indicators provide visibility into project status.

influence diagram A risk analysis technique useful in structuring a decision model and hiding the details.

infrastructure The organization policy and standards that require the use of risk management on projects.

innovation style An approach to the creative process that is based on individual preferences for thinking; to think of new ideas by envisioning, experimenting, modifying, and exploring.

integrated risk management Performing routine risk management by distribution into regular project activities.

internal view The part of a process definition that describes the activities that transform inputs to outputs.

issue An unresolved matter with possible negative effects.

L^2 A notation for risk exposure that measures the risk by multiplying likelihood times loss.

leading indicator An indicator that has predictive capability (e.g., requirements growth may be a leading indicator for software size).

Living Lifecycle Model A tool that predicts project completion using actual measures to update the project cost model.

loss Something lost; a missed opportunity.

Measure A discipline for comparing expected and actual results.

measure A standard unit of measurement to determine the dimensions, quantity, or capacity. Lines of code is a measure of software size. Note that a measure is a standard unit (e.g., lines of code), whereas a metric is a historical composite measurement (e.g., 20 lines of code per day).

measurement process The activities to define, collect, analyze, report, and interpret measurement data and metrics.

methodology A set of methods and underlying principles particular to a branch of knowledge.

metric A historical norm used in planning and scheduling. Metrics are guidelines or rules of thumb that are a composite of measurement data taken over time that are used as standards to measure against. The software productivity metric was 20 lines of code per day. Note that a metric is a historical composite measurement (e.g., 20 lines of code per day), whereas a measure is a standard unit (e.g., lines of code).

mitigation plan   An action plan to reduce the probability and/or consequence of a risk.

mitigation stage   The second stage of the Risk Management Map, which details the shift from crisis management to risk management.

net income   The difference between revenues and expenses that determines the profit, loss, or break-even point.

nominal group technique   A consensus-based prioritization scheme used to rank risks.

opportunity   The chance of a good outcome.

opportunity cost   The loss of a missed opportunity.

opportunity stage   The fifth stage of the Risk Management Map, which is a positive vision of risk management that is used to innovate and shape the future.

P^2I^2 Success Formula   The major factors that affect risk management capability: people, process, infrastructure, and implementation.

paradigm shift   A change in a pattern of thinking.

Pareto analysis   Analysis based on the Pareto principle that 20 percent of the sources cause 80 percent of any problem. The result of Pareto analysis is a Pareto chart that provides focus on key risk areas by showing their relative frequency or risk exposure in a descending bar graph.

Personal Risk Management Matrix   Describes an individual's behavior (with respect to risk) for each discipline in the 6-D Model as an individual progresses through the five stages of the Risk Management Map.

Plan   A discipline for mapping available resources to requirements derived from project goals and objectives.

policy   An administrative procedure or guiding principle designed to influence people to a particular course of action.

portfolio theory   A theory that diversification reduces risk.

prevention stage   The third stage of the Risk Management Map, which is a transitional stage where the approach changes from avoidance of risk symptoms to identification and elimination of the root cause of risk.

proactive   For action, not reaction; favorably causing action or change.

proactive quality assurance   A quality philosophy for problem prevention through use of risk management methods.

proactive risk management   Attacking risks; acting to identify, assess, and manage risks to prevent problems and create opportunities.

probability   The likelihood of risk occurrence.

probability theory   Defines probability as a degree of certainty and uses a quantifiable probability to forecast an outcome.

problem prevention   Avoidance of problems to eliminate their result: problem detection cost, rework cost, and opportunity cost.

problem stage   The first stage of the Risk Management Map, when risk identification is not seen as positive, and crisis management is used to address existing problems.

project management   The management team responsible for the execution of the project; the process of planning, organizing, staffing, monitoring, and controlling a project.

project profile   The characteristics of a project that make it unique.

prototyping   A technique for reducing risk by buying information (i.e., risk research). Knowledge is gained through creating a physical model without adding the implementation details.

quality assurance   The practice of ensuring that quality standards are met.

quality control   Methods by which quality is measured, reported, and improved.

quantitative process improvement Numeric perceptions of practice performance and importance that yield objective measures through statistical analysis.

quantitative targets   Best-in-class metrics; success criteria expressed quantitatively.

return on investment   A ratio of savings to cost used to evaluate the effectiveness of management.

rework   The cost of not doing something right the first time.

risk   A measure of the probability and consequence of an unsatisfactory outcome.

risk abatement   The process of reducing the amount of risk. *See* risk reduction.

risk acceptance   A strategy for risk resolution to choose to live with the risk consequence.

risk action plan   The objectives, constraints, and alternatives for risk resolution. The risk action plan documents the selected approach, triggering mechanisms, resources required, approval authority, and resolution results.

risk analysis   Estimation and evaluation of risk with respect to its probability of occurrence and consequence at occurrence.

risk assessment   A process that identifies, estimates, and evaluates risk based on established criteria and prioritizes the set of risks.

risk attributes   Characteristics of probability and consequence that describe a risk.

risk averse   A conservative risk attitude with a preference for secure payoffs.

risk avoidance   A strategy for risk resolution to eliminate the risk altogether (e.g., no-bid a proposal for a risky fixed-cost project).

risk checklist   A list of risk areas that relate to the checklist topic (e.g., a list of items on the critical path can be used to identify schedule risk).

risk context   The collateral information that further describes a risk. Supplements the risk statement by describing additional detail surrounding a risk.

risk control   The process of developing risk action plans, monitoring risk status, implementing risk action plans, and correcting for deviations from the plan.

risk database   The repository of identified risks and associated information.

risk database schema   The design of the fields for the risk database.

risk drivers   Those variables that cause risk exposure to increase significantly.

risk ethic   The rules of conduct that characterize a proper risk management philosophy.

risk exposure   The product of risk probability and consequence. *See* L^2.

risk forecast   A projection of risk exposure for all risks whose time frames for action are short.

risk identification   The process of communicating known risk and sources of risk.

risk index   *See* risk management index.

risk leverage   A rule for risk resolution that reduces risk by decreasing the risk exposure. Risk leverage = (Risk exposure$_{(before)}$ – risk exposure$_{(after)}$)/ risk resolution cost.

risk list   An inventory of active risks.

risk management   A general procedure for resolving risk.

risk management capability   The range of expected results that can be achieved by implementing a risk management process within an organization.

risk management champion   An individual who acts as a change agent to facilitate transfer of risk management technology.

risk management committee   A group of people with responsibility for directing risk management activities.

risk management form   A mechanism for addressing risk systematically through a fill-in-the-blank template.

risk management index   The summation of risk exposure values as a percentage of planned project cost.

Risk Management Map   A practical guide to understanding how the major factors of the P^2I^2 success formula evolve, thereby increasing the ability to manage risk by transitions through five stages: Problem, Mitigation, Prevention, Anticipation, and Opportunity.

risk management plan   The documented goals, strategy, and methods for performing risk management.

risk management process   A systematic and structured way to manage risks that includes the activities and mechanisms used to transform project knowledge into decision-making information.

risk manager   A person with responsibility for coordinating risk management activities.

risk neutral   An impartial risk attitude with a preference for future payoffs.

risk planning   The process of determining and evaluating alternative approaches to resolving risk and documenting the selection in a risk action plan.

risk practices survey   An appraisal method to obtain perceptions of risk management activities.

risk preference   Attitude toward risk, categorized as risk averse, risk seeking, or risk neutral.

risk protection   A strategy for risk resolution to employ redundancy to mitigate risk (e.g., incorporating a fault-tolerant disk in the system design).

risk reduction   A strategy for risk resolution to decrease risk through mitigation, prevention, or anticipation.

risk research   A strategy for risk resolution to obtain more information through investigation.

risk reserves   A strategy for risk resolution to use contingency funds and built-in schedule slack.

risk resolution   Resolving a risk by one or more of the following strategies: acceptance, avoidance, protection, reduction, research, reserves, and transfer.

risk resolution alternatives   The set of options that may resolve risk if implemented.

risk resolution cost   The cost of implementing the risk action plan.

risk resolution strategy   The approach to using acceptance, avoidance, protection, reduction, research, reserves, and/or transfer to resolve risk.

risk scenario   The projection of events and conditions that can lead to risk occurrence.

risk seeking   A liberal risk attitude with a preference for speculative payoffs.

risk severity   Determines relative risk priority by mapping categories of risk exposure against the criteria of time frame for action.

risk statement   A concise declaration of risk in a standard notation: Issue • probability • consequence. For example, "Requirements instability • will likely • delay the design review."

risk status   Progress made against a risk action plan.

risk taxonomy   A hierarchical classification scheme used as a structured checklist to identify and understand risks.

risk tolerance   An input parameter used in sensitivity analysis that determines how risk averse a utility function is. Larger values of risk tolerance mean that an individual can tolerate more risk.

risk tracking   The process of monitoring and maintaining risk status.

risk transfer   A strategy for risk resolution to shift the risk to another person, group, or organization.

ROI$_{(RM)}$ Risk management return on investment is the ratio of savings to cost that indicates the value of performing risk management.

savings   The return for each managed risk. *See* cost savings.

selection criteria   Documented rules for choosing among a set of alternatives.

sensitivity analysis   To identify the most critical factors in a decision model. This analysis changes an uncertain variable to its extreme values, while keeping all other variables constant. Tornado diagrams are a graphic representation of sensitivity analysis.

silver bullet   A panacea for the software crisis.

simulation   A technique for reducing risk by buying information (i.e., risk research). Performance capabilities and limitations are determined through development of an analytic model of system behavior.

Six-Discipline Model   A management model based on a requisite set of disciplines required to manage product development successfully. PM-WIDE is an acronym for the six disciplines of Plan, Measure, Work, Improve, Discover, and Envision.

software crisis   Problems in the software community that have led to late and over-budget software systems that do not satisfy the intended user community.

software engineering   Establishment and use of sound engineering principles in order to obtain an economical, reliable, and efficient computing system.

software measures   A dimension, attribute, or amount of some aspect of software; a measured quantity such as earned value.

software process risk   A major category of software risk that describes risk associated with the practices used to develop and maintain software.

software product risk   A major category of software risk that describes risk associated with the intermediate and final software work products.

software project risk   A major category of software risk that describes risk associated with the project constraints.

software risk   A measure of the likelihood and loss of an unsatisfactory outcome affecting a software project, process, or product.

software risk management   A practice of assessing and controlling risk that affects the software project, process, or product.

Spiral Model   A risk-driven life cycle model of software development and maintenance.

standard process   A minimum set of procedures defined and approved for use by an organization.

systematic risk management   An approach to assess and control risk methodically using a system of checks and balances that perpetuate the process.

tailoring To modify a process, standard, or procedure to match process or product requirements better.

technical performance measures A class of system engineering metrics that describe the quantitative targets for system performance.

Ten-Point Game Plan A procedure that uses a metaphor for playing golf to illustrate how to increase your skill level at managing risk.

threshold A value that defines the inception of risk occurrence. Predefined thresholds act as a warning level to indicate the need for action.

time frame How soon action is required to prevent the risk from occurring.

Top-*N* Risk List The most significant risks to the software development effort.

trend A time series of metrics data (e.g., the trend in productivity is up from last quarter).

trigger A device to activate, deactivate, or suspend activity (e.g., the trigger activated the risk action plan).

uncertainty That which we do not know; potential outcomes with unknown probabilities of occurrence.

uncertainty theory A theory for decision making that uses probability to model unknown, uncertain, or subjective decision problems.

utility A measure of the consequences of an outcome in valuing risk.

utility function Captures a decision maker's risk preference.

utility theory A theory for decision making that incorporates risk preference as a decision criterion.

watch items Issues (or risks) that tend to be long term and may be resolved by the normal engineering process.

weighted multivoting A consensus-based prioritization scheme used to rate risks.

Work A discipline for implementing a plan to produce a product.

work breakdown structure A structured hierarchy that organizes project activity (requirements analysis, product design, etc.) down to the level necessary for cost reporting and control.

INDEX

Other Titles from the SEI Series in Software Engineering

Introduction to the Personal Software Process℠
by Watts S. Humphrey
0-201-54809-7 • 1997 • Paperback • 304 pages

This workbook provides a hands-on introduction to the basic discipline of software engineering. Designed as a programming course supplement to integrate the PSP into a university curriculum, the book may also be adapted for use by industrial groups or for self-improvement. By applying the book's exercises, you can learn to manage your time effectively and to monitor the quality of your work.

Managing Technical People
Innovation, Teamwork, and the Software Process
by Watts S. Humphrey
0-201-54597-7 • 1997 • Paperback • 352 pages

This insightful book—drawing on the author's extensive experience as a senior manager of software development at IBM—describes proven techniques for managing technical professionals. The author shows specifically how to identify, motivate, and organize innovative people, while tying leadership practices to improvements in the software process.

A Discipline for Software Engineering
by Watts S. Humphrey
0-201-54610-8 • 1995 • Hardcover • 816 pages

This book scales down successful methods developed by the author to a personal level for managers and organizations to evaluate and improve their software capabilities. The author's concern here is to help individual software practitioners develop the skills and habits they need to plan, track, and analyze large and complex projects and to develop high-quality products.

Managing the Software Process
by Watts S. Humphrey
0-201-18095-2 • 1989 • Hardcover • 512 pages

This landmark book introduces the author's methods, now commonly practiced in industry, for improving software development and maintenance processes. Emphasizing the basic principles and priorities of the software process, the book's sections are organized in a natural way to guide organizations through needed improvement activities.

Other Titles from the SEI Series in Software Engineering

The Capability Maturity Model
Guidelines for Improving the Software Process
by Carnegie Mellon University/Software Engineering Institute
0-201-54664-7 • 1995 • Hardcover • 464 pages

This book provides a description and technical overview of the Capability Maturity Model (CMM), with guidelines for improving software process management. The CMM provides software professionals in government and industry with the ability to identify, adopt, and use sound management and technical practices for delivering quality software on time and within budget.

Software Architecture in Practice
by Len Bass, Paul Clements, and Rick Kazman
0-201-19930-0 • 1998 • Hardcover • 480 pages

This book introduces the concepts and practices of software architecture—what a software system is designed to do and how that system's components are meant to interact with each other. Architecture is, increasingly, a concrete part of a software organization's business strategy because it is a reusable asset that can be reapplied to subsequent systems.

Developing Software for the User Interface
by Len Bass and Joelle Coutaz
0-201-51046-4 • 1991 • Hardcover • 272 pages

The authors of this book explain the concepts behind the development of user interfaces both from the end user's perspective and from the developer's perspective. The book provides a categorization of the levels of abstraction of various tools and systems.

Software Design Methods for Concurrent and Real-Time Systems
by Hassan Gomaa
0-201-52577-1 • 1993 • Hardcover • 464 pages

This book provides a basic understanding of concepts and issues in concurrent system design, while surveying and comparing a range of applicable design methods. The book explores two object-oriented design methods for the effective design of concurrent and real-time systems and describes a practical approach for applying real-time scheduling theory to analyze the performance of real-time designs.

Other Titles of Interest from Addison-Wesley

The Mythical Man-Month
Essays on Software Engineering, Anniversary Edition
by Frederick P. Brooks, Jr.
0-201-83595-9 • 1995 • Paperback • 336 pages

Fred Brooks blends software engineering facts with thought-provoking opinions to offer insight for anyone managing complex projects. Twenty years after the publication of this influential and timeless classic, the author has revisited his original ideas and added new thoughts and advice, both for readers already familiar with his work and for readers discovering it for the first time.

Electronic Commerce
A Manager's Guide
by Ravi Kalakota and Andrew B. Whinston
0-201-88067-9 • 1997 • Paperback • 448 pages

This book is a clear overview of electronic commerce for business managers and professionals, as well as users who want to keep abreast of the latest trends in management practices affected by electronic commerce technology. Highlights include a specification of the business uses and technology directions of the Web and a description of electronic commerce applications and challenges in banking, retail, and publishing.

Safeware: System Safety and Computers
A Guide to Preventing Accidents and Losses
Caused by Technology
by Nancy G. Leveson
0-201-11972-2 • 1995 • Hardcover • 704 pages

More than ever, software engineers and system developers—as well as their managers—must understand the issues and develop the skills needed to anticipate and prevent accidents before they occur. Nancy Leveson examines what is currently known about building safe electromagnetic systems and looks at past accidents to see what practical lessons can be applied to new computer-controlled systems.

Object Technology
A Manager's Guide, Second Edition
by David A. Taylor
0-201-30994-7 • 1998 • Paperback • 224 pages

At a time when many of the world's largest companies are making the transition to object technology, David Taylor has updated this book to address the important issues facing the growth of object technology and provide a glimpse into the future of this evolving paradigm. In updating this seminal work, the author has retained his signature conciseness and clarity of discussion that made the first edition so popular.

Register
Your Book

at www.aw.com/cseng/register

You may be eligible to receive:

- Advance notice of forthcoming editions of the book
- Related book recommendations
- Chapter excerpts and supplements of forthcoming title
- Information about special contests and promotions throughout the year
- Notices and reminders about author appearances, tradeshows, and online chats with special guests

Contact us

If you are interested in writing a book or reviewing manuscripts prior to publication, please write to us at:

Editorial Department
Addison-Wesley Professional
75 Arlington Street, Suite 300
Boston, MA 02116 USA
Email: AWPro@aw.com

Addison-Wesley

Visit us on the Web: http://www.aw.com/cseng